P9-DVU-039

Fog Valley
CRUSH
Love at First Bite

Fog Valley Crush

Love at First Bite
At Home in the California Farmstead Frontier

Frances Rivetti

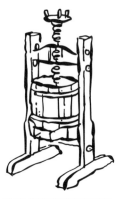

FOG VALLEY PRESS

Copyright © 2014 by Frances Rivetti.

All rights reserved.

For permission to reproduce or transmit any section
or photographs in this book other than in the form
of a brief excerpt for review purposes, write to:

Fog Valley Press
40 Fourth Street, #226,
Petaluma, CA 94952
fogvalleycrush.com

ISBN 978-0-9904921-0-8
"First Vintage" Edition 2014
Printed in China

For Timo, Rocco, Luc and Dominic

"I firmly believe, from what I have seen,
that this is the chosen spot of all this earth
as far as nature is concerned."

Luther Burbank, Horticulturalist, 1875

contents

Prologue

Google image search "Italian Mother" for any wild or random reason and whose mugshot pops up on the third line, poised for time immemorial in some sort of faux desk-functioned activity, intended to capture an air of casual professionalism? Mine.

There I am, arms crossed, decked out in my favorite asparagus-green sweater, me with my 100 percent British bloodline lined up, much to my astonishment and bemusement, amongst an entourage of far more authentic Italian mamas, most of whom are, in contrast to myself, comfortably captured in frame, accessorized not by bauble and bangle, but with various suitable gadget culinari.

This is a title that has, I assume, been generously, though rather bewilderingly bestowed upon me by the assumption of modern social media's putting two and two together and making five. And though it is true that I do have a suitably Italian last name (thanks to that old fashioned option at the altar) I certainly never set out to strive for notoriety of the Italian mama variety.

Not only have I succeeded in stumbling over the line from (mostly) mild-mannered English country girl to full-fledged, vociferous British

American, but now, in my late forties, finding myself ranked on the World Wide Web as a prominent de facto, spicy-meatball-making matriarch of a large Italian American family! How on earth did this happen?

A lot of things that led to this had to do with my chance meeting of a young British-Italian man. At that time, I'd reached the tender age of 21. A lot of other things that transpired along the way have contributed in equal parts to my newfound 15 minutes of fame on the aforementioned great wall of Google Image Italian Mama line-up.

Most of this has to do with a keen fascination, appreciation and ongoing exploration of food, and wine — a tri-cultural, Anglo-Italian-American sense of curiosity and experimentation in the merits of a good, solid meal, my love of food and feeding others.

On the subject of titles, where they spring from, what they mean, *Fog Valley Crush* is the story of my journey as an immigrant, seeking the nourishment of community and home. It might have started with a crush, but years of traversing a reporter's beat along the wild and wonderful wind and fog tunnel that defines southern Sonoma County out west to the Pacific coastline, has, in truth, evolved, in that deep, slow, smoldering sort of way as one of life's most ardent love affairs. I've found home in a quiet, unassuming little patch of northern California — one of the richest places on earth in terms of gross regional happiness and one that has allowed my past to shape my future.

When I married an only slightly Anglicized (despite his being British-born) Napolitano, I wasn't much more than a child bride. I had absolutely no idea of the degree to which I'd be called to adapt, not just in a multi-cultural marriage, but one that would take me clear across the world, far from family and friends. I had been perfectly happy with my life as a young, provincial English newspaper reporter. Fresh-faced and newly wed, my modest aspirations for travel had extended little further than out and about on the continent, be it for work or the occasional holiday. My culinary repertoire wasn't very extensive, either. Up to that point, my cooking skills consisted of a rotating range of sandwiches, salads, boiled eggs and toast. I had every confidence that my dashing Italian mate must have fallen for and fell in love with me for myself alone, he certainly hadn't been hoodwinked by any early indication of hidden kitchen talents.

My trim, traditional, English mother, no doubt suspecting that Timo, her spirited, self-starting and ambitious new Italian son-in-law, might have a few other plans up his sleeve than a sedate marital set-up close by in the East Anglian countryside, made it a priority to warn me not of any impending cultural challenges we might anticipate, more of the perils of a pasta-heavy diet. Up until I'd met this swarthy, persuasive suitor, my cultural ideal of a spaghetti dinner had consisted of little more than the dubious contents of a can of Heinz "Spaghetti Rings," heated and served on toast.

These tiny wonders, bathed in convenient, can-shaped slurps of cheese and tomato sauciness, are the Heinz manufactured British version of Campbell Soup Company's iconic SpaghettiOs, which had been introduced to the meat-and potato market in the UK in 1965, just in time for my introduction by high-chair at the familial tea table across the pond.

Remarkably, it had taken an American convenience food to translate even this most basic of Italian staple to the tea table of the provincial Brit. Back in the 1960s, traditional Italian spaghetti had yet to make an appearance on the family meal roster, at least not in small-town England.

A quarter century on and a trans-Atlantic distance apart, I distinctly remember my mum's polite "chat" about the perils of pasta. Despite these words of warning, a curious revelation of discovery in the delights of my new mother-in-law's delicious and authentic Neapolitan spaghetti dinners put an abrupt end to the pasta-free diet of my entire childhood and youth. I guess I was, unbeknownst to me, and, as my mother had feared, on my way to de facto Italian mama-status, myself!

Lest I sound like a total defector or a Brit-food-bashing ex-pat (heaven forbid — Yorkshire pudding, trifle, scones and sausage rolls being my specialties), it has been in partial heed of my mother's early warnings, that I have kept an open mind to careful balance and sensible economy in figuring out how best to feed an Anglo/Italian-meets-Californian fast-paced, modern family of five. Much as we devour it, pasta appears on the table once a week. Well, maybe twice.

I had visited Southern Italy for the first time, with Timo, to meet his grandparents, aunts and uncles, before we were wed in the UK. The visit made a lasting impression in that it was clear to me that close family and friends around the table, on a regular basis, make for some of the happiest households anywhere in the world. Once our basic needs are met, all the money in the world doesn't make a dent in contentment stakes. Compassion, caring and gratitude is well met over shared mealtimes. I recognized in an instant, the quality of life obtainable in Sonoma County. Intent to live well is not tied to an excessive bank balance but rather in gifts from the garden for family, friends and neighbors.

My household grocery bills and I instinctively prefer the time-old approach of making the most of what's available, by season and locale. Lucky, then, that the challenge of reinventing my cultural mix of culinary influence on arrival in a far away continent, happened to take place in one of the world's most tastiest of farming regions.

Still, cooking for a family is relentless. Admit it. Anyone who has this primary role in any manner of populated household knows this. No matter how much a person loves to have the clan over for a slow-cooked pot-roast, over decades the chore of grocery shopping, daily prepping, cooking and those inevitable piles of dirty dishes is monotonous, even a bit soul-destroying at times.

An early American mentor of mine, an amazing, creative woman who scared the pants off most anyone she met, told a wide-eyed me (following the birth of the second of my three sons) that having children was the single worst thing for a creative woman to do. Period.

The late, great, Phyllis Patterson, educator, entertainment innovator and creator of the original California-based Renaissance Pleasure Faire, was, herself, a major "mother figure" for several thousand actors, artists, craftspeople and other creative types (many of whom went on to have extraordinary careers of their own in Hollywood, the music industry and beyond over a half century).

A grandmother, her honesty was as it was intended, to not hold back, but to motivate and challenge in her peculiar brand of igniting and nurturing the creative process. Phyllis fully encouraged me as a young, immigrant working mother without extended family support, to push my boundaries, work and flourish in a fast-paced, festival environment, often with babies in tow.

We've all witnessed the struggle of parenting vs. career and/or creativity; many have experienced this more than we'd probably care to admit. But staying the course and finding inspiration in the "doing of it," especially with regards to the family meal, is, I believe, the glue to creating and maintaining a solid, cheerful and sustainable, family or shared life.

In the words of Julia Child, no less: "The only real stumbling block is fear of failure. In cooking you've got to have a what-the-hell attitude."

Can we have it all? Only with a food philosophy that is fairly simple to follow. I think of this as the sort of skill base essential for the long-term management of a small hotel. In my case, a boarding house for hungry male lodgers, a sort of modern-day, West Coast American Fawlty Towers — swept up in a transatlantic hurricane and plopped down, somewhat haphazardly, inland a little bit off the northern California coast. When the food is consistent and good, all the other chaos tends to fall into some sense of place. I grew up with the philosophy that a cup of tea fixes all ills. Add a decent dinner to the daily grind and life starts looking up considerably.

This is an account of my attempt to balance mothering, multi-cultural marriage and professional life, through the exploration, understanding and appreciation of the farm-food environment and community in which I landed.

It's also about change, but mostly about change in the way that myself as a transplant as well as my friends and neighbors are sourcing our food.

We increasingly seek out small-scale farmers, get to know our food producers and, together, contribute to the building of a community that places health, harmony and wellbeing as a priority. From my perspective as a freelance journalist, food and wine blogger and Girl Friday in my family's backyard, hobby vineyard, to boot, I have crafted a sort of literary stone soup of my experiences — an insider's portrait of a place that chefs are calling the New Provence. Also, in large part, a love story, this is a collection of my own peculiar observations and passions as an outsider, having fallen, hook, line and sinker, down the rabbit hole into the pulse of a personality-packed, hyper-local real-food community that provides much of the ingredients featured on America's most lauded restaurant menus.

America's preeminent food writer, Michael Pollan describes the region I call home as: "One of the most vibrant local foodsheds in the world."

Likewise, Alice Waters declares all over the place in print, that the coastal reach of this rustic region is precisely where she wishes her legendary Berkeley, California restaurant, Chez Panisse could be.

At a time when we all want to know where our food and drink comes from, along with the stories of the people who farm, produce, cook with and champion it, I invite you, intrepid reader to join me on my ramblings along the back roads and farm trails of my adopted homeland — rustic southern Sonoma County and neighboring, coastal west Marin. Here, you'll meet some of the artisan foodies and farmers, beer makers, cheese and wine producers who are busy reinventing and preserving old-world farm-to-table practices, in the midst of today's otherwise fast paced, globalized marketplace.

From the proprietor of the "littlest cheese factory in California" — a utilitarian cheese-making facility, consisting of several carefully converted shipping containers, positioned between a farmhouse house and milking shed, to sophisticated former executives-turned biodynamic farmers, the real people of Petaluma and its farm-to-coast neighboring communities make a compelling case for a more sustainable life.

Featuring United States artisan food industry leaders such as McEvoy Ranch Olive Oil, Cowgirl Creamery, Lagunitas Brewing Company, Straus Family Creamery and Baker Creek Heirloom Seed Company — each anchored in the Petaluma area, this is a region shaped not just by its agricultural past, but, I believe, by its potential as an international role model for the future.

Over the past two and a half decades, I've self-appointed myself the task of exploring the best of what this quirky, personality-packed micro-region has to offer, dishing up an unspoiled region of coastal California for feature articles and blog posts. While other American writers have sought experiences settling in far-flung, otherwise famously food-centric parts of the world, mine is a reversal of sorts, a British/American putting down new roots in one of the most intriguing agri-tourism destinations in the United States, a place where celebrity chefs and global tastemakers are sourcing some of the world's best new artisan foods.

This book does not pretend to be a wine country compendium, nor a complete history of the region.

It is here in Sonoma County that I've raised my British/Italian/American brood of three sons (at the time of writing this book, Rocco is aged 23, Luc 19 and Dominic 16), fed an ever-revolving door of friends and neighbors, visiting family and assorted wine country critters as well as having apparently, made my mark, albeit to my own amusement as a Google-worthy, top-drawer Italian Mama! My exploration of this rustic and peculiar slice of American life continues to unfold as the sustainable food movement evolves.

In these pages, help yourself to a great, big, hefty serving of the warmth, beauty and deliciousness that I've enjoyed best in southern Sonoma County and coastal west Marin. I firmly believe that the simplicity of living at a less manic pace has made for a rural, rambling idyll in the sourcing, serving and eating of some of the best farm food in the world.

This is a portrait of my observations amidst a region of red barns and rolling hills, pastures studded with cattle and vines. Here I have taken strides to bridge a cultural culinary gap within my own family's curious dual-heritage blend. I am celebrating the coming-of-age of the organic food movement in my adopted community.

I hope to have opened a door into the northern California heritage and countryside that inspires you, too, to cook and eat fresh, seasonal farm raised foods, to make a point of selecting local products from small-scale producers and at the very least, think twice when tempted to open that last can of SpaghettiOs, gathering dust on the pantry shelf!

History weaves itself into the heart of this pastoral paradise of down-home goodness. It practically drips with it. Hours spent in the Petaluma Museum and library history rooms revealed a heritage of original regional recipes, many of which quite perfectly illustrate the timeless simplicity of eating local. I've included several, as well as a lot of my family's own favorites. I couldn't resist paying homage to a few popular Country and Western songs for my chapter titles. They seem to fit the pace of life here, off the beaten track of the wine region's more tourist-filled highways.

Nature's foraged bounty in all its beauty.

Chapter 1

keep my skillet good and greasy

British multi-media's domestic darling, and Food Network doyenne Nigella Lawson claims: "How we eat and what we eat lies at the heart of who we are, as individuals, families, communities." I couldn't agree more.

Connecting with the farmer takes this premise so much farther. Knowing the breed of the animal whose meat we are about to eat, what it was eating, where it was raised and slaughtered and what its tastiest parts are, takes good cooking techniques to a new level. Today, environmental factors are increasingly taking center stage in a chef or home cook's pondering of dairy products, fruit, vegetables and libations. Most anything edible has a history and we want to know its story.

French-born chef and restaurateur Alain Ducasse insists that 85 percent of cooking is about the ingredients — where they come from, how they were raised or grown and how ripe they are. If we take a tip from the chef, a handful of simple foods, sourced from a rich, natural, chemical-free environment make for home meals every bit as tasty as world class cooking in one of his fine dining establishments.

A revolution based on such a simple mantra is afoot in many regions of the United States, with Sonoma County and west Marin, ground zero as best of the West.

The first issue of an invitation to cook and dine with friends Suzanne and her husband, Bill, arrived with a series of strings attached. The promise of tucking into a multi-course menu of farm fresh, hand-crafted fare from late afternoon and into the wee hours sounded like a prospect no food lover in his or her right mind would possibly turn down.

This scene from an evening of sensory overload serves to set the stage for the smorgasbord of foodstuffs available in this farm-rich region. A rally call to participate in each season's newest culinary game, staged at the couple's modern-ranch-style home with its sparse, spacious, semi-industrial farm kitchen is a nod to the hostess's inventive designs — an evolving series of domestic soirees, masterfully purposed to teach and reclaim the comforting, nostalgic rhythms of our community's rich, farm-to-fork heritage.

Yet, I must admit to an undeniable "fear-the-call" to this particular table that is part and parcel of daring to accept a seasonal, extreme food revolution dining challenge, such as Suzanne tends to have up her sleeve. This was not a run-of-the-mill, couples get-together for communal dinner. I should make note, at this early stage of the game, reader, that I'm not sharing these rarified tales in an attempt to turn you into a crazed, elitist foodie, but rather to give you an idea of just how fun and fantastical the home cooking arena can be.

Suzanne's free-form experimental, collaborative communal dining designs are so completely out-of-the-box, an unconventional pre-dinner agenda issued a week or two in advance proved, as expected, an event in itself.

This particularly daring, elaborate call to dine is a fashioned and erratic, visually breathtaking, locally sourced (largely by the guests), seasonal feast at laden trestle tables in a reconstructed ranch home straddling the grassy, outer rim of the small, northern California riverfront wine country gateway city of Petaluma that we call home.

To accept her matriarchal challenge is to knowingly join forces and willingly surrender to the concept of communing in the kitchen with a knife-wielding, apron-clad, colorful cast of characters, an eclectic gathering of foodies and farmers armed and ready to play Suzanne's ever-evolving micro-civilized game of tribal feasting.

The e-vite read:

"If you are feeling daring save Saturday, May 12 (starting at 4:30 pm) for a foodie experience like no other: A Tribal Dinner prepared on-site @ the ranch, with food gathered and hunted."

"In a nut-shell: Bring three pounds or more of a vegetable or protein that you've gathered or hunted. Your money may not be exchanged or used in its cultivation."

Each course was to be inspired by local wines. As guests, we were instructed to select two identical bottles of one Sonoma County wine worthy of a feast. This would require dollars. The rest, preferably not.

Guests would be divided into two "tribes" and tasked with using the offered ingredients to create a three-course meal paired with wine. Not all tribal members would need to cook, each tribe determining how to best engage its talent.

Each tribe would be expected to create its own identity and story related to its food offerings.

A second email, delivered into my inbox a couple of weeks later further outlined Suzanne's Tribal Dinner concept. It took me more than a few concentrated minutes to absorb the guidelines:

"You've all answered the call and are about to experience a wild culinary adventure!"

"Gather, forage or hunt three pounds or more of a vegetable or protein (quantity can be more less depending on the ingredient — to feed 16 @ 4 ounces each) — money may not be exchanged or used in its cultivation — the story is a part of the offering. Food must be brought as a raw ingredient to be used by the tribes as they see fit. Do not come with recipes or preconceived notions. This means do not hide a juicer in your car, spices in your purse or tequila in your pocket — I reserve the right to frisk."

Those brave souls who had risen to this particular season's challenge were advised to bring along offerings and tokens in the form of musical instruments, more wine, poetry, even more randomly, beads and treasure (in the spirit of the region's first people) — anything that might be been deemed useful should the need for courting of favors arise.

"It is possible that you may have to go beyond the ranch gates to get what you need," advised Suzanne, *"and for this too you will have to barter or trade — again, no money may be exchanged. There will be cooking utensils, basic pantry ingredients and fire; you may want to bring an apron and knife, but it's not necessary."*

The schedule, subject to change, read:

4: 00 pm-ish	*Arrival*
4:15 pm	*Tribal Roll Call*
4:30 pm	*Tribe Planning Pow-Wow*
5:00 pm	*Cooking and Preparations Begin*
7:00 pm	*Final Touches and Clean-Up*
7:30 pm	*Dinner*

For my part, I turned to George, a retired San Francisco firefighter friend, and avid outdoorsman, who had generously agreed to barter me three pounds of prime duck that he'd hunted in an untamed, neighboring Colusa County, in return for a couple of bottles of Timo's pride and joy — his micro-managed production of backyard, cool climate, heavy-duty 2009 vintage syrah.

Admittedly, I was stoked about my trade, banking on a hunch or a hope that no-one else in on Suzanne's Spring Challenge would likely have bartered, or worse, actually gone out and hunted wild duck. The wine challenge was easy, at least for me, with a half acre of hand-planted hillside vines having transformed the backyard of our suburban home into a vine-cypress-and-olive-tree-studded vineyard; wine from our yearly 64-gallon barrel is picked, crushed, fermented, pressed, barreled, bottled and stored just feet from where the grapes grow.

I suppose I was feeling a bit smug that this was all falling into place without a lot of trouble.

As intrepid home winemakers for more than a decade, we'd learned by now to stash at least a small reserve of the good stuff that Timo had painstakingly, though with a lot of trial, error, pain and pleasure, learned to craft. Bartering our prized, home bottled treasures was fair game, after all, and made for a quick deal.

Suzanne's participatory dinner theater extravaganzas, I've discovered, may never be (deliciously deliberately) less than mad making in detail, yet, once submitted to, are outrageously fun, tantalizingly tasty and always tempting enough to jump on in, again and again, hungrily and with enthusiasm. Certainly not for the unadventurous.

Of course, extreme hunting, gathering, cooking is not for all, in reality not for many, even in the farmstead frontier. Suzanne's parties might be best described as the epitome of a locavore's feast — life well lived in the American slow food movement's westernmost reach — a meeting of the territories' instinctive side — a modern day aesthetic of fire-roasted wildfowl on a white tablecloth. You know the sort of drool-worthy feature articles emblazoned on the pages of gourmet food magazines, the hippest of the food movement captured in a series of improbably casual glam-grunge-dining scenes that we couldn't possibly conceive of pulling off at home. In reality, Suzanne's boho-gourmet gatherings actually serve to open the door in deconstructing much of the mystery and allure of the modern dinner party and are a lot more fun and enlightening.

Our curious, creative, crafty host knows precisely how to spot a potential guest. As a former Farm Trails promoter, backyard farmer and passionate proprietor of Free Range Provisions and Eats (her popular, little store in historic downtown Petaluma) this super-charged, wildly-creative mother of three won't risk the plunge of any one person into the heat of her self-invented melting pot unless she thinks there's potential for some degree of fun-loving, food-forward originality and energetic participation.

Prospects of mischief, merriment and lots of wine tend to keep things sweet and seal the deal for those, such as myself who might otherwise be alarmed at the depth of clarity and regularity of Suzanne's punctual series of sporting pre-dinner emails.

Keeping on top of these electronic missives is crucial, I've discovered, paramount once signed up for a fantastical feast of plenty at Suzanne's place.

In fact, an hour before the big Spring Feast commencement, a message pinged via email, instructing players to arrive a half-hour later than scheduled and be ready to begin the tribal selection process immediately upon arrival. No small talk, no dilly-dallying, no California-time typical late arrivals.

Fifteen slightly anxious guests were duly assembled by the kitchen window, huddled in a collective haze of late afternoon sun, aprons tied, brown paper bagged offerings lovingly cradled for a ceremonial unveiling of all things gathered, foraged or hunted.

Dr. Gary was first to share with three pounds of gamey, wild turkey sausage, hand ground with bay leaves and other natural, wild seasonings.

"I hunted the wild turkey, plucked and prepared it, ground the meat into sausage with just the right amount of natural seasonings," announced the doctor, somewhat nonchalantly, I thought, considering the degree of dedication to the cause in clarifying precisely where his food was sourced from. I'm sure I wasn't alone as my heart took a swift nosedive down into my stomach. Clearly, I'd signed up to play with the serious, the pros. When not taking the lead in tribal dinner parties, I learned Gary is chair and founder of California/Colorado-based Mountain Education Project and as a consequence, no slacker, no stranger to the land.

Here was a man whose life work is to improve the quality and availability of education in mountain regions around the world. I sized him up as a compact, ruggedly fit-looking, mid-life dynamo of a contender, comfortable cannonballing down a mountain, if called for, with an al fresco, campfire dinner on the cards.

For added good measure and first impressions, he'd brought along a photo of himself wrestling the wild turkey with its wingspan in full regalia.

Deer, wild turkeys and quail roam our city's grassy perimeter in herds and flocks. I'm frequently accustomed to having to wait for a rafter of cackling turkeys to cross the road when driving home during both day and night time hours. Keeping an eye out for a spontaneous deer leaping into the path of traffic is a given, but the wild turkey population is currently giving the deer a run for their money and when driving, are harder to spot.

I had, several times, wondered at the potential of these stringy looking turkeys as a food source, but that's about as close as I'd ever come to actually envisioning one plucked and prepared and served at table. I suppose that is evidence enough of how far removed we are from our food sources. A plump, farm raised turkey is our vision of the holiday feast with very little connection to his scrawny, free-living counterpart roaming our region's back roads and hillsides in unfettered abundance.

Next up at the altar of the evening's sublime offerings, and no less of an early intimidating contestant, was food writer, chef and roving cooking class instructor, inimitable west Marin county native, Mel. As a long-time kitchen collaborator and fellow scribe, I, more than most anyone else in the room, knew Mel to be the real deal. In she came with two, young and chubby, free-range chickens of which she then informed us, had been newly slaughtered and plucked by her own hands. How could my pre-cleaned, wildfowl barter even remotely compare?

In order to complete this calculated barter, magnificent Mel further elaborated the previous day's actual "processing" of a total of 10 chickens at a friend's backyard farm. She'd apparently "opted for the preferred method of putting each chicken into a paper bag, holding it by the legs and cutting its head off with a machete." Old-fashioned neck wringing, in Mel's mind, was somewhat of a less humane thing of the past. Endearing, effusive and big-hearted she might be, but Mel's in it to win it when the stakes are high.

Here's a girl whose first claim to culinary fame was nothing less than winning one of Martha Stewart's baking competitions with a batch of melt-in-the-mouth maple scones — launch pad for vigorous, contagious enthusiasm for outlandish culinary aspirations to come, back then in her early 20s.

Mel lights up not just a room, but an entire building with her can-do, pioneer-woman meets modern-urban-farmer, forthright charm. These were skills, innate and developed and finessed in the wilds of her own free-range, coastal childhood in and around the mysterious hamlet of Bolinas, where she and multiple siblings rambled blackberry-studded hills, gleaning fistfuls of ripened bounty from the quirky community gardens of coastal west Marin.

Hers is a potent, unfiltered earthiness, and a natural aptitude for copious, super-enthusiastic cooking, canning, back and front yard farming, that can't be taught. By adding the grounded, mother-of-two into the mix, anyone else's foolish notions of ruling this specific culinary roost, were really, in my mind, already unofficially over.

Mel and I met as featured bloggers back when our local newspaper, the *Petaluma Argus Courier* launched its first online site in the mid 2000s. Focused on equally prolific streams of food and lifestyle pontifications and postings, any sense of rivalry soon gave way between us, as we readily agreed it was far more delightful in the edibility stakes to collaborate and employ a sense of camaraderie in the enjoyment of one another's food related discoveries, online ramblings and face-to-face tea and cake times.

Here's where Suzanne's crafty guest selection process had its most potent impact. By pairing all of the known Type A personalities in the room with Mel, I detected a palpable sense of tribal balance shifting gears to bring a Lord of the Flies-like dimension to the kitchen. Demon-eyed competitors challenged to work on Team A were entertaining and alarming in equal measure, as I keenly observed from my vantage point on the opposing side.

By letting the weightier personalities duke it out amongst their own tribe, my substantially more mellow Tribe B was busy taking calculated stock in stealth fashion, devising a plan to outwit the go-getters in a three-course-menu that would incorporate the best of presented offerings on display.

Another of Suzanne's longtime friends and secret weapons, David, owner and founder of an established Sonoma County-based natural food product company, struck out next, with an impressive, winning pitch to lead the alphas of Tribe A into battle, taking it in turns with the betas of Tribe B to barter for specific offerings laid out amongst a glistening array of ceremonial food offerings on the kitchen table.

After the rigors of an intense, 30-year career building high-tech telecommunications equipment, it had occurred to Dave's proven business savvy that since so many people were telecommunicating with each other around the region and beyond, the next thing they'd need, logically, was a really good pickle. Combining the north Bay native's lifelong passion for food with a hobby of making pickles from his homegrown cucumbers, Dave had duly created Sonoma Brinery (formerly known as Alexander Valley Gourmet). His company never uses any artificial food preservatives, colorings or flavorings and encourages sustainable agricultural practices in its provision of all sorts of all-natural pickles and sauerkraut to stores and restaurants throughout the west. So we were talking professional. Another head start for David and Tribe A.

Here was a guy who had clearly come to the party primed and ready for some serious action complete with professional chef's knives wrapped up in one of those real-deal, heavy-duty pro-chef knife belts. There was little doubt amongst us hangers-on and hopefuls over in Team B that Dave had his trained eye on the more involved of the meatier offerings and we'd have to take turns in bartering for it to score in that department.

His mother, Dave explained, was a naturalist and he'd been raised in the San Francisco north Bay eating just about everything edible growing wild in the area. "I think of cattails like palm hearts, just great with vinaigrette," he shared, during the evening's pre-cooking, ingredient presentation ceremony, in which he'd unveiled to the astonishment of most of us, an armload of the roots of those sausage-looking shoots that grow around ponds and wetlands. Native Americans and pioneers were prolific foragers of these ancient cattails, stripping away the fibrous green of the roots' exterior to reveal a more promising, white meaty flesh, surprisingly packed with protein and other nutrients — suitable for steaming or pickling, or using in salads during springtime.

These multi-faceted roots were also used for centuries as hardy roofing material and for weaving mats and baskets. The common cattail, Dave further explained, takes a quite forceful yank to get it out from the ground and only after the first rains. "By pulling the inside leaves, a tube of root, when bitten off and flattened, makes for a whistle, or, peeled from the bottom to the top, a wonderful natural food source," he'd said. Right. Naturally.

Though not nearly convinced, I must have shown sufficient a degree of intrigue towards the peculiar root to find myself duly tasked with the painstaking job of diligently and finely shredding (without complaint) Dave's extensive loot for what would eventually emerge, dressed with a homemade tartar sauce, as a surprisingly crisp and zesty bedding for Tribe B's third course presentation of freshly breaded, pan-fried, wild-caught sea bass.

The *Hunger Games* literary trilogy sprung to mind as I mused my allocated task. I'd seen the movie and fancied myself in this particular scenario as a sort of grown-up Katniss, a forty-something forager-warrior protagonist named after the edible aquatic arrowhead root, which, like the cattail, is a part of the genus Sagittaria family. I wondered, are millions of teenagers around the world now pondering the lost art of foraging for their potential survival should the future shape into the brutal fantasy land depicted in Suzanne Collins' post-apocalyptic novels? If so, they really ought to know about the versatility of the common cattail.

The highly-charged tribal turn-taking selection process for matching of raw ingredients with each tribe's on-the-spot, conceptual menu plan ensued. Up for grabs alongside our bartered duck and Dave's cattails were local free-range, extra large duck and chicken eggs, venison, expertly plundered (also by Dave), wild porcini mushrooms, front yard artichokes and pathway nasturtiums.

After all of the wild and wonderful ingredients were assembled, full access was granted to the hosts' peerless pantry for herbs and seasonings, spices, flour, butter and cream. A swirling, whirl of gustatory activity set the scene with various individuals emerging as a cast of unscripted, zealous players trying quite politely not to trip on toes while stealthily positioning for stove top space, an oven rack or in line for a flammable al-fresco cooking station.

My focus on task at hand was met with considerable distraction. I found the flour-clouded rival-tribe dynamic, the most enthralling, entertaining element of all. But then I'm a people watcher at heart. Don't tell Suzanne, but I've never really been the competitive type.

Herbs and the ripest of juicy, young strawberries emerged from some previously unseen spot in our hosts' two-acre back yard, along with other similarly scrumptious berries scrounged from a few good-spirited, pre-warned neighbors' gardens.

Tribe B's Peter, a tidy, bespectacled, highly efficient technical engineer, admirably took supplemental rummaging to new heights in the surrounding streets. Wisely deciding against the temptation to plunder a nearby elementary school teaching garden, he targeted a more forgiving neighbor property. Here was a man quite impressively intent on the incorporation of a fist-full of prize-foraged, bright orange nasturtiums. These robust, little orange edibles duly graced the top of a rock-salted, Waldorf-style roasted chicken salad, served over Tara Firma Farms' fresh greens — Tribe B's first course presentation at table once the feast finally began.

Peter's wife, Martha, was every bit as keen and quietly commanding as her husband. I found this to be encouraging, as our mellow tribe had clearly shown its starting colors, early on, as underdog.

Put on the same team as her mate, Martha came to table with proven, stellar negotiation skills for bartering favors within the community. Fresh from the role as a founding force behind the substantial renovation and expansion of a neglected, old teaching garden at the nearby junior high school, she had identified and successfully fulfilled a dire need for bringing the school's garden back to life in a way that reflects the dynamics of our region's lively food movement.

Husband and wife team Trinity and Frank had already more than proved themselves serious contenders at several of Suzanne's earlier, exploratory dinner gatherings. This time, thanks to participant placement, the dynamic duo was focused on out-cooking one another on rival tribes. I'd partnered with elementary school teacher Trinity, on a separate occasion and had not forgotten her formidable, on-the-spot culinary prowess with an unforgettable carrot reduction sauce that had materialized seemingly out of nowhere (without a lot of input from me, except for wide-eyed interest) as our base for a scene-stealing, seriously delicious dish of fried green tomatoes.

Grouped together in Tribe B, the potent combination of Trinity, Martha and Gary as unspoken leaders of a stealth unit of seven would prove fruitful in our plot to outwit our uber-competitive opposition of Tribe A.

Frank and Dave were clearly taking things a whole lot more seriously than any one else. Mel and Timo (who generally considers himself a genetically-pre-destined, commander of the home kitchen at whatever stage of a meal's preparation might be already well underway) had clearly met their match of über team members amidst a smoky, simmering backdrop in which the smells of rich, raw and half-cooked food only served to salivate and up the ante for the fiercely competitive types.

Gary had prepped Mel's chicken offering in no more than the first two or three minutes of tribal activity — setting the scene with a flurry of robust labor, an abundance of rock salt, fresh rosemary grabbed from the garden and an oven roasting at highest possible heat. I'd long since been impressed by what I'd considered privately as Suzanne's anti-statement in her run-of-the-mill kitchen stove, in an otherwise state-of-the-art kitchen. The sort of stove you would have expected to pick up in Sears, maybe 15 years ago. Actually, the exact same sort of stove I've relied on to cook for my own family for the past decade and a half, given that I've yet to realize a state-of-the-art kitchen, myself. Each of these stoves have been used and abused by as many years of cooking for families of five.

In its place, though, here in Suzanne's kitchen, that evening, a professional-grade Viking range had apparently sailed into dock. Not one to be suckered into springing retail prices for luxury goods, Suzanne has a track record of sourcing some impressive domestic appliance and furniture bargains online. This gently used super stove transpired to be one such savvy score and a significant boost to Suzanne's mad culinary antics, finally usurping the dear dutiful old General Electric in her busy kitchen. It was bound to happen some day, but refreshing to me to learn of its journey to this Petaluma kitchen.

So many cutting-edge kitchens are utterly unused. Timo, in his life outside of being a *garagiste* (Collins English Dictionary definition of which is: a small-scale entrepreneurial wine-maker, especially one who does not adhere to the traditions of wine-making), a golfer and down-to-earth gourmand, makes his living selling real estate. More often than not, he reports, the fancier the kitchen appliances in a property for sale, the least likely they have ever been used. What a crying shame to have a top-notch range and oven and never switch it on. Suzanne's was, by contrast, before and after the advent of a Viking Range, a cook's kitchen if ever I've seen one.

By the time we were half way through each tribe's elaborate interpretations of three-course delights, Mel and Gary's prized, flash-roasted birds were set out to cool, scenting the entire house with that unmistakable, mouthwatering, sensual aroma of those Sunday dinners at grandma's that we remember so well.

Four crazy hours of slicing, sautéing, stirring, broiling and baking ensued, until, following a shuffling of tables and a run to Suzanne's clean laundry pile for a giant stash of crumpled Indian-print napkins, a fleet of mind-blowing, beyond delicious small-plate courses was carried to table, inspected, debated, paired with local wines and in turn, entirely devoured.

Tribe B's second course following on from the chicken Waldorf salad we presented in the form of a delicate duck egg omelet nestled in a casing of pan-fried wild turkey sausage patties (a sophisticated take on sausage and eggs), topped with the most decadent reduction of wild turkey fat gravy.

A third course followed. Pan-fried fish in breadcrumbs perched atop my tart little salad of Dave's intriguing cattails. Painstaking trimming and stripping of the peculiar cattail root had been my idea of a perfect chore for the people-watching I'm so fond of and paid off in spades in small plate presentation and originality. Yes, I was let off lightly this time, but happily, it both looked and tasted (refreshingly tangy and intriguing) far better than I would have imagined.

By the time pumped-up Tribe A took center stage to present its fanciful fleet of competitive fare, contenders were visibly beginning to show signs of languishing, wilting under the weighty fare and such diverse taste experiences of multiple courses.

A citrus-dressed watercress salad with duck crackling, shaved leeks and parmesan crisps snapped our collective taste buds back to attention, successfully bridging the gap between tribal offerings and cleansing the palate with a series of zippy, fresh, unforgettable flavors.

If you are starting to wonder at the sanity of accepting such an invitation to dine, you're not alone. Tribe A's next spectacle was a dish of deboned, seared duck breast with porcini mushrooms followed by a third and final savory presentation of flash-seared venison in a drop-dead delicious, zinfandel reduction sauce.

Both tribes conjured last degrees of waning energy and inspiration in the mustering up of dessert dishes from found items in Suzanne's pantry, fridge and fruit bowl. Smoky, sultry, bittersweet chocolate brownies a contrast to master baker Mel's wonder of a whiskey-soaked, dried fruit and rhubarb galette.

Someone or other eventually nods off at table during dinners at Suzanne's and this particular evening, as dinner stretched out languorously into the dark, quiet hours of post midnight, was certainly no exception. Running into fellow guests around town in days and weeks that followed felt, I thought, a little like having survived one of those crazy reality TV chef shows, down to the final cut. There was no real competition, the prize being what we had each taken away with us.

For me, it meant a heightened appreciation of the endless range of bounty available at hand if we actually take the time to look. The lost skills of foraging, bartering and hunting for fresh, seasonal foods are still there, somewhere in our capabilities. Here was a group of people united by the common bond of living in a community in which the tallest building in the city center remains, to this day, a grain silo.

It is said that the tallest structure in a place depicts the community's values. Where a church is tallest, religion is paramount, where a bank is tallest, money's the key. In Petaluma, farming is paramount.

Potato warehouses and grain mills gave Petaluma its reputation as the county's predominant market town in the 1850s. I felt, at the end of this extraordinary feast, that the ghosts of the region's rich farming history would have most certainly approved.

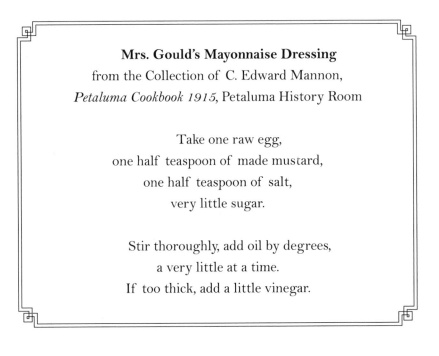

Mrs. Gould's Mayonnaise Dressing
from the Collection of C. Edward Mannon,
Petaluma Cookbook 1915, Petaluma History Room

Take one raw egg,
one half teaspoon of made mustard,
one half teaspoon of salt,
very little sugar.

Stir thoroughly, add oil by degrees,
a very little at a time.
If too thick, add a little vinegar.

*Hunt & Behren's Feed Mill & Store standing sentry
by the Petaluma River since 1921.*

It is easy to envision the unspoiled, sweeping vistas of the Coast Miwok Indians from "The Big View" at Wilson Hill, a large expanse of pristine topography at the border of Sonoma and Marin Counties.

Chapter 2

wide open spaces

Many rustic outposts positioned within a forty-mile journey inland by foot from an unspoiled, coastal precipice mark the locations of the region's first inhabitants. These are verdant valleys and pastures of the ancient hunting/gathering lands of the Coast Miwok. The Pacific coastline, the early people thought of as perched on the very edge of the world.

It is one of the most prolific of nature's foodsheds, a place where rolling hills of craggy pastureland, rivers, streams, creeks, lakes, bays, oak woodlands, eucalyptus and redwood groves meet the dramatic beaches of northern California's Pacific Coastline.

Sonoma County is the northernmost and largest of nine counties in the San Francisco Bay area. Neighboring Marin County, sitting to its south, reaches out west and up along the coastline to border Sonoma County's southern gateway city of Petaluma and the surrounding countryside.

This is an area blessed with an unapologetic abundance of nature's gifts. From rugged coastline to flat lands, rolling hills and mountain ranges, large expanses of watery marshland, coastal scrub, grasslands and woodland combine as an enduring nirvana for hunting, fishing, raising livestock, dairy farming, growing grapes and olives, fruits, herbs and vegetables.

Climatically, its microclimate is at the mercy of a defining, twice-daily dose of intense wind and fog. When inland valley air heats up in warmer months, cooler coastal air is sucked through an actual "gap" in the coastal range mountains.

As anyone who has spent even the briefest time in these parts will testify, a robust wind blows from the ocean between Tomales Bay and Bodega Bay, building speed as it funnels through the "gap" billowing over the rolling landscape of southern Sonoma County to ultimately empty itself of its gusto into San Francisco Bay.

Most every day (except for the rainy season from November to March), those of us who call this home are, whether they particularly like it or not, treated to a natural air conditioning cool blanket of this most familiar fog.

By the time late morning rolls around (for most of the year), the sun usually manages to make a point of blessedly chasing the proverbial fog away. According to the time of year, temperatures climb up by the mid-day hour, reaching a peak by early afternoon.

Generally (by my British standards) tea time at my house — 4:00 pm, cool breezes are back, flowing from west to east, gathering speed as the afternoon morphs into evening and the fog blanket unfolds at dusk.

It is usual for the temperature to swing forty to fifty degrees during the standard stages of a west Marin/southern Sonoma County day, creating just the right environment for nature to do what she does best in bestowing the region's abundant fields, orchards and vineyards with the season's bounty. It is important to have a good grasp of the influence of the climate and its role in our lifestyle here. I've come to appreciate these extremes, despite being frequently envious of our neighboring, inland city of Sonoma's balmy summer evenings.

Though so familiar at first impression to early settlers from Mediterranean parts, extended Indian summers and the cooling effect of the Pacific are the region's defining factors. Instead of the maritime warmth of its European counterpart, this clockwork chill of clifftop ridge and valley makes for unique and distinctive growing conditions.

Before I delve deeper into the farm-to-table history of southern Sonoma County and west Marin (during its formative years in the Gold Rush era), a time when European settlers started what would evolve into a rich history of agricultural diversity and reinvention, let's journey deeper into the past.

We must start at the beginning to fully comprehend the legacy of the land that provided every single ounce of nourishment that the native tribes of Coast Miwok people needed to survive along the shores, hills and valleys of west Marin, coastal Sonoma County and inland to river's edge of Petaluma, for a staggering five thousand years.

Archaeologists estimate, prior to the shocking decimation of these peaceful first people during early European settlement, there were around 2,000 Coast Miwok people at any one time in the region's native history.

Indians had, for thousands of years, lived in harmony with the land, hunting, gathering and fishing in and around some 44 villages. Known as "tribelets" and each consisting of up to 100 people, these villages were dotted along the coast from Bodega Bay to the hamlets of Tomales and Marshall and inland to the what would become, over time, the cities of Novato, San Rafael and Petaluma.

Historic documents describing the waterway known today as the Petaluma River point to evidence of significant Miwok settlements along its banks, slightly upstream of the city's downtown. Tributaries that still today bring a freshwater mix with saltwater flowing up from the San Francisco Bay with the tides would surely have been a major factor in driving factions of the Coastal tribe to settle inland for its bounty of wildfowl and fish available year round. When out at the coast on a particularly chilly, fogged-in day (and that also happens a lot in warmer months, inland), I think about the hardiness that the natives possessed.

Petaluma derives its name from one of the Miwok villages located east of the river — Péta Lúuma(meaning hill backside — in reference most likely to Sonoma Mountain to the east). Additional riverfront villages known as Wotoki, Etem, Likatiut and Tuchayalin were also located close to downtown — with the villages of Tulme and Susuli positioned at the north of today's city limits. With current emphasis on celebrating the city's official founding in the Victorian era, its ancient heritage has sadly fallen into the shadows of the big boom of the Gold Rush days — a tiny blip, yet an explosion in time when measured against centuries of the Miwok's unchanged landscape.

A few miles to the south west of Petaluma, more small Indian villages were known to exist in a scenic, lush outpost known for the past three quarters of a century as Chileno Valley. The name derives from a 1930s settlement of Chileans in the area. Villages of Ameyelle and Meyela were located along the abundant fresh water San Antonio Creek that forms part of the boundary between Sonoma and Marin Counties through Chileno Valley, today.

The Coast Miwok considered their interior homeland as center of the world, believing that earth began with land formed out of the Pacific Ocean. "Coyote" the Miwok ancestor, inspired a lifestyle philosophy of "animism" — living without walls, treading lightly on the land, leaving little footprint and apologizing to Mother Nature or the animals whenever these gentle people had cause to disturb the balance of the wilderness.

We would do well today to pay renewed attention to the ancient ways of the Miwok. They maintained small enough communities to maximize the natural resources surrounding their settlements of huts made from redwood tree bark (shaped rather like upside down ice cream cones) — without any need for the sort of destruction wrought with so much of our modern development.

The Miwok lived without the need for pottery, fabric, seeds or captive animals. An intimate, spiritual relationship with their surrounds rewarded these first people with centuries of harmonious living that left the landscape unscarred but for the arrival of our western ways.

Men of the region hunted deer, seals, sea otter and sea lions year round and were experts at fishing. Seafood was available in abundance year 'round, including abalone, oysters, mussels, clams. Around one third of the Coast Miwok diet consisted of fish. Salmon in season was plentiful as was an abundance of rabbit, duck and seafowl.

Nowadays it's a familiar sight to spot groups of kayakers in the waters that once accommodated fast and easily maneuverable boats made from tule reeds, sufficient in size to carry eight to ten people. Double-ended paddles were used in deeper waters, long poles in shallow waters.

During winter months, Miwok men made spears, bow and arrows, drums, rattles, reed flutes and bone whistles while the women constructed watertight baskets decorated with beads and feathers, preparing animal skins for capes and ceremonial dress.

The Miwok calendar revolved around autumn's acorn harvest, during which hundreds of pounds of acorns would be gathered from the region's prolific oak trees, sorted, prepared and stored in cylinder-shaped acorn houses called "Chukas" and made from cedar and California laurel, built on legs about three feet high to protect this most valuable, nutritious commodity from insects and deer. Buckeyes (nuts related to the horse chestnut) and seed crops, roots and leaves rounded out the varied diet of the healthy Coast Miwok.

In spring, Miwok women gathered abundant greens to supplement their diet, including nettle, clover and the spade-shaped native winter purslane (Indian lettuce), later to be known as miner's lettuce (due to its popularity amongst Gold Rush miners who ate it for its Vitamin C in order to prevent scurvy).

Native greens were, intriguingly, picked and placed near red anthills. A strange, vinegar-like substance exuded by the ants as they walked over the greens apparently acted like a sort of Miwok salad dressing. Kelp was gathered in the warmer months, dried and stored for winter. Though coastal stinging nettles are a fashionable fixture as topping greens in farm-to-table restaurant fare of today (picked with long gloves and frozen or steamed to de-sting), I've yet to come across the Miwok salad dressing as a modern menu option.

During summer, seeds from wild flowers were collected for use as the main ingredient in Miwok bread making. Blackberries and strawberries would be eaten in season and later, one of our most sought-after wild treasures, chanterelle mushrooms. The wilderness provided everything the Miwok needed. Work and play were not differentiated and whole tribes, from the youngest children to a family's most senior elders, participated in the daily process of domestic life.

It's interesting to note that young farmers and ranchers returning to family land in the region of late, are busy figuring out ways to make their work more enjoyable with an emphasis on sustainability back at the forefront in providing economic stability for multiple generations to coexist in harmony, just as the Miwoks were able to do for thousands of years.

Deer head masks were used for hunting, which took enormous preparatory effort, with sweat lodges built to rid the human scent. Bows and arrows were pulled through the smoke and bodies of hunters were rubbed with mugwort and angelica.

Cooking was primarily undertaken in water-resistant baskets with heated rocks, mush and water. Fowl, meat and fish were broiled over open fires.

An archaeology research project by the National Park Service United States Department of the Interior investigating sixteenth-century cross-cultural encounters in Point Reyes National Seashore further illuminates local lore of our indigenous coastal hunter-gatherers as they first meet Spanish and English sea voyagers in the late 1500s.

It is equally fascinating to learn that the Miwok were not considered an isolated people, due to their communications in complex trade networks with inland tribes. Yet, it is clear that the Coast Miwok's unprecedented introduction to sixteenth-century Europeans was the turning point in time, resulting in significant cultural change and forever altering one of the world's most ancient, sustainable and dignified ways of life.

To carry out their project, researchers from the National Park Service and the University of California, Berkeley in partnership with a restored tribe serving Sonoma and Marin counties, the Federated Indians of Graton Rancheria are currently utilizing historical anthropology, original excavation field data from the 1940s to 1970s, historical documents, ethnography (cultural study) and native oral tradition to understand how the Coast Miwok people first fashioned reproduction versions of ceramics and other material goods salvaged from the ship wrecked Manila galleon San Agustín, an occurrence that took place in the present day Drakes Bay, along what is now the Point Reyes National Seashore in 1595.

Although Sir Francis Drake and his crew had spent five weeks amongst the Miwoks preparing his iconic wooden galleon, *The Golden Hinde* for its Pacific crossing and return to England 16 years before the galleon from Manila, it was the impact of the San Agustín being driven ashore during a storm shortly after its crew arrived along the coastline that would make the biggest impression on daily life in the region.

This was the earliest recorded ship wreck along the Pacific Coast and though it would be the last recorded contact with Europeans until Spanish colonialism reached the area almost 200 years later, material remnants since discovered beneath the seashore in coastal village sites and middens (mounds of shell and animal bones), paint a compelling picture of how a diverse cargo of Chinese luxury trade goods bound for Mexico, made its lasting impression on an indigenous culture.

The Coast Miwok likely used salvaged bowls and plates as models for food storage, porcelain for scrapers, setting themselves apart from other indigenous groups by establishing what was, in effect, the first early European-influenced settlement in the West.

Intrepid Spanish Franciscan missionaries followed, coming through the area in 1776, introducing European agricultural practices and converting the Coast Miwok to Christianity.

The Spanish, in dire need of laborers to tend cattle lands, undoubtedly weakened the immune systems of the Miwok with this radical change in lifestyle, leaving them desperately vulnerable to Western disease.

By 1822, Spain had ceded its control of the area to Mexico. By this time, the Petaluma area had become a part of a sprawling 66,000 acre Mexican land grant of 1844 by Governor Pio Pico to General Mariano Guadalupe Vallejo called Rancho Soscol.

It would be Mexico's turn to surrender the area to the United States in 1848 during the Mexican-American War, bringing about further changes that would inflict even greater peril to the natives.

Hard-scrabble émigrés to rural Sonoma County and west Marin next arrived on the scene, in the mid-1800s, primarily hailing from faraway Chile, Croatia, China, Scotland, Switzerland and Portugal, attracted, I'm sure, not unlike myself, by the agricultural potential of the region and its many topographical similarities to home.

Tragically, a huge proportion of the Indian population in the area died of smallpox in 1838, with a second bout reportedly hitting both natives and Chilean settlers in the Chileno Valley area, in 1868. Sealing the lid on the coffin of native rights, Congress passed Public Law 280 in 1953, turning over law enforcement on California reservations to state and county agencies.

By 1958, the federal government had fully terminated any recognition of the Coast Miwok people.

Some four decades later, the Coast Miwok were finally federally re-recognized as a 1,300-member tribe. Back in December 2000, legislation was signed that granted the Federated Indians of Graton Rancheria, previously known as the Federated Coast Miwok (incorporating the Southern Pomo Tribe), the full rights and privileges that were afforded other federally recognized tribes elsewhere.

Today Coast Miwok tribal members live within the modernized world of this region, determined to keep their history and at least some of their traditions alive.

The past hundred and fifty years have all but obliterated much of the every day reference to the honoring of the region's first people. As we continue to embrace the culinary customs and traditions of those who followed, the truth and beauty of what these lands will bear is no better illustrated than by those who preserved its bounty for so much of history.

Ironically, the Federated Indians of Graton Rancheria may have had the last laugh on latest human impact on the area.

"How's that line from the movies go?" asked Bay Area ABC news on November 5th, 2013. "If you build it, they will come." It certainly came true at the Graton Resort and Casino in Rohnert Park, where thousands of people showed up for the controversial casino's grand opening."

The casino, the newest of some 60 casinos throughout the state of California, with its 3,000 slot machines, 150 gaming tables and 13 restaurants was a decade in the making (and at the time of my writing, was still being contested by irate citizen groups, with a court case pending).

Tribal Chairman Greg Sarris reportedly shelled out some $800 million dollars in building the casino, staffed by 2,000 employees. Describing it as a project for his people, he has pledged that millions of revenue dollars will go back to the state.

Residents of southern Sonoma County were infuriated by clogged freeways with hoards of casino-goers madly rushing north for a hopeful lucky break during the casino's opening week. I'm not a gambling girl and had little desire to check the place out, for myself, but I don't have the heart to join its ranks of opponents. Though it doesn't fit the origins of these peaceful, outdoor people, and, for many, is an awkward duck-out-of-water, it does represent a hefty dose of poetic justice.

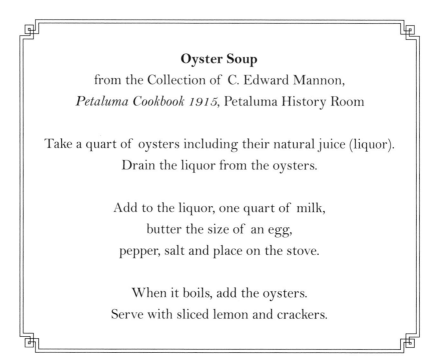

Oyster Soup
from the Collection of C. Edward Mannon,
Petaluma Cookbook 1915, Petaluma History Room

Take a quart of oysters including their natural juice (liquor).
Drain the liquor from the oysters.

Add to the liquor, one quart of milk,
butter the size of an egg,
pepper, salt and place on the stove.

When it boils, add the oysters.
Serve with sliced lemon and crackers.

*Timo's al fresco Italian–American Sunday dinner
with family and friends, Sonoma County style!*

Chapter 3

home on the range

Cooking with locally sourced foods in my northern California kitchen makes for the perfect celebration of the family's Italian side. The region's Mediterranean-like climate closely enough mirrors that of my mother-in-law Giuseppina's native southern Italy, providing us with just about everything that also grows so well in the part of the world where she learned to cook.

Italian/Portuguese/Swiss influence in Sonoma County and west Marin long-since shaped the region's predominant cultural cuisine, with Italian-style meats and cheeses, pastas and locally produced sauces widely available throughout the area's various grocery stores and delis.

Some of my first dining experiences in the region were at the several long-established, traditional "family-style" Italian eateries, both in town and on the road to the coast.

During our short winter, my family welcomes the reappearance of more of the hearty English foods of my upbringing, roast dinners,

Yorkshire pudding, shepherd's pie, bangers and mash, but for the majority of the year, the Italian influence fits in so well with our climate.

The food on my table has been one of my top priorities in household spending since signing myself up (one foggy New Years Eve in the 12th Century Abbey in the small, English town where I was raised) for married life with a man of large, Italian appetite. Though I recognize that I have been fortunate to have been able to afford to steer clear of most-things processed in my feeding the family fresh, regional foods, the value of having raised three sons with a strong sense of what makes for the mainstay of a healthy life has been the most rewarding.

When Timo and I arrived in California, we started out with the grand, collective sum of a modest fifteen hundred dollars, with which to find a place to live, furnish it with garage sale finds, feed ourselves and figure out our first mode of transportation. My large and meticulously curated, solo suitcase never did arrive, lost in transit somewhere over the Atlantic. There was no preconceived idea of grandiose in our assimilation to a new culture. It took time, penny-stretching, entrepreneurial diligence and sufficient a degree of determination that oft accompanies the immigrant spirit, along with a lot of experimentation in the kitchen to establish a path for our family. Food and nourishment have always been a top priority.

One of the best things about our joint efforts to recreate my Italian mother in- law's old country culinary specialties (as well as my best-of-British favorites), has been the inter-connectedness it brings to table. Nonna Rivetti stands at her kitchen counter, thousands of miles away, back in the old world, yet here she is, right here with us, at the same time, a presence in our kitchen, on a near daily basis, with the fullness and flavor of our recreation of her most nostalgic dishes.

A big, slow, sit down, west coast country version of a frequent, old-world Sunday dinner anchors us, reinforces us as a family.

These family meals serve as a reminder to slow down and commune. To celebrate the best of what the land has to offer, here, now and hopefully, having planted the seed of the importance of a robust home life in the next generation.

To pull off a family-style Sunday dinner, complete with the pre-requisite six hours of food prep, Timo sees it as an opportunity to retreat from the hectic pace of his workaday life in real estate and, in past years, our constant rounds of creative and sporty sons' activities.

Since the advent of the smart phone, his mastering of the art of stirring sauce and closing deals at the same time has proved fruitful enough to have helped make our move to the California countryside a permanent one.

Though it has been largely up to me, as a home-based writer, to juggle and manage the production line of varied, seasonal meals, three times a day for the past twenty three years of parenting (I've always made a point of packing brown bag lunches, ever since the boys were in part-time nursery and pre-school), the bigger, sit-down, boisterous bonanzas at the dining table are mostly, thankfully, my capable cook of a husband's forte.

Roaming around, as a food and lifestyle writer I've spent a considerable portion of the past two decades getting to know (and eating with) a colorful cast of neighboring characters, pioneering craft food producers, farmers, cheesemakers, bakers, beer and winemakers with whom I share the common bond of home.

These hard-working, highly-focused folk are reinventing and preserving old-world farming practices with a collectively modern and increasingly appealing approach. Although I'm keen to follow news reports of similar food-centric communities around the United States, it's hard to imagine any one other region having quite the natural resources in play that continue to shape this part of the world as one that is so outrageously edible.

I find this quirky, distinctive little place to be peopled by a disproportionate, thoroughly interconnected body of fiercely individual farmers and craftspeople, families and groups whose energies and vision have brought about a vibrant farm town-and-country revival set amidst one of the more down-to-earth micro-regions north of San Francisco's famed Golden Gate.

I recognize these folks; I was born into a family of small market town greengrocers, newsagents and corner storekeepers. I consider myself a country girl through and through. Raised with newsprint on our fingers and the sensibility to sniff out a good story within our community, its not surprising that myself and my sister, Kerry, two out of four siblings, pursued careers in journalism. What is surprising is the ground we would cover, given our small-town starting point. Kerry, an Australian citizen, has boomeranged from London to Sydney several times in her career.

We were raised in, what we'd felt, especially as teens, the isolated far reach of the back of beyond. Britain's ancient, marshy, mysterious and super fertile East Anglian Fenland and my starting point in this story, has, since time began, retained its solitary status as far, far off the beaten track.

As austere in name as in its infrastructure and architecture, the insular Fenland market town of Crowland, with its small, struggling commercial center, straddles the bleak and desolate, yet, hauntingly beautiful borders of the lesser-tamed counties of Lincolnshire and Cambridgeshire. In his 1951 book *A History Of The Fens*, author J. Wentworth Day described the Fens as a place where there are no half measures: "You either love them, or you are appalled by them," he wrote. It is a half land of earth and water, a place of piece and quietude, with, as Wentworth eloquently penned: "over-arching skies, where clouds sail into the North Sea in high armadas."

Despite my long-since defection from the immense sense of space within the primitive, multi-generational pull of my birthplace, replicating such early sense of place proved a tough act to follow in my young adult wanderings and search for a subsequent, surrogate home.

My paternal family is made up of several generations of market town shopkeepers, greengrocers and newsagents by trade, depending upon locally produced food to stock the shelves as well as supply a rural daily delivery route. An appreciation of the farmer as key in managing and protecting the environment and economy was, undoubtedly in my blood from the beginning. My great, great grandfather, a farm laborer, established the family in the Fens having migrated internally in Britain from the South East.

His son — my great grandfather, my grandfather, my dad, uncle, two of my three siblings and myself inherited a distinctive Anglo-Saxon gene that is quite apparent in a familial robust stature, tall height, sandy hair and green/blue eyes. The Anglo Saxons of South East England lived, for centuries following their piratical raiding of post-Roman Briton, a largely rural existence in family farmsteads and small hamlets of the descendants of tribal settlers from Germanic regions of Europe.

Seafaring pagans were dominated by earth-related Druidism, until Christianity took over in the mid fifth-century. A later era of intense human movement saw well-entrenched families with Anglo-Saxon origins eventually mass migrating from the region into other parts of England in the 18th and 19th centuries, as fields and common land were enclosed, larger farms created and laborers condemned to low wages and squalid living conditions.

Historic Lincolnshire was the second largest county in the country, but only six or seventh largest in population in the mid 1800s. Walled in by flood banks and for centuries, largely made up of inhospitable marshland, Anglo-Saxon blood, with its strong brows, high cheekbones and pronounced jaws, had, until this time, largely given the region a wide berth. Hiring fairs in market towns would, eventually attract farm laborers to the same ag-rich region from which many of the county's earlier inhabitants had emigrated to New Hampshire as Pilgrims, from Lincolnshire's Boston port town, in the mid-sixteenth-century.

When my great-great grandfather made his way north to the Fens during the mid-eighteen hundreds, he would have found himself a remote, yet food-rich wonderland where punts were taken out early morning to shoot ducks that settled on the reed-filled marshes. Eels were caught in abundance using wicker traps and eel forks would have supplemented pike, pheasant, rook pie and root vegetables in his diet.

Geographically, 10,000 years ago, the Fens were joined to northern Europe and the four Fenland rivers, the Witham, Welland, Great Ouse and Nene, all originally tributaries of the Rhine. Five thousand years ago the Fens were separated from the rest of Europe by the rising North Sea. The region's uniqueness, whose first sea defenses and changes to the landscape were made by the Romans, was captured in what is widely considered one of the best modern British novels, *Waterland*, by Graham Swift (and acclaimed 1992 movie version, with Jeremy Irons, Sinéad Cusack and Ethan Hawke).

I still am able to remember as a mere toddler, being bundled up for frequent morning rides in the passenger seats of one of the family's business delivery vans in order to give my mum, Elaine, a bit of time to run unhampered errands for our household of six.

One of my mum's favorite tales to tell at family gatherings is the time that my dad, John, arrived home for lunch at the end of his rural delivery route, without a certain small person in tow. "Did you forget something?" phoned the little, old farmer's wife who I've been led to believe, considered my visits to her crumbling, stone cottage, a highlight of her otherwise isolated week. Fenland folk are known for their blunt character. Good thing she'd had a telephone installed in her lonesome North Bank location. I don't suppose my dad would have remembered his delivery companion until dinnertime. I wonder if these rural routes and regular social visits formed the part of my character that compels me to explore, to get to know people, to connect. I'm pretty sure they do.

My mum, on the other hand, an only child, had been raised by a single mother who sent her, at several stages of her childhood to live with various relatives, friends and an occasional boarding school in any one of a number of post second world war cities throughout the UK. For her, the ideal of a joyful family life with kids to farm out couldn't have been more different from how she was raised. When she first met my dad, as a young ward of court and a trainee nurse barely out of her teens, she took a bus out into the Fens from her nurse's home in the region's cathedral city of Peterborough.

"I was shocked at how remote it seemed," she'd tell us, growing up in a small town community, regaling us with stories of how many times she found herself in a panic, hopelessly lost, driving one-track country roads seemingly leading to nowhere, for some time after she'd married and moved from the city.

My mum never has really taken to the Fens, preferring city life to this day. Her bloodline runs thick with that of the Welsh Britons. A feisty, brunette, darker-skinned Celt (passed on genetically to my sister, Kerry) to balance out my and my other two siblings (Stuart and Lindsey's) steely Anglo Saxon lines. Though the Celts withstood thousands of years of intrusions from Germanic, pagan, Viking, Norman and of course, English invaders, my maternal great-grandparents, as with so many impoverished Welsh people, finally gave in on the fight when they turned to earning a decent wage in post-Industrialized England. My mum and my dad still live in the house in which my siblings and I were born, a house my dad built before he met his bride, anchored and entrenched in his beloved Fens for life. It's the house that I return to when visiting family in England, awaking to the comforting, familiar sounds of medieval Abbey bells chiming in a Sunday morning, a rooster making his timeless dawn chorus on the farm next door.

During my childhood, my extroverted grandfather, Frank (and later, my dad), was, as chairman of the town council, unofficial mayor of our town of three thousand staunch descendants of Fenland's early marsh men and women. He was a ruddy-faced, barrel-tummied fixture, a product of twice a day pints of Guinness on tap at the George and Angel.

There wasn't a soul he didn't know and a soul who didn't know Frank. Tweed jacket and a trilby hat were his trademark business attire as this large, jovial old man rambled around town and the surrounding countryside with his car door, typically half ajar. "I'm getting out in a few miles," he'd once told a neighboring village bobby, who'd pulled him over in the midst of a rural grocery delivery route.

Frank was an expert and perpetual veggie trimmer, constantly tending produce to maximize the lifespan of his and other locally grown assortments of salads and vegetables.

There was no such thing as out-of-date produce in his book and the sorts of extravagant, sorrowful waste we see in stores today. Though he passed away when I was 17, I still picture him in my mind's eye with his green grocer's paring tool that he kept in his jacket pocket, expertly slicing away at the browning folds of a cabbage during mid-stream banter with his customers.

During World War II Frank had served (matched by his talents in bartering for small production fruits and veg, dairy products and meat) as a Provisions Officer for allied troops first in Africa and later, in Salerno, Italy, After the war, he returned home to the Fens to expand his one-store grocery business into a family-run chain of small corner stores. He never left the country again. For the rest of his life, Frank's daily van delivery service supplied farms and remote homesteads with newspapers and groceries within a 10-mile radius from Crowland.

My grandfather grew much of his own produce in long, narrow glasshouses behind the home that he shared with my grandmother, Clarice. The memory and smell of picking his plump, deep red hothouse tomatoes in the English summers of my teens is one that I'm instantly reminded of each time I pluck a vine-fresh tomato from my kitchen garden, here in sunny California. Similarly, strawberries, tiny and crimson and perfect, June's juicy jewels we picked from the black, peat earth fields of the Fens will forever serve as a standard and for the innocent summers of my youth.

I learned to drive in one of the family's rickety grocery delivery vans under wide horizons, out in the middle of nowhere along the longest, straightest, loneliest Fenland roads.

With farm parcels dotted a good distance from one another in this flat, expansive, endless landscape and traffic few and far between, conditions were ideal for a teenager learning to drive. When I managed to deliver the goods on time and intact to patiently waiting farmwives, it proved a win-win!

Rhubarb, gooseberries, crab apples, asparagus, leeks and potatoes — seasonal, mud-encrusted, farm fresh and familiar, were neatly packed into cardboard boxes alongside newspapers, magazines, tobacco, dry goods and basic pantry staples.

Stacked boxes jostled and slid with each of my wobbly, early maneuvers and frequent false starts. Food in the fens before the advent of the deep freezer chest cabinet was, as I fondly recall, mostly fresh, simple, traditional and tasty.

After my granddad passed away I sort of inherited his long, white, hatchback, station wagon (some form of modest payment gleaned from my meager savings and to teach me the value of vehicle ownership went back into the family business).

Each time it rained — and it rained a lot in my childhood and the more vivid years of my late teens (or at least it feels like it did from my current sunny perspective) — an aroma of smelly old cabbages permeated the car. I liked to think that Frank was looking over me as I careened around the Fens, in search of the sort of art, culture, fashion, music and merriment that a small town/dying to be cosmopolitan seventeen/eighteen year-old was inclined towards in the mid 1980s.

Though my designs were on broadening horizons, in truth, I had little conscious intention to permanently decamp this primal landscape, let alone look for a new one, clear across the world.

A few short years later, every bit as charismatic and unconventional as my grandfather had been, Timo stepped boldly on the scene, swept me swiftly off my otherwise grounded young feet and deftly derailed any ideas I'd had of rising through the ranks as a rookie regional newspaper reporter in the Fens.

I must have seen something in him of the exuberant, irrepressible Frank, who would tease me as a child that we would one day travel to America with the weekly takings. Little would I have guessed, a year after marriage, at age twenty-three, I would arrive in the United States.

Timo had sold the plan as a brief, six-month stint to help an ex-pat friend launch a fledgling San Francisco test commercial studio. It was a big-world, short-term opportunity too good to pass up. We'd intended to take our new-found knowledge and international findings back home, where my boss had kindly held my job open for me for half a year.

A six-month taste of northern California, constant wide-eyed discoveries and several consecutive years of complicated paper shuffling birthed a much debated, though mutual decision to stay put and remain in the States.

It took time, but I was able to eventually persuade my more cosmopolitan husband that it would be the very real presence of cows in fields around the borders of a greater Bay Area city to seal the deal if I agreed to stay.

After a more urban start, the bucolic Sonoma County/west Marin scene was so soul-speaking to me, I considered it a sign that this was the perfect place in which to put down permanent New World roots — the sense of community I'd left behind and that I had been coveting, the pervading factor.

Our first, two-year-long U.S. address in the sprawling, bustling, east bay had failed to meet my requirements in any soul-satisfying way, especially in my search for surrogate landscape and community in which to call home. "I can see cows," I'd declared, when a move to a rural community became a possibility.

The first time I set eyes on the Victorian riverfront city of Petaluma was from the misty coastal west, driving into historic downtown via quaint and charming D Street, its well-preserved Queen Anne and craftsman homes a classic Thomas Kinkaid picture of Hometown Americana come to life. As I remember it, that late weekend evening, almost two and a half decades ago, Petaluma struck me as the sort of town its people must like to come home to — the sort of place where families gather at the table come evening time and neighbors chat on the porch. I didn't know it at the time, but I'd been chasing my muse in the American west and I'd found it.

What unfolded for me after moving to the earthy, grounded northwestern reach of the greater Bay Area, was a deep appreciation for the creative and industrious, quirky and unpretentious foodies and farmers of southern Sonoma County, the characters I have honed in to in my search to establish a replacement hometown community in Petaluma and its surrounding hamlets.

My transplanted provincial reporter and country girl's roots are by now, deeply and firmly entrenched in the soils of my adopted beat on the edge of the American west. Having felt the constraints of early motherhood and work without any extended family back-up available, I picked up my camera, my notepad and pen and set about crafting a way to make sense of it all, to do what I love in order to be a happy, fulfilled person and mother.

In exploring the area's multi-layered largely European agricultural heritage, I surprised myself, staunch English ex-pat in so many ways, in the depth of my affection and admiration for this extraordinary little place.

Timo's Italian Sunday Dinner

Anti Pasti

Timo would tell you to always make sure your guests are well aware that this is just for starters. It's quite easy to eat an entire plateful of scrumptious marinated veggies, melt-in-your-mouth mozzarella balls, salami and prosciutto (in our case natural-meat company, Zoe's Meats) with a slice of the best fresh, locally-baked bread and call it a wrap.

The idea at all times when partaking in a home-cooked, traditional Italian dinner is to pace your appetite. Timo serves home-marinated mushrooms and artichoke hearts, oven-roasted red, yellow and orange peppers, meats and zippy little peperoncinis with a glass of house wine to get things going.

Neapolitans know that less is more when it comes down to it and the best example of this mantra is the basic, flavorful, fresh and homemade marinara sauces, staple of Nonna's cucina and the base of most authentic Italian dishes cooked up in our California kitchen.

Marinara Sauce

1/4 cup olive oil

2 large garlic cloves, crushed

splash of vermouth

2 pounds of ripe plum tomatoes, crushed
(or one 28 ounce bottle of preserved, crushed tomatoes from last season)

salt

10 big basil leaves, torn apart

Sauté crushed garlic in olive oil in a large pot over medium heat for about four to five minutes. Pour a splash of vermouth and reduce the alcohol. Add tomatoes and salt, bring to a simmer and cook, stirring frequently until sauce is nice and thick. Stir in basil leaves. Cook for at least 30 minutes or more. Serve over a big bowl of spaghetti, ravioli, crespelli or cannelloni.

Nonna's Ragù Sauce

Add 1/2 chopped onion and one pound of lean, ground beef to the marinara ingredients. Sauté garlic and onion in olive oil, brown beef and drain off fat, add a splash of vermouth and reduce. Add tomatoes and basil, salt and pepper, bring to a boil and simmer for several hours.

Polpette

2 pounds of ground sirloin

1 cup of grated parmesan cheese

1/2 cup of chopped parsley

1 teaspoon of minced garlic

2 cups of fine, fresh breadcrumbs

2 large eggs

1 teaspoon of salt

1/2 teaspoon of pepper

olive oil

Combine all of the ingredients in a large mixing bowl, saving a small amount of the breadcrumbs to roll the meatballs before frying. Shape three-quarters of mixture into medium (golf-ball) sized meatballs and bake or fry. Add to the sauce. Make smaller, marble-sized meatballs with remaining mix. Bake or fry and set aside.

Braciole
3 pounds of flank steak
2 teaspoons of minced garlic
1/2 cup of chopped basil
salt and pepper
parmesan cheese
splash of vermouth
twine for tying up the braciole

Tenderize flank steak evenly. Add garlic, basil and season to taste. Sprinkle with a small handful of parmesan cheese. Roll up flank steak tightly and secure with string. Brown the flank steak in a pot with olive oil and a dash of vermouth, rotating until browned on all sides. Remove from the pot. Add ragù sauce and polpettes and braciole and simmer for three to four hours.

Lasagna
3 eggs, hardboiled
2 packages of no-boil organic (ideally fresh) lasagna strips
4 cups of fresh mozzarella, sliced
small-sized meatballs (made from polpette recipe)
1 cup of parmesan
Nonna's ragù
salt and pepper

Chop the eggs into small pieces. Pour ragù on bottom of baking dish, layer with sheets of lasagna. Add mozzarella, meatballs, eggs and more ragù and sprinkle with parmesan. Repeat layers three or four times, topping with sauce. Preheat oven to 375° F and bake for 30 minutes. Let rest for five minutes before serving.

Serve meatballs and braciole after lasagna with a green salad dressed simply with olive oil, lemon juice, salt and pepper, fresh Italian herbs.

No great Italian feast ends without the hosts' party trick of setting alight a few espresso beans dropped into tiny glasses of Sambuca. Grappa is another option, one for the die-hard diners who don't mind a bit of a delayed start come Monday morning.

Morning fog lifts over historic west Petaluma.

Chapter 4

small town USA

From the perspective of an avid (senior) citizen-photojournalist friend (another) Frank, a retired lawyer who moved to Petaluma from Illinois back in 1985, his general consensus as to just how good we have it in grocery stores, farmers markets, cafes, restaurants and at home in this particularly small corner of wine country can be summed up in one of his frequent cross-town email missives: "The 'food scene' here in Sonoma and Marin is unique," he shared. "When we venture beyond to San Francisco, Napa, or Mendocino, it really tends to degrade. By the time we reach Sacramento, we are back in Peoria when it comes to food." No offense to anyone reading this in Peoria.

To appreciate my adopted northern California community (population 59,000) in its wider context, let's return to its heyday, when the small city of Petaluma basked in the limelight of a quirky marketing mantle: "Egg Basket of the World." Today's still relatively compact, yet productive Victorian riverfront city and surrounding unincorporated areas remain agricultural to the core. So much so that its highlight of the year (and largest community event of its kind in the San Francisco North Bay) is the aptly named Butter & Egg Days Parade.

It was emboldened promoter and Chamber of Commerce Manager Bert Kerrigan who had coined the rather lofty claim of World's Egg Basket for Petaluma, back in the prosperous days of 1918. Petaluma was busily basking in the glow of nationwide renown as the auspicious birthplace of the innovative egg incubator and home to the world's first chicken pharmacy.

Marketing whiz, Bert seized this spirit of ingenuity by instigating an initial eight-year series of elaborate, annual egg-themed parades that weaved their festive way (despite the otherwise dampening effects of Prohibition), through the city's ornate iron front downtown.

"It was Bert who first coined the famous quote, 'Milk from contented cows' which actually put Carnation Milk on the map," explained my oft-Victorian costumed friend, Susan. British-born past president of the Petaluma Historical Museum, and board member for the non-profit annual Salute to (in honor of the cult movie) American Graffiti, Susan is one the city's annually recognized, official "Good Eggs" and avid collector of Petaluma historic ephemera.

Susan's rambling, Victorian country farm home's interior décor transforms by season and special occasion and during frequent "Ladies of the Long Table" elaborate pot-luck dinner group gatherings and costumed events.

This long table in her large dining room is one of those unique pieces of furniture, unrivalled in tales, could it talk, it would gleefully retell. Hand hewn by British Columbia native, *Reclamation Road* show media personality Michael "Bug" Deakin (Susan's fellow *American Graffiti* classic car parade announcer) of Petaluma-based Heritage Salvage, this is a dining table that serves as a rotating centerpiece for many an impromptu, character-filled, plough-to-platter themed communal feast. It's one of my favorite dining tables to have the pleasure to pull up a pew at.

Susan's knowledge of Petaluma's history and popular culture never ceases to enthrall. Between 1900 and 1920, the city's population doubled from around 3,000 to somewhere in the region of 6,000 resident citizens. "A huge influx of Russian and Ukrainian Jews, Danes, Irish and Swedes had migrated further north from San Francisco following the Great 1906 Earthquake," she informed. "Transplants who found opportunities aplenty for hard working hired hands were able to save enough in as short a time as three to four years to buy a little five-acre chicken farm of their own."

Petaluma's poultry industry had begun in earnest in 1878 when a young inventive Canadian genius, named Lyman C. Byce recognized the region's even climate, sandy soil and extraordinary market potential as ideal for chicken raising. After Byce started manufacturing what were the world's first chicken incubators and brooders, much of Petaluma's industrial efforts rushed to embrace the building and operations of feed mills, commercial hatcheries, box factories, packing facilities, incubator and brooding factories.

By the early 1900s, a flotilla of low wooden chicken sheds studded the valley. Newcomers were greeted by a giant painted chicken, which stood sentry at the entrance to the city. Among the thousands of chicken farmers drawn to the area at that time, were a couple of hundred Eastern European immigrant Jewish families, young socialists and intellectual idealists from the sweatshops of New York's Lower East Side who had heard about the little city of Petaluma and its agricultural opportunities for hardworking young optimists looking to escape the stinking factories of the Big Apple.

"In the early twentieth-century, the Petaluma Syndrome was a psychiatric term coined for urban transplants struggling with the transition from vibrant city life to rural farm existence," wrote Marlene Goldman in a feature on the city in *San Francisco Chronicle's* online SFGate.com. "The syndrome hit a slew of East Coasters who had flocked westward, not for gold, but rather Petaluma's ovular fortunes. Hundreds were inspired by ads placed by Petaluma's egg industry in East Coast newspapers touting the benefits of country living and egg ranching."

By the 1920s, the small city that could, was shipping an astounding 10 million eggs a year at a price of 30 cents a dozen. Mansions continued popping up along leafy, tree-lined streets leading out of town, as egg mania in turn dramatically transformed the city's downtown in the funding of essential improvements such as sewers, schools and paved roads.

A newly-formed Chamber of Commerce had considered its options carefully to attract new and diversified industries to participate in the boom. Marketing man Bert Kerrigan was once again called upon to study the city's dairy and chicken industries and all that had been bringing in the big bucks.

Armed with a reported $50,0000 ad budget said to have rivaled a New York Bloomingdale's campaign of its day, the showman set about his study. After a mere couple of months, the recommendation that he put to the Chamber was to stick to its smarts and embrace what it did best. Bert was given the go-ahead to spend huge amounts of his budget attracting film crews to a series of spectacular, giant egg stunts, adorned with the sorts of glamour girls that Hollywood newsreels loved.

"So started chicken mania. No stunt was too loony or outlandish and all the film crews from the newsreels were invited and lured to Petaluma," said Susan, during one of many of our off-topic chats on the bleachers of Petaluma High School's historic Durst Field (keeping one eye a piece on our respective, then soccer playing sons, of course). I've learned a lot, as I'm sure has any curious conversationalist, about a whole slew of interesting subjects outside of the realm of sports from random bleacher conversations over the years.

On hold for over a half century, Petaluma's annual egg-themed parade would eventually make its reappearance, at first fairly quietly, but over the past three decades, to the delight of street-lined throngs of crowds attracting up to 30,000 strong. Then Downtown Association promoter Alice Forsyth and merchant Linda Buffo revived the 1920s themed parade in 1981, adding Butter to Eggs in homage to the region's stronghold of the dairy industry that had followed a decline in egg ranches and hatcheries.

Despite its appearance in the movies over the years (Hollywood loves a well preserved, authentic American downtown), there is nothing superficial to be found in this particular outpost of the Golden State.

Cafes, bakeries, restaurants and creameries in Petaluma's downtown boutique district lure out-of-towners and locals alike for some of the most honest-to-goodness, award-winning wine country offerings to be found in a highly competitive region.

Authentic, wholesome and more affordable than elsewhere in wine country, locally-sourced menu items in a burgeoning selection of eateries continue to put Petaluma on the map as one of northern California's most up-and-coming real-food dining destinations. Farm stores and tours, cult-micro-breweries and small wine tasting operations offer tastes at the source.

Close your eyes and picture cruising the boulevard in the coming of age movie classic, *American Graffiti*. Co-written and directed by George Lucas in 1973, the film, starring Richard Dreyfuss, Ron Howard and Harrison Ford is arguably the most famous of several major movies putting sweet Petaluma on the silver screen for something other than chickens.

Each May, since 2005, thousands of classic car enthusiasts as well as movie buffs visit from all over the world for the annual Salute to American Graffiti weekend. A wander through this annual nostalgic scene is another essential part of the annual calendar for a southern Sonoma County die-hard.

It was this same landmark downtown locale that took on the look of a Times Square West on a September Sunday in 2012. An historic ticker tape parade welcomed home Petaluma National Little League super team, that made it all the way through to place third in the International Little League World Series, in Williamsport, PA. I stood amongst a crowd every bit as big as that for the Butter and Egg Days Parade, as confetti blew through the familiar iron-front streets. It seemed that day that the rest of the world was entirely sealed off. A community bubble for a couple of hours, captured past, present, future, everything a hometown should be.

Though many of today's back-to-the-land, multi-generational south county farming families have little free time for Hollywood's bright lights and lure (baseball's a different matter), many of these thoroughly entrenched farm families have gradually succumbed to the region's better known attraction, the rush to crush.

Crops of premium, cool-climate winemaking grapes have ever-so-gradually usurped a large portion of the region's half-century, drawn-out demise of costly, traditional dairy farming.

For those who have thus far stood their ground on dairy farms, resisting the call of the grape, the old farming ways of post World War II have taken a back seat in favor of a widespread race to embrace organic farming methods. In doing so, a palpable sense of the area's wholesome, earlier identity has re-emerged. So much so, that a large percentage of America's best new artisan cheese and ice cream, premium milk and cream is being produced in this compact and inter-connected, action-packed and progressive micro-region.

Biodynamic farmers in the area have literally cropped up in swift course with a consecutive wave of demand for the supply of much of the most sought-after, succulent greens, fruits, poultry, fish, oil and meats, not just to savvy locals, but in supply for discerning, top-notch restaurateurs. Chefs clamor for the best of the west, the taste, quality and appeal of the American rustic ideal.

This is not (neighboring) Napa County. Let's get that clear from the outset. Outsiders unfamiliar with the nuances of wine country find it a surprise to learn that Sonoma County is actually three times the size of its manicured "frenemy" next door.

Premium food production amidst the down-to-earth, hardworking and countrified ag-communities of Sonoma County and west Marin is developing at a reassuringly steady pace.

Sweeping Spanish land grants of 1846 created an ideal economic and social center for the area's first pioneers. In 1836, the last of the conquistadores, then 24-year-old General Mariano Vallejo built, with the blood, sweat and tears of hundreds of indigenous people (two years before smallpox wiped most of them out), as well as Mexican colonists in the area, the largest ranch house in California, the still standing Petaluma Adobe. Vallejo had been ordered to settle here to prevent Russian fur trappers making inroads into the area from the coast.

By 1845, the general's 50,000 head of cattle produced an extraordinarily valuable trade commodity known as "California banknotes" — hides that were sold to Yankee traders for $2 a piece. Sadly, since there were no refrigerators in those days, a vast amount of skinned steer meat was left to rot.

The end of the Mexican era was to come abruptly with the 1846 Bear Flag Revolt. Most of Vallejo's land and influence was lost. By the time James Marshall discovered gold on the south fork of the American River, in 1848, hunters and fur trappers had established winter camp on the Petaluma Creek. This would be one of the primary sources of valuable wild game supply (primarily deer, ducks, rabbit) for bagging and shipping to a soon-to-be booming northern California population.

Set, ideally, amongst a grassy topography of hills to the south and west and a valley floor in which the river divides the center of the city in two, Petaluma as a city was founded in 1852 and chartered in 1858. For almost 100 years, this bustling, agricultural city was dependent on its waterway for commercial security.

It was a port of entry for the north counties. Regularly scheduled small boats known as packet boats and schooners (designed for domestic mail, passenger and freight transportation and common in Europe in the eighteenth and nineteenth-centuries before rail) ferried settlers in search of land from San Francisco to Petaluma. Prior to the 1840s, the only visitors to Sonoma County had arrived via rickety stagecoach, traveling north as far as The Geysers (the world's largest geothermal field drawing steam from more than 350 wells, located in the Mayacamas Mountains, some 72 miles north of San Francisco). On their return journeys, the first little boats were laden with lumber, hay, barley, eggs, butter and other farm fresh products destined for a clamoring city market.

Mark Twain lectured in Petaluma in 1866 and likely arrived by the waterway. Author Jack London and his wife Charmian frequented steamboat transportation along this, California's third busiest waterway, in the early 1900s, when traveling between homes in the East Bay and the London's famous Beauty Ranch, in Glen Ellen, in the northeastern part of Sonoma County. The *Red Jacket* was the first steamer to be introduced to this busy waterway back in in the early 1850s. Half a century on, one of my favorite images to envision is that of Charmian London riding her husband's prized black stallion off a steamer at the Petaluma Wharf and solo onwards for some twenty-five or more miles to Glen Ellen. For a Victorian-era woman, this spoke volumes for her as soul mate to one of the world's greatest adventurer writers.

After years of visiting with, getting to know and writing about many of the most innovative and determined personalities who make these parts such a vital, international showcase of understated rural idyll today, it continues to strike me as a place in which its fairly recent history plays an extraordinarily powerful part in the deliberate return to its early focus on being the best of the west when it comes to food.

A writer friend (and fortuitously, my editor) Elaine made her own emboldened move to a small house in the countryside close to Petaluma from New York City, far more recently than I. Elaine shares pearls of unbridled wisdom when we meet for tea. I like to quote to newcomers her delighted revelation that she couldn't toss a stone without it targeting a compelling someone or other in our adoptive hometown.

New York, Austin, Los Angeles, Portland, Seattle, San Francisco and San Jose are celebrated as some of the most fertile breeding grounds of the contemporary American food movement. But it is small, agrarian cities, such as Petaluma, particularly in this part of the country, that are fast becoming renowned as magnets for artists and designers, aesthetes and inspirational, original thinkers, as well as the rapidly multiplying ranks of artisan food, wine and beer producers dedicated to clean, healthy food, healing the land, growing a new generation of young, organic famers and having fun while doing it.

Life in these parts is, on the whole, not about making the most money, but about crafting ethical, sustainable, happy lives in which whole communities, including young families may thrive and are encouraged to stay in the area to raise their own kids.

When I first set foot in what was then not uncommonly considered the more unglamorous northern reach of the Bay Area, at the start of the 1990s, I felt a palpable element of division between the remnants of the region's legendary, laid back hippy contingency, the stauncher ranks of old school, fourth generation largely Italian, Swiss and Portuguese farming families and the upwardly mobile newcomers who'd settled for Sonoma County when neighboring, tony Marin proved too pricey. What has emerged, in the mix, like the phoenix from the ashes of the 2007 recession, is a trending back to more of the region's pioneering values of the mid 1880s.

It's impossible not to absorb this widespread appreciation of the land and its natural resources. A sweeping, mainstreaming acceptance of the farm-to-fork mentality continues to lead to the escalation of small production artisan food, beer and wine making and a dwindling emphasis on big box goods, material excess and large homes.

The America I first experienced in 1990 was very much still of the post World War II industrialized production of the manufactured-foods-mindset. Factory foods were deemed to be the norm.

Thankfully, today, at least in this countrified region, though we might not be ready for a complete return to the primitive life, the general populace does seem to have taken the time to absorb the benefits and bounty of being in step with the seasons and the natural harmony of working towards a locally grown, greener economy, food and otherwise.

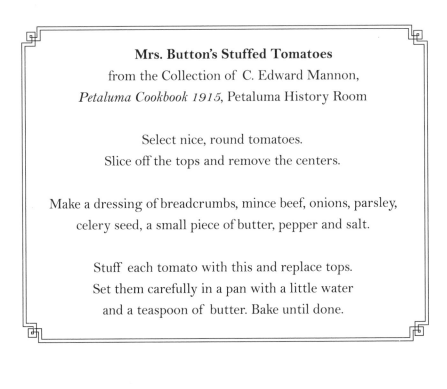

Mrs. Button's Stuffed Tomatoes
from the Collection of C. Edward Mannon,
Petaluma Cookbook 1915, Petaluma History Room

Select nice, round tomatoes.
Slice off the tops and remove the centers.

Make a dressing of breadcrumbs, mince beef, onions, parsley,
celery seed, a small piece of butter, pepper and salt.

Stuff each tomato with this and replace tops.
Set them carefully in a pan with a little water
and a teaspoon of butter. Bake until done.

Fruit is picked in the early morning hours
of an October grape harvest on Rivetti Mountain.

Chapter 5

family tradition

Lively and mercurial, Timo is fully immersed in the real estate business when he's not making wine. Over the past sixteen years, he has knocked on innumerable doors and has proven himself as one of the most consistent at property sales in the region. He is tenacious, a maestro of survival and natural-born salesman. Ironically, the task of finding a nest of our own has never been the slam-dunk, easy deal you'd think it would be, due in large part to our peculiar personal criteria being not so easily quantifiable.

After several years of renting homes in the Bay Area and for the first few years after heading north to Sonoma County, our initial search for settling in a first home of our own in the U.S. might be described as the real estate equivalent of producing a slow food meal. You'd think that a pair of European transplants might likely be stuck on the notion of replicating the notion of home in the old country, in our case, perhaps to snap up the first house with some sort of features that might echo my small market town upbringing in the English countryside. For Timo, a rustic, Italian-style acreage reminiscent of his grandparents' hard-scrabble, hillside subsistence farming would fit the bill.

In making our way as an immigrant family of four (at the time), we'd found ourselves neither under illusions of grandeur nor being over-flush with down-payment funds. Somehow, by sheer will, optimistic spirit and determination, we'd cobbled together a sufficient down payment to buy a home in west Petaluma, when the first two boys were five years old and one. Five years later, a millennium year move from a smallish, but charming, creaky-stair Victorian in the city's heritage home district was designed as more of a practical, lateral move, cost-wise, with the magnificent prospect of a sprawling backyard for now three boys (all under ten) in which to run and roam.

What had been a long search had led us, much to our surprise (as neither had any predisposition toward anything other than an old, character home), to the very last lot in a new home subdivision, nestled on the edge of town. Its seemingly gargantuan, backyard acre hillside reaches up into the fold of an old oak forest in Helen Putnam Regional Park.

The day I looked at the property for the first time, not a single fence line delineated the bare hillside from the forest beyond. It was a suburbanite's dream come true — a mother-of-three-boy's affordable fantasy for tree forts and secret trails, teddy bear picnics, fishing expeditions into the park, scavenger hunts and backyard camp-outs. What I hadn't banked on was the imminent blossoming of the Italian man's previously unspoken dream and physical welfare. Like generations of his ancestors before, he was about to become a backyard grape farmer.

I'd taken the instinctive liberty to reserve the house on the spot, much to the bemusement of the sales lady, who questioned me politely on Timo's status as a well-known real estate agent in town.

"Oh, he'll agree," I'd told her, assuring her that I'd bring him by the next day to confirm.

Together, that evening, after the sales office had closed and construction workers were gone for the day, we hiked the hillside behind the newly framed house, each feeling like we'd won the lottery in terms of a piece of the California landscape to call our own. "We'll plant grapes," the man declared. And that was that. Just a few months later, after testing the soils for the best suitable cool climate varietal, we were the proud owners of 550 young syrah grapevines grafted onto newly planted rootstock.

This large, open hillside reminds Timo of his maternal grandparent's property just outside of a small town named San Michele di Serino, in southern Italy, a half-hour's drive inland toward the city of Avellino from Salerno on the Amalfi coastline. "The freshness of the place, the greenness in spring, hills, space, valleys and vistas ground me in San Michele and here in Sonoma County," he said. We have lived in a lot of places since we have been together, on both continents. An exuberant youth, Timo himself had moved at least once a year, since leaving home at age 16. He'd weathered, hardily, an early, roller-coaster career in the music industry as band manager of Brit-band Curiosity Killed the Cat, in his 20s. It had been a wild and inventive period for him and I think it's fair to say that by the time we wound up in Petaluma, we were both ready to put down roots.

Timo's relationship with winemaking, now twelve years into the annual backyard harvest is a part of his core. The doing of it has been such a constant undertaking that it has taken my writing of this book to prompt our delving deeper to talk to one another about the lifestyle we've developed as one that is its own way, uniquely our own. "Coming to a new country, starting from scratch, gaining a new identity, a new perspective and developing my learned art of winemaking has helped me rediscover my roots," he said. Sitting down and talking for the first time in years on the paradox of Italian character and our journey as immigrants, Timo was finally able to celebrate his background without a sense of displaced shame that had been his from childhood — the first-born son of working class immigrants in what had been a highly class-conscious UK.

Forgive my generalization, but from my vantage point as more of a cool, calm Brit (there are other ways to describe my culture, I know!), the Italian character, on the other hand tends to be widely prone to emotional extremes. Winemaking, I have found, captures the Italian soul in a way that nothing, other than the art of la cucina, could possibly come close to.

If you were to ask me what the primary factor behind our decision to decamp the more rigid social structures of the UK and test the waters of a new world as a young, newly-married cross-cultural couple, I'd tell you the simple truth. My handsome, olive-skinned, outgoing Anglo-Italian husband, with his (still) strong English accent, had sensed a warm and generous welcome in a first, short stay in the USA. It was such a contrast in a culture's positive embrace. Despite the inevitable hard work of starting again from scratch, this, as with many more Italian men before him, called for following his instinct, working tirelessly, slaying a few dragons and flourishing.

Immigrant status times two has eradicated a deep-rooted sense of Timo having not felt he fitted in anywhere, as a child. If we had stayed in the United Kingdom and not made the move to the United States, I am sure that my husband's youthful angst would have dissipated over time, as it did do, I'm happy to report, for the two of his siblings who have remained in the UK. Many of his fellow Anglo-Italian school pals are today some of the most successful self-made business magnates in property development, construction, restaurant and nightclub ownership and in more recent years, political office within and beyond their old Italian neighborhood in the UK. Their parents had escaped the chaos that was post World War II Italy, with its dire lack of raw materials and a booming population. Prior to that time, over 55 percent of Italians lived in the countryside. It was the proud poor who flooded into the UK, Germany and Australia in the 1950s. Had my in-laws stayed in Italy, the odds against their offspring having the chance to spread their wings even farther afield would have been astronomically low.

Of course, many more immigrant groups settled into Great Britain at various intervals in time after the Italians of post World War II. To be an Anglo Italian in the UK today is to be third and fourth generation. Integrated, accepted, celebrated even, for their spirit, their direct approach, sense of family, hardiness of race, but most of all, their food culture. Britain of the post millennium is a vastly different place than it was in Timo's formative years of the 1960s, 1970s and the 1980s.

Finding our place at the foot of a northern California oak forest-topped hill, on the cutting edge of the new American food movement, gave us common ground in which to express ourselves, our strong family values, as Brits, as an Italian and as modern day naturalized Americans with all of our various cultural life experiences in tow. Timo claims that in his 20's, he would have gone to the moon had he had the opportunity. Coming to California in his early 30s, my 20s, falling pregnant with our oldest son, Rocco, a few short months later, was, for both of us, a game changer. Those would be the toughest, most challenging, at the same time, fun and rewarding years. "That's when we had to prove ourselves," Timo recalled. "That's when I knew, for the first time, what my own father had experienced," he said.

It was by the side of Timo's dad, Michele, that the alchemy of winemaking had first come into his life. "I was fifteen or maybe a little younger, the first time I helped my dad to make wine," he recalled.

"Nonno" Michele passed away in October 2013, aged 83. His working life had been spent at the coalface, not literally, but figuratively, working first for London Brickworks hauling thousands of newly baked bricks each day during Britain's major post-war rebuilding, later, with four small children at home, traveling the UK on grueling labor of railroad reconstruction, and, by the time, I came on the scene, he was a factory floor machinist.

For Michele, making wine was a breath of fresh air. He and Italian friends, neighbors, co-workers from his brickwork days pitched in with what would have equated to around a week's wages each to commission a truck load of late harvest Italian (varietal likely unknown, other than whatever red grew rigorously in their home region) wine grapes to be delivered to the front doorstep of small, tidy, inner city, terraced Victorian homes in an immigrant neighborhood, on an unspecified day each September.

Timo's first taste of wine, at his dad's side, was at around five or six years old, each week at the family's formal Sunday lunch with friends, heavily diluted with water or Sprite. Wine at the Italian dinner table was (is) to its culture, the tall glass of ice-cold milk at a Midwestern farming family meal table. Festive occasions called for refills, a weekday dinner, for grown-ups, a glass, or half glass at most. My mother-in-law's grandmother, Francesca, had famously lived well into her hundreds on bread and house wine alone, at least her last decade or more.

Michele and Giuseppina had been under considerable pressure in raising four children in a country whose language they had yet to master. I think it's fair to say, given all the stories I have heard, that this was somewhat of the scenario in which "the inmates were running the asylum" in so far as a bunch of bright, young, first generation Brits (Timo and siblings) at least gave it their best shot to rule the domestic roost by way of translation. Still, the Rivettis ran a tight ship. Four kids in six years were impeccably turned out for school, church and any other rare family outing. Dinner was on the table promptly at six every evening — homemade Italian-style, from scratch, five days a week, plus Sunday lunch and "English food" (bangers and mash, fish and chips...) on Wednesdays.

As soon as the kids were school-aged, my mother-in-law went to work in factories in order to make the family's increasing ends meet. She hurried home each lunch-time to prep that evening's meal. Left-over breaded chicken, veal, cold meats and roasted peppers made their way into Michele's packed lunches for his weekday lunch. Family and friends fondly recalled these tastiest of tributes to Michele, during the celebration of life his offspring organized at the Italian Community Center, after their dad's funeral service at the dedicated Italian/Polish Catholic Church in Peterborough city center.

My mother-in-law's tiny, spotless kitchen in her long-time terraced, London Road home remains at the heart of the family, as it has been for decades. The fabulous food emerging daily from this kitchen is hard to beat at any cost, in any Italian restaurant in the world. Giuseppina, "Nonna" of six, has cooked up a delicious homemade feast in her small kitchen every single day for over half a century.

She drank a cloudy, homemade white wine, very sparingly. But for Michele, the red wine of his region spoke of home, of family, of tradition. The Rivettis returned to Italy to visit both sides of the family on few occasions over the years, voyaging by sea and train at what must have been enormous expense to the family budget. Timo's dad's family, from Caserta, an industrial, commercial, agricultural center, 21 miles from Naples, live more of an urban lifestyle than his mom's family, further out in the countryside. His dad was tickled pink when he first told him over the phone from California that he was planting his own vineyard. "I couldn't wait to get in there and dig and produce," said Timo.

Early recollections of rare childhood visits to his mother's family in southern Italy were of donkeys, pigs, chickens, turkeys, outdoor-only dogs roaming around the humble hillside property. "I watched as my grandfather buried a litter of newborn puppies alive," he recalled. "Later, when I thought that nobody was watching, I went out onto the hillside and uncovered them. I doubt, now, that the family had the means to support so many dogs. They most likely didn't survive."

Michele and Giuseppina's new reality as immigrants in England of the late 1950s was marked with a stark contrast in climate and topography to their sun drenched, though impoverished roots. In search of any sort of work after the war years, one of their toughest adjustments was figuring out how to feed themselves and a growing family in their traditional manner with zero access to the sorts of fresh fruits and vegetables, olive oil, robust meats and cheeses of the southern Italian subsistence culture.

Though food was scarce during the Second World War and afterwards, whatever humble produce was grown (meager livestock or poultry raised) on any small patch of land behind their respective homes, had made for fine ingredients in the humble and delicious regime of peasant culinary fare. Give my mother-in-law a chicken carcass, a potato, some leafy greens and a handful of dried beans and she'll hand you the best bowl of steaming broth you're ever likely to taste.

This was not New York. Or London. At first there wasn't a single Italian storefront to be found anywhere in East Anglia (located some 100 miles north of the capital), despite a flood of immigrants setting up neighborhoods around its provincial industrial city centers. A small truck brought the first of pasta and basic staple deliveries to the region, dropping off and picking up orders, door to door. "It took time to build community," said Timo. After around five years, when it became apparent that the Italians were there to stay, the first of several Italian corner stores opened their doors in the most populated immigrant neighborhoods. "A network of consumers within these Italian hubs organized grape deliveries from Italy, a bit of a stretch given the distance and conditions of transportation, but a way for them to romanticize the culture that they had left," said Timo.

Michele's share of the annual grape delivery was around 50 cases, producing enough juice to fill two to three glass demijohns. Equipment was rudimentary — calling for little more than a hand crusher and a home-constructed press. The process was basic, old school, without any testing, added yeasts or oak. "My dad relied on the natural fermentation process to turn his crushed grapes into wine," said Timo. "Looking back, I'd say that the young wine typically underwent an extremely limited fermentation process in glass containers before bottling and imminent consumption." Dago red, it was widely referred to. Though no one in their circle had developed much of a palate for fine wines, they were well aware of less favorable descriptors for their humble house wines. Paint stripper being the worst, acidic and tart at best. It was, however, authentic alright.

Wine making is a messy endeavor in which it is essential to have a clean, protected open space in which this splashy, colorful ritual unfolds. My father-in-law, Timo and his younger brother, Mick, made for a three-man team under a makeshift shed roof in the back yard. One would handle the grapes, one the hand cranking of the crusher and one to negotiate capturing the juice in a large, plastic container. Old cardboard and newspaper covered the floor. The winemaker wore old overalls, his apprentices a lively assortment of any outgrown clothing.

"There was such a sense of pride in this labor," says Timo. "It was one of the happiest times of the year at our house and the hours spent over a couple of weeks, in a cold, damp climate, crushing, fermenting and racking wine into demijohns encouraged camaraderie and appreciation of carrying out our cultural tradition despite the change in scenery."

Hundreds of years of Rivetti family winemaking tradition, now in turn, takes place in our own garage, today. "It continues to be an active, productive family time," said Timo. "Making wine with my dad has helped me to be myself, to know who I am based on my lineage. It gave me my voice so that I make my own wine today, to the best of my ability given the bountiful advantages of my environment."

Bountiful indeed. We are able to grow our grapes in ideal terroir, tend them throughout the year, prune, pamper and talk to them, monitor conditions and pick at optimum conditions based on sugar content and sophisticated testing techniques. Our grapes are hand carried 100 feet down the hillside into our garage, and crushed within minutes of being plucked from the vine. After fermentation of a week or so, hand pressing with a traditional Italian hand press and nurtured through a secondary fermentation process (called malolactic), each harvest season's young wine is racked into oak barrels and stored in our backyard wine shed for 18 months of premium aging, then bottled on the spot and stored in the coolest part of the house. When Timo and I take a bottle of our Que Syra to a dinner party, this is the farthest the bottle will have traveled from the vine.

Multiple gold medals for winemaking hang in the wine shed, in testament to Timo's fortitude, patience, passion and allegiance with assorted, benevolent wine industry allies who have bailed him out on many an occasion when nature's meddling has messed with ideal conditions. Early and enduring relationships built with wine country friends, confidantes and outstanding professionals such as Bob Peak, partner in Santa Rosa-based The Beverage People (suppliers of all things brewed and fermented) and enology expert Maggie McBride, lab manager extraordinaire of Petaluma-based Scott Laboratories, have saved his skin along with that of the season's vintage, multiple times over the years.

Early rains, noble rot on a crop of late hanging fruit, yellow jacket infestations, all sorts of unforeseen conditions may occur around harvest time in a vineyard, some seasons calling for extraordinary measures in the harvesting and winemaking process.

The crush is made more efficient with the loan of neighbor Steve's stainless steel Italian-made electrical grape crusher/destemmer.

Here's when it starts to get a little hairy for me, as second-in-command by proxy. — Girl Friday of the winemaker's lair. Though grounded and stoic and calm when faced with a good deal of life's potential calamities, for some reason that I'm not completely sure I could explain, I find myself to be not nearly as patient with the heavy-duty, labor intensive process of raising grapes and turning them into wine, as I am, for instance, with raising multiple sons. As with parenting, a lot of things can and sometimes do go wrong in the growing process. The fine art of remaining upbeat and undefeated in the vintner's role does not come as naturally to me as taking three very individual transitions of boy-hood into teenage-hood. I never knew I had it in me, but I've found parenting the best job in the world. Winemaking assistant has been somewhat more of a stretch.

Winemaking has at many times felt like the most outrageous responsibility. There's a magnitude of overwhelm that has a tendency to emerge when walking the burgeoning vines come summertime.

Others see spectacular, leafy vines and perfect bunches of young, green grapes beginning to take shape. Oh, the sheer romance of it all. I see weeks and weeks and hours and hours of intensely focused work — a year and a half of ardent and impassioned nurturing before a drop is to be drank. On the other hand, Timo is invested, culturally, viscerally, in this thing we do that is a full-on grape harvest. One that happens every October, whether I am ready for it or not.

Actually, I should say that this is something that happens *almost* every October, as our 2011 vintage taught us well. Funky weather conditions throughout the growing season that year culminated in unseasonably cool daytime temperatures during what should typically have been the warmest of late Indian summer weeks. A slow, painful ripening process dragged itself out as we watched and tested and waited for the sugar content to rise to even a respectable level. An extreme for September, three inches of precipitation fell from the heavens, much to the added chagrin of rightfully worried winemakers throughout the region. Humidity duly followed the rain when finally the sun decided to make its late appearance.

Yellow jackets arrived in swarms of unbridled enthusiasm from what must have been nothing short of hives from hell (secreted in Helen Putnam Regional Park's oak forest), amidst acre upon acre behind our vines. After so many extremes, grapes had begun to burst open, an invitation no self-respecting yellow jacket in the region could possibly ignore. We'd had plenty of experience with yellow jackets at this time of year, hanging traps throughout the vineyard each late summer and picking before the heat of the day at harvest time. But nothing had prepared us for this onslaught.

The later the grapes hung, as we hoped against hope for a last blast of sunshine to raise the sugar levels (Brix) of our fruit, the more we diced with sudden death for the year's entire vintage. Within a couple of days of reaching a satisfactory sweetness, our entire crop would suffer the indecency of being sucked dry by every last yellowjacket seemingly known to southern Sonoma County. Shriveled skins hung in sad, droopy bunches of depleted grapes, row upon row of destruction and loss.

Timo had invited his Italian conversation dinner group over for a gathering and post-meal tour of the vines. He was nothing short of devastated to walk a group of six or seven wine lovers through this decimated sight. I'm not sure if he explained nature's cruel offering in his native tongue or not, that evening, though I think, in retrospect, probably not. Some disappointments, even though a learning curve, are better dissected in the "keep calm and carry on" pragmatic mother tongue.

There was nothing to do but cut our losses, cover the crusher, move on emotionally and wait out another 12 months to see what the following season would bring.

For every perfect harvest (or maybe two or three in a row, if Mother Nature's feeling benevolent), challenges inevitably arise and are part and parcel of having experience in trials and tribulations of tending a vineyard. Noble Rot being one that most grape growers fear in unpredictable weather patterns in which early rains make a whole load of mischief for the winemaker. If rains are persistent and there's not enough of a break in between showers for the breeze to roll through, moisture is trapped in the clusters of ripened grapes and a fungus known as Noble Rot infects the fruit at the point when dryer weather hits. Grapes begin to shrivel and raisin.

A motley crew of the staunchest grape sorting pals had stepped up during our 2010 harvest to help us in the meticulous task of hand sorting through each and every cluster of our affected crop in order to salvage the premium fruit. This proved, over time, to be one of the finest, multiple Gold Medal winning wines to emerge from our humble hillside set-up. Without the faith and persistence of Timo as increasingly learned winemaker, almost all would have, once again, been lost.

Earlier on in our winemaking endeavors, back in the fall of 2005, he had inadvertently utilized a different type of yeast than had proven successful in his first attempts at fine wine making. The whole thing with fermentation is that it is controlled spoilage and in choosing to make a one hundred percent natural wine, we soon discovered the very real risk of the production of too much nitrogen entering the picture as a bi-product of uncontrolled fermentation.

After a couple of days post-crush, as the grapes began to ferment, the entire house, from the garage up suffered the unfortunate, creeping onset of a stink of rotten eggs. He'd also opted not to add nutrients, hoping a more primitive approach would suffice. The direct result of this was an overwhelming ransacking of the fermenting must by bad bacteria.

Wine making pros suggested we add a couple of copper pennies to the pressed grape juice, as copper sulfate removes hydrogen compounds. This seemingly simple solution had little effect in the remedy of this particularly off-putting stinky egg problem. Despite being in a state of understandable distress, Timo came up with a grand plan to concoct a copper plate contraption that he eventually placed over a plastic barrel. The young, stinky wine was racked and pumped over the copper plate contraption multiple times in order for the liquid to be fanned out and aerated. This did the trick, for a time. After three weeks in the barrel, the smell came back.

Timo, at the time, was taking a wine sensory course at the Santa Rosa Junior College, with Dr. Barry Gump. "We were studying chemical analysis," he recalled. "He had equations on the board. My wine that year was a classic example of one battling the presence of SO2, sulfur dioxide, and just what can go wrong when it presents itself."

Barry's class diagnosed the problem in our garage. Sulfur dioxide, a toxic gas with a pungent, irritating and rotten smell, is, we were relieved to learn, generally treatable by adding up to .06% copper solution to the barrel. One fellow garagiste winemaker, whom we shared equipment with at harvest time, had advised Timo to throw that year's wine away.

"Being the stubborn Italian that I am, of course, I didn't do that," admitted Timo. After adding the copper solution in the correct amount, paired with the undertaking of yet more barrel racking sessions, each lasting three to four hours, over the next couple of months, Timo was eventually able to resolve the rotten egg smell. His 2005 vintage aged beautifully in the barrel and was entered into the Marin County Fair amateur wine competition 18 months later. It won a coveted Double Gold.

Together we have come to the conclusion that it is these tests of determination, muscle and maintenance that differentiate the hobbyist from the serious winemaker, never mind if he or she sells their wine or not.

Picking fruit at the optimum time comes first on the list of stellar winemaking musts and it has taken us over a decade to figure out the full ramifications of precise timing. Second is controlled fermentation to avoid a myriad of pitfalls at a critical stage. Thirdly, careful attention and storage will seal the deal on how well a wine shapes up.

Our 2012 harvest brought with it even more lessons to be learned. Going against our better judgment, we'd picked at least a couple of impatient weeks too soon, rushing Mother Nature to cooperate for a harvest party that would coincide with Timo's October birthday. We'd done this successfully for his 50th birthday, despite my almost having a nervous breakdown at the time. Friends and family were flying in from the UK and elsewhere, staggered, international arrivals that called for reunion pre-birthday celebration-harvest suppers on multiple nights in a row. The boys and I dubbed it "Festa di Antimo" as its seven-day extravaganza brought to mind the sorts of feast weeks Italy is famous for. Though I'm a fan of the lighter, lower alcohol, sweet violet-infused vintage that would emerge from this second, not so well scheduled birthday/harvest pick, the winemaker himself would have much preferred it at its full-bodied potential when left to hang to the extreme. Lesson finally learned —no more birthday/harvest festivals unless the stars are in complete alignment, as they were, so fortunately for his 50th.

Yet more to follow in the ever-expanding learning curve of the winemaker's lot. Anxious to avoid the 2012 rush to crush, we picked the following 2013 crop so very late, two weeks after Timo's dad had passed away. The fruit was spectacular and suffered not a bit from its extended hang time. It was the later season's cold evening temperatures that would creep up on us and impact the fermentation timing of this big, bold, bombshell of a newly-crushed wine. What had shaped up to be the perfect harvest, tons of incredible fruit, perfect weather, had, naturally, fallen by the wayside when news of Nonno Michele's passing had reached us in California. Timo was on the first plane back to the UK, I wasn't far behind him and the grapes, well they were left to hang for our return.

"My mind wasn't at all on that harvest," recalled Timo. Picking in the very last week of October at a record 28 Brix sugar count, this extra hang time would boost alcohol level to a whopping 15% from its standard 12%. Attempts to keep evening temperatures during secondary fermentation to a steady 67 degrees and involving the (not unusual) use of aquarium heaters interfered with the process to the degree that the wine started smelling of burnt rubber. Timo and his winemaking partner of the past couple years, Mike, godsend of an all-round great guy with suitable (East Coast) Italian heritage too, were collectively having a freak out after hours and hours of heavy manual labor in the garage and on the lawn outside of the wine shed, as they continually racked the wine off its lees (the sediment at the bottom). I thought this one might, in fact, be doomed, given this alarming level of despair.

"Looking back," said Timo. "I was in mourning and in a somber mood. It reflected in my winemaking. After re-inoculating for secondary fermentation three times and blending with a little of the 2012 vintage, the wine would finally come around. "I was very lucky to have another great Michael in my life at this time," said Timo. A framed photograph of Nonno Michele oversaw the harvest and winemaking that took place so soon after his passing. The wine is doing wonderfully well in French oak re-cooped barrels as it continues its aging process. Nonno would approve.

I continue to find the annual rush to crush to be as daunting as it is exciting. During the first few years of our winemaking escapades, the boys were young. Consequently, most of our friends also had kids of a similar age group. These friends, as with ourselves, were easily seduced by the prospect of participating in their first few neighborhood grape harvests. Who wouldn't? For about an hour, at least. Or less. Rising at dawn, dressing in layers, donning work boots and traipsing up and down two sets of steep, stone steps, hauling heavily laden tubs of newly plucked grapes is a tremendous fun for the first 15 minutes. Over the years friends have come and gone, many, thankfully, return, but the need for a professional picking crew on hand to do the real heavy picking became apparent fairly early on in our hillside's harvest history. Once in a while the offspring of a volunteer grape harvester surprises everyone by undertaking the task at hand with tenacity, enthusiasm and longevity.

In most cases, kids are not too keen. What they did prove terrific at, in those early, first few years, was a distribution of the wealth — trampling purple skins and perfectly squished grape seeds in a crazy trail throughout the house, up and down stairs, in and out of bedrooms. Everywhere. Madness. I wouldn't say that I am excessively house proud but a few years of fall season grape harvests cured me of any tendency towards heading in the direction of domestic clean freak.

As the grown-ups huddled over hot coffee and freshly baked pastries in the chill morning air of an open garage, various offspring busied themselves constructing circular purple pathways on my carpeting, culminating in an elaborate series of bouncy cushion forts in my family room. In between the myriad tasks of assisting the winemaker, directing first-time enthusiasts and orchestrating a makeshift outdoor hospitality table laden with fresh fruit, coffee and baked goods, indoors, the pantry and refrigerator were being stripped bare by marauding troops of youngsters, gleefully unsupervised for several high-energy hours. Repeat this over a period of years and a pattern begins to emerge. That of yours truly doing her best to keep timing of the grape harvest from leaking out to anyone other than those with a proven track record of actually being useful. That strategy worked well for a couple of years. Facebook arrived and a "Support Your Local Winemaker" t-shirt wearing Timo broadcast an open invitation to the world.

Those who know me well, know that the home winemaking lifestyle and I have a love-hate relationship. If something as unpredictable as a grape harvest happens in your backyard, heck, inside your home for the large part, you'll likely relate. Like any farming endeavor, large or small, it has been a huge responsibility, involving substantial time and energy commitment, not to mention space allocation for equipment, barrels, bottles, cases, corks... During the recession years, when real estate and freelance journalism paired amongst two of the riskiest professions for a self-employed family of five, costs of upkeep for even the most sustainable of vineyard operations, plus all the actual winemaking paraphernalia required each year, took a chunk of our annual household budget and turned it into purple liquid. Lots of it.

Before a person takes the plunge to plant a significant number of grape vines in his or her back yard, real costs of this, even at the hobby level, might well be more than bargained for. Soil analysis, water management (in drought years, we stress our fruit with reduced irrigation), pest management (in our case Marley and Phoebe, brother and sister Manx cats), cover crops, pruning, netting.

These are some of the many essentials in vineyard management. Though the best fruit is sourced from vines that require the least resources, vines left unattended will never bear a quality winemaking crop.

I like to remind Timo that we might have alternatively built up an impressive and substantial wine collection over the past twelve years had we not planted and instead spent weekends wine tasting our way through the region. He nods and smiles. But I know there has been nothing as rewarding as this experience for him. Of course, there is little more satisfying for a wine lover than sampling the fruits of his or her labor, especially when the winemaker has planted the vines, grown and tended and hauled down the hillside, too. I simply can't picture my husband not making wine. Wherever we may roam, if we move from this first vineyard property, which, being world travelers that we are, home base will be somewhere in the heart of southern Sonoma County. A place to make wine. And I will cover the carpets.

I once read that the Napa Valley's Opus One wine mogul, California Hall of Famer and New World wine industry's leading, late philanthropist Robert Mondavi and his Swiss-born second wife, Margrit shared a bottle of wine with dinner each and every night of their 28-year marriage.

The fact that Mr. Mondavi died peacefully at his Yountville home in 2008 at the ripe old age of 94 to me speaks volumes for the couple's shared enjoyment and ritual of dinner with wine. Considering their extraordinary wealth and access to the best of the fertile Napa Valley and its global access and influence, here was a pair that clearly preferred a home-cooked meal for two than a lavish restaurant lifestyle of the rich and famous.

When not at home, painting at a counter top in her kitchen, with a pot of soup on the stove, Margrit Mondavi is reportedly still going strong into her late 80s, traveling the world in her role as a wine ambassador and international woman of taste.

Dinner at my house, whether it is a simple pasta dish, soup, a summer salad from the garden or something, quite frequently, more elaborate, is never a rushed affair. Wine, especially when homemade, enjoyed in moderation, anchors the dinner hour in a wonderfully relaxed way.

Backyard Bounty Zucchini Frittata with Blossoms
8 whole eggs

4 large egg whites

1/2 cup of milk

6 ounces of crumbled ricotta salata

pinch of salt and pepper

1/4 of a chopped, medium sized onion

1 garlic clove, minced

2 teaspoons of fresh oregano

1 tablespoon olive oil

1 1/2 pounds of zucchini, grated

1/4 cup shaved parmesan

6 large zucchini blossoms, trimmed to remove stubs

Preheat broiler. Whisk eggs, egg whites, milk, ricotta salata, salt and pepper. Sauté onion, garlic and oregano in olive oil over medium heat in an ovenproof pan until tender. Pour egg mixture on top of zucchini and continue to cook over medium heat, releasing the edges of the frittata with a spatula. Sprinkle shaved parmesan on top and set blossoms in an even arrangement on top, pressing in lightly. Broil until golden, puffed and set, around four minutes. Cool for a few more minutes. Slide onto a plate to serve warm, in slices with a green salad.

The "garagistes" at work. After fermentation,
the wine press comes into play, along with youthful muscle.

Chapter 6

sixteen tons

When asked what winemaking fundamentally entails, I turn to the venerable center of the universe, here in Northern California Wine Country — the hallowed halls of educational research institution, University of California, Davis. Don't be fooled that the ten following processing operations most common in the making of a red (or white) wine make it a doddle to whip up a premium vintage just like that. Including the wine-making process in this book is intended to give those who might like to know a bit more of what it takes to make a good wine, a new level of respect for anyone who manages to call themselves a pretty decent winemaker.

I've fiddled around with the operational descriptions to form an outline of what seems to work best in my garagiste's lair. Each of these processing operations I have adapted to reflect winemaking as experienced over the past dozen years, first hand. If you'd like to have a go at winemaking yourself, I'd recommend you take a class or two at your nearest college, get to know winemakers in your neighborhood to pool equipment resources, elbow grease and experience and seek out several more detailed winemaking texts. As discussed, a lot of things can go wrong and are quite likely to. It's what you do next that counts.

Step One

Determining sugar and acidity of the grape juice really is the foundation for all good wine. Whether growing your own grapes or sourcing from a neighboring vineyard, a winemaker's first priority pre-harvest is to figure out the direct correlation between the sugar (Brix) present in the fruit and its ability to be turned into wine. The precise right time to harvest depends on the ripeness of the fruit. Winemakers utilize a simple piece of portable equipment called a refractometer.

Step Two

After harvesting the fruit (and this is one of the most time intensive parts of the process, requiring gloves, portable plastic bins, grape shears, friends and a lot of patience), stemming and crushing separates stems from grapes and breaks the skin of the fruit to free the glorious juice. The mixture that forms juice — skins, seeds and pulp is commonly referred to as "must." For this process, you, as winemaker will need a crusher/destemmer machine and sufficient lightweight, easy-to-sanitize, half-ton plastic fermentation bins to contain the flow of must. Sugar content is tested again to insure sufficient levels exist for the fermentation process to kick in. If not, you're going to have to add sugar and you don't want that.

Step Three

Next on the agenda is a winemaker's insurance against the growth of spoilage organisms and nasty oxidation. Precisely calculated quantities of sulfur dioxide SO_2 have been used in winemaking since the golden age of the Roman Empire in the second century BC.

Trust the Romans to have figured out that burning a sulfur candle inside an empty wine vessel would maintain freshness and remove any lingering vinegar smell. Given the advances in New World winemaking, it's comforting to know that many of the basic rules of wine stewardship have remained the same for so many thousands of years.

Managing sulfur dioxide is a complex part of the winemaking process and absolutely essential in the production of a high quality wine. I ask a lot of questions on the subject. I find it particularly complex, not being much of a scientist. Timo patiently explains SO_2 management in brief as: "One of the most important things a winemaker needs to learn." He says that effective management of sulfite levels in his wine protects it during the aging/storage process and is an on-going necessity during the making of a wine. If at any stage of the wine's maturation process, prior to bottling, testing indicates an insufficient level of sulfur dioxide, Timo adds additional SO_2 to protect his wine.

Step Four

Though there is an interest in harnessing "natural"' yeasts amongst a handful of winemakers in this area, by far the most common practice to insure quality control in the fermentation process is to add pure wine yeast starter cultures early on. In its no-nonsense overview of winemaking document, U.C. Davis describes the addition of pure wine yeast starter cultures as: "facilitating a clean, consistent and complete fermentation."

Step Five

Yeast converts sugar to alcohol and carbon dioxide during the fermentation process, which is known as maceration. "Basically, this is the conversion of must and juice that creates the end result. It's a culmination of initial harvest and once you add the yeast, the race begins. Millions of bacteria are fighting each other out," Timo explains. "A good winemaker knows what he or she wants from the grape and this is the stage in which the art of winemaking takes on its own unique form — an individual's signature style in punching down the cap, measuring the temperature and monitoring the chemical outcome of what is, in effect, a controlled spoilage." The grape cap is formed when crushed grape skins riding carbon dioxide bubbles float to the top of the fermentation bin. The cap is punched down into the juice, by foot in olden days, or more typically, today, by plunger, mixing the grape skins and must back into the juice.

A lot of things that go wrong in the winemaking process happen during the fermentation process. Unnatural yeasts have a desire to invade and if they do, they may halt the entire process. Off-odors from a lack of nitrogen in the grapes pose problems for some winemakers. Fertilization of the vines is an essential practice to avoid the sorts of problems arising from there not being enough nitrogen in the fruit to start with. Up to about 70% of a wine's alcohol level will be present by the end of primary fermentation. It's up to the winemaker to decide on the temperature to maintain in the fermentation environment; too warm may speed things up too rapidly, too cool may result in an extra long process and a far less fruity, robust wine. Getting it just right is not just trial and error, a lot depends upon the weather conditions if making wine like we do, in a natural environment.

Step Six

After the must has successfully gone through its initial fermentation process, taking anywhere from five to fourteen days usually, depending upon those varieties of conditions, pressing is the next all-important stage and one that requires the most willing muscle and goodwill clean-up crew! "Hand pressed in a 50 gallon Italian basket press is the most authentic way to make a premium, handcrafted wine," says Timo. Trust me, it's a massive, messy, gloriously purple affair that requires sheets of tarp to protect the ground and most other surfaces in our small garage, each fall. Skins and seeds are now separated from the juice of our red wine. Huge, peculiar looking, compressed cakes of dry skins (like huge purple wheels of cheese) are discarded after extracting the young wine.

This is the stage of harvest season in which I tend to start losing my composure. For the neurotic, I'd say, volunteer a neighbor's garage for home winemaking adventures.

Step Seven

Once this spectacularly hued, freshly-pressed young wine is transferred into an assortment of temporary (in our case plastic) barrels, glass carboys and jugs, next on the list for the winemaker — after a period of secondary fermentation known as malolactic fermentation — is the "racking" of the new wine from its lees. First spoken of in the fourteenth-century, the Middle English term "lees" is defined as the sediment of a liquor (in this case, wine) during fermentation and aging. During the malolactic fermentation, which may take just a few days or as long as a couple of weeks, the hard, green, apple-like malic acid in a young wine undergoes a conversion into softer, butter-like lactic acid. Timo, much to my bewilderment, generally helps this process along by creating an elaborate tent-like structure over his barrels to keep the heat in and to help speed up the typical slowing down of the final 30% of fermentation.

Foam disappears and little bubbles begin to appear on the surface of the wine. Here's where a lot of the myriad bits and pieces of equipment needed for winemaking are essential to have on hand — testing kits, stoppers and airlocks, tubing and siphoning, sanitizers to keep all this paraphernalia spotlessly clean. Airlocks bubble every 30 seconds or so after the malolactic fermentation process has taken hold. Keeping a close eye on this is imperative as every harvest season brings its own unique vintage, varying sugar content and fermentation conditions that call for specific timing and care.

By siphoning the wine off the lees into yet another sanitary container, dead yeast cells are removed before they have a chance to break down in the wine and rot. This must be done every three to six months throughout the wine's aging process, prior to bottling. The more barrels of wine a garagiste has in play, the more of a physical performance this is. The idea of a wine aging in a toasty oak barrel in a darkened cellar for a year-and-a-half is a romantic notion that in reality, requires far more hands-on regular and exhaustive racking than the average wine drinker would imagine.

Step Eight

Adjusting the SO_2 content each and every time the wine is racked is essential in the prevention of spoilage, improving a particular wine's aging potential. Blended wines are popular in today's market, but unless each wine has been controlled in the same, closely monitored conditions, differing levels of sulfur dioxide present in the various components can really screw things up as a blended wine ages.

Step Nine

Another thing the winemaker must always have on hand is a good quantity in reserve of more of each wine than the amount estimated to fill its aging barrel. During the fermentation process, through evaporation, as well as each time the wine is racked, some of its volume is lost. This is rather sweetly, considering the stealth involved, coined as the "Angel's Share."

Topping up during aging is imperative to maintaining proper conditions. Anywhere from one to two gallons per 50 gallons of wine generally require topping up each year. Ignoring or slacking in the topping up process after the angels have had their share, allows for the dastardly chemical reaction of reddish-brown oxidation to take hold and with it, the growth of vinegar bacteria in the vacant air space.

Red wines particularly benefit from aging in oak barrels and take from one to two years depending on the varietal (18 months for syrah), the size and age of the barrel and the style and taste of the individual winemaker.

Cloudiness in a wine may arise from microbial growth or "haze forming" components that are removed by an experienced wine-maker by fining or filtration. It's critical to keep an eye on the clarity of a wine, as well as any off-odors or off-tastes throughout the racking/aging process. Timo spends much of his limited downtime pottering around with wine maintenance.

Step Ten

A wine is ready for bottling when the winemaker says so. After satisfying the various standards for maturity in clarity, stability and style, a final check of the wine's SO_2 content prevents a risk of spoilage after bottling.

Devices that work best for bottling act to minimize aeration and prevent oxidation after the cork goes in. Bottling tools and accessories, sanitized bottles, corks and seals fill the garagiste's lair at this important juncture in the winemaker's calendar. Cleanliness and organization is key. Once a wine has been bottled, the proper storage conditions call for placing cases of bottles upright for the first three to five days, before storing on their side at 55 degrees Fahrenheit for red wine, for at least one year.

Most wines in the Petaluma Gap growing region have been typically run into French oak casks and, in recent years, American oak. Initial use of American oak and oak from several other countries was widely reported to yield less than stellar results — too much flavoring overwhelming the wines.

Further experimentation in the actual preparation of the oak and the way that barrels are constructed, splitting wood and aging it in the French manner, as opposed to sawing it, have fortunately made it much more of a viable option today for American winemakers to bring in more affordable barrels. Limited exposure to oxygen in the air through pores in the wood helps the wine to mature.

"Mighty Oaks from Little Acorns Grow" — so says a fourteenth-century proverb. For Native Americans and European settlers to North America, acorns were the most reliable source of warmth, shelter and food. It's fitting, then, that American oak barrels are becoming such a viable commodity in the aging of our wines.

With a winemaker in the family, summer time never passes without some serious head scratching as to figuring out the barrel situation for oncoming harvest.

With record harvests throughout northern California wine country in 2012, there wasn't a barrel to be had without dropping any less than a shocking sticker price of $1,500 for a brand spanking new beast, be it premium American oak or one from some fancy sounding French cooperage.

It was no secret in the winemaking community that there was some widespread, serious wheeling and dealing going on between wineries big and small in order to accommodate the premium juice from that year.

Small time winemakers such as ourselves were extremely lucky if they managed to score one or two recooped barrels from around the region, or simply had to make do with storing aging wine temporarily in stainless steel vats or old fashioned glass carboys.

Generally one step ahead of the game, Timo had his order in for two beautiful, sustainable and comparatively affordable barrels from a great local resource, ReCoop Barrels, a west county Sebastopol company, just in the nick of time.

The close to quarter-century-old company's director of business operations, Lori Marie Adams spoke to me of being swamped with lines as long as 20 multiple barrel-buyers at a time during record harvests in both 2012 and 13.

"After turning so many customers away during last year's bumper harvest season, it was our main goal to put our locals at the top of the list this year, " said Lori Marie. "I call it eco-socio-economics — taking care of our community." Good thing for Sonoma County wineries and small production winemakers, that companies such as this take care of their neighbors, as thousands of ReCoop's barrel stock are sent out of the state during peak demand.

During 2012's rush to crush record loads of fruit and during the post-harvest production period, many of the region's premium wineries were scrambling to find solutions to excess barrel needs. Several attempts were made to buy back the same barrels sold earlier in the year for recooping. Lori Marie explained how only the best barrels are bought by ReCoop, doubling their useful life while ensuring the ability to produce excellent wine. Barrels that have housed white wines are the most sought after. Once recooped, a barrel sells for under $300.

Nearby Russian River vineyards were ripening at a clip and flatbed trucks were already pulling in on site during my visit in the late summer of 2013. "Harvest in this area is likely to be four weeks early," said Lori Marie. "Once its starts, it's amazing to see the fruit stripped from vines 24/7, until it's all off."

An early pioneer in the business, the small team at Recoop uses specially designed machines to plane the wood with the grain, removing a quarter inch of the interior to ensure that all wine-penetrated wood is removed while maintaining the wood's integrity and allowing the stave to once more contribute its flavor and oxygenation benefits.

Recoop recommends completely filling the barrel with warm, clean, unchlorinated water for one to two days in order to hydrate it. After draining, a recooped barrel must be filled with wine straight away.

Balleto Vineyards, Hanna Winery, Hart's Desire and Sebastiani Vineyards are amongst the many wineries in the region that have adapted to greening their practices and recooping barrels.

Timo and I took the country corners carefully, enjoying the scenery, while driving back from Sebastopol with a couple of barrels in the back of the old Suburban.

Que Syra Syrah Barbecue Sauce
1/2 a white onion, diced
2 garlic cloves, minced
1 jalapeño pepper, diced
1 cup of syrah wine
1/2 cup of ketchup
2 tablespoons of red wine vinegar
1 tablespoon of soy sauce
1/2 teaspoon of cumin

Sauté the onion in olive oil over medium heat. Add garlic and jalapeño after it begins to brown. Cook for another couple of minutes. Deglaze pan with wine. Reduce until only a third of the wine remains. Add ketchup, vinegar, soy sauce and cumin. Stir. Bring to a gradual boil. Remove from heat and store in an airtight container in the fridge for up to five days.

The author's view. Hillside grapevines provide the perfect backdrop for thousands of hours spent chronicling the surrounding area.

Chapter 7

I think
I'll just stay here and drink

Though much of this distinctive area's robust, early wines were made from the contraband root-stock smuggled into the country in rucksacks of European immigrant settlers, poultry and dairy farming undoubtedly served as the primary draw for homesteaders first arriving in the area.

Unimaginable prospects for the humble grape emerged from smuggled stock, as early winery pioneers in the 1870s led by the example of one particularly enterprising exiled Hungarian soldier, named Agaston Haraszthy established the first commercial vineyards in Sonoma and Napa counties.

Agaston, soldier/turned merchant and promoter was the first to launch a full-scale operation in pursuit of "purple gold" by planting vines from many of the greatest European vineyards, in his now historic Buena Vista Estate, located around 15 miles to the east of Petaluma, on the edge of neighboring Sonoma.

Through the subsequent years of the 1800s, resilient Swiss, Portuguese, German, French and Italian first generation families toiled the many thousands of acres of meticulously hand-grafted, fertile vineyard land throughout the county that would be lauded as amongst the finest in the world, today.

While legions of chicken ranches and dairy farms were flourishing around the bustling young riverfront city, pre-prohibition era vineyards in the Petaluma area filled steamer boats with vast quantities of red wines for transportation down river to San Francisco and distribution around the country. A major wine market had, at the same time, opened with expanding hoards of seemingly quenchless 49ers, no doubt taking a fancy to something more refined than firewater, ale and cactus wine served in the booming mines of the Sierras beyond.

According to an intriguing article in the archives of the *Sausalito News* (October 26th, 1907), quality control of waste product from wineries in the area often left a lot to be desired: "Petaluma — Fish feed on wine when the tide is high and become so thoroughly intoxicated that they forget to go home when the waters recede. Being left on the shoals they die by the hundreds until complaint to the board of health has been made. It is alleged that the Apple Vinegar Works and Lachmann Jacobi Winery are responsible, through dumping refuse along the edge of Petaluma." Hard to imagine this sort of unregulated activity these days.

Around the transformative time of the late 1870s, an infestation of the ruthless, root-born aphid Phylloxera was devouring the French wine industry by attacking its heritage vines. Enterprising northern Californians snapped up vineyard land like no tomorrow, in the hopes of capturing the prized French market. By the early 1900s, more than one thousand acres of land had been planted with vines in the Petaluma area alone.

Tragically, just as these industrious early grape growers were gearing up to take advantage of their sudden market share, Prohibition ushered in an immediate stop to operations, ruthlessly grinding a highly promising, regional enterprise to an abrupt and sudden halt. A double blow followed hot on prohibition's heels when a state-side battle with the deadly Phylloxera *(Daktulosphaira vitifoliae)* ransacked the region and brutally wiped out, in one fell swoop, more or less all of Petaluma's largely imported vineyard varietals.

Though a few big name early pioneer wine families elsewhere in the county somehow managed to survive the double whammy of Prohibition and the ruinous Phylloxera plague (largely as shrewd suppliers of the country's sacramental wine stock), an entire century would pass before the sight of neatly planted, vine-studded rows ever-so gradually reemerged along the foggy landmark of Petaluma's south county hills and valleys.

Today, pioneering modern-day members of a decade-strong Petaluma Gap Wine Growers Alliance have rolled up their sleeves once again in the compact little area's production of thousands of tons of premium cool climate grapes now grown in dozens of vineyard properties, ranging in size from backyard plots to hundreds of hillside acres.

Over the past dozen years, vineyards have slowly replaced more than 3,000 acres of redundant dairy, sheep and chicken ranches, dotted throughout this inland approach to the lauded Sonoma Coast region.

Though not yet governed under its own official appellation (in the works), the idiosyncratic Petaluma Gap is rapidly gaining a prized reputation amongst sommeliers and wine connoisseurs for its distinctive, robust and exclusive Rhone Valley-style fruit, highly identifiable within its parent Sonoma Coast Appellation and now widely appreciated for the hearty, cool climate characteristics of some of the world's most outstanding, character-filled pinot noir, chardonnay and syrah grapes.

Hardy stewards of the land, Petaluma Gap growers are tending towards farming sustainably, with organic viticulture increasingly widespread. Wines from Petaluma Gap-grown fruit are high quality and delightfully, appealingly distinctive at the same time, exuding the vital characteristics of the area's distinctive little terroir.

It is interesting to consider, that, according to the Sonoma County Grape Growers Association, one single acre of the typical Sonoma County vineyard averages a hefty 10,000 pounds of grapes. In turn, 10,000 pounds of grapes yields 13.5 barrels, sufficient liquid for 3,985 bottles, or some 15,940 glasses of wine.

Considering that one bottle of wine contains almost two-and-a-half pounds of grapes, you'll have a good idea of how many vines it takes to make even the smallest wine production.

The age-old process of making a good red wine is very similar to that involved in a white wine, except for the fact that a red wine's grape skins remain in contact with the fermenting juice, providing a more intense flavor and color. Fermentation tends to last longer for reds than whites, at a higher temperature.

Much of the character of red wines made from fruit of the Petaluma Gap derives from tannins — chemicals in the grape skin and seeds that play a major role in the aging process.

A deep appreciation of the oft-grueling perils and earnest satisfaction of farming a premium product, has provided me a rare insight into the character of the individuals and families forging ahead with farm to table principals, focusing on a healthier, more wholesome and sustainable future for themselves, their families and community. Though sometimes seen as a romantic alternative to the rat race, small-scale farming takes guts and determination. Beards and boots optional.

And with more award-winning local wines on the market than ever before, competition is getting tough. Growing ranks of innovative winemakers are producing a wealth of intriguing cool climate vintages, each with its own distinctive personality and ubiquitous sense of place.

It's an exciting time for Petaluma-Gap-grown grapes, as each year, a new plethora of complex, rich and expressive wines emerge from this unique geographical area, as yet, tagged on along the cutting edge of the lauded Sonoma Coast appellation.

While the average American wine consumer likely thinks first of France and Italy in terms of the world's winemaking heritage, scientific evidence unearthed in the past few years dates wine being made over 7,000 years ago, during the Neolithic Period, in the Iranian Zagros Mountains.

According to reports in *National Geographic*, U.S. leading scientist Patrick McGovern, a University of Pennsylvania expert on origins of ancient wine continues on with his life's detective work in attempting to prove that the wild Eurasian Vine, found from Spain to Central Asia and the mother of a wide range of varieties of almost all of the world's wine, was actually originated even earlier, in Turkey.

Still, chemical analysis of pottery unearthed in the remote mountainous region of Iran is, until proved otherwise, as old and as good as it gets. The very first wine-tastings were likely slurped (after studiously observing birds as they merrily gorged on fermented fruit) from naturally fermented wild grapes, in animal skins, pouches or crude wooden bowls.

It's a side of Iran that, sadly, we don't hear much about these days. The country was a hotbed of rich food and wine, arts, letters and culture prior to the Islamic Revolution. Its ancient city of Shiraz, city of poets, literature, wine, flowers and gardens, is perfectly positioned at an altitude of 1,600 meters — an enviable, ideal climate and terroir for its historical vineyards and grapes. The city's namesake dense, smoky, spicy red wine (also known as syrah) had been a large part of its heritage for centuries.

In 1999, a study by geneticist Dr. Carole Meredith, head of the Department of Viticulture and Enology at U.C. Davis, revealed a surprising DNA testing as proof that that the shiraz/syrah grape is in fact, a product of two French native grapes, dureza and mondeuse Blanche and likely established not in Shiraz, but in the French Rhone Valley in the latter part of the Roman occupation. How the vine made its way to one of the oldest cities in Persia remains a bit of a mystery.

Having produced excellent wines, amidst a rich tradition of legend, for millennia, the region around Shiraz was celebrated for having hundreds of wineries prior to the 1979 revolution. Despite being punishable today by physical torture, fines and imprisonment, thousands of illegal, underground Iranian winemaking operations are indeed still determinedly at work, as has been the case for so much of the region's history, in the ancient art of wine production of some degree.

I have a special interest in the syrah grape, its leafy vines frame my view as I write. It doesn't matter if I'm sitting at my kitchen table, typing or pondering prose in the family's home office upstairs, syrah, in whatever season of ripening or repose, steals the scene from every window. The closest neighboring vineyard to ours is that of Iranian/American couple, Kamal and Pari Azari, proprietors of the commercial Azari Vineyards and Estate. The Azari family's Persian traditions flourish in its adopted corner of Sonoma County wine country.

Though certainly not underground, it's fitting that theirs is, at least for now, still one of the best-kept secrets in wine country. Tucked into the golden ridgeline of Spring Hill Road to the west of Petaluma heading out to remoter parts of the Sonoma coast, the couple has created a private, peaceful Persian paradise — an oasis of calm and tranquility — a Mediterranean-meets-Sonoma County style compound they've dubbed their "cross-cultural oasis."

Pari, an artist, and Kamal, a political science and Iranian studies researcher, author and PhD, stumbled upon the rambling, romantic property back in 1988, while taking a family drive through the back roads of Sonoma County from their then home in neighboring Marin.

Pinot noir vines planted under the spell of the salty Pacific maritime stream of the Petaluma Gap made most sense for the property, but they naturally, couldn't resist the planting of a secondary crop of cool-climate shiraz, in tribute to Kamal's family's roots.

Where so many growers in the area opt to sell their fruit, the Azaris built their own custom winery down the hill a few hundred feet from their home. An elevator in the Persian-styled house they also built on the property, takes friends down to an additional wine cellar, built into the cool ground beneath the house.

Heavy wooden doors open into an intimate tasting room that leads to the wine cellar. It's a fairy-tale setting for an estate wine owner and certainly for one of Iranian heritage. The opportunity to recreate the harmonious, centuries old culture of the ancient shiraz winegrowing region in a tucked-away corner of northern California was a dream come true for the Azaris. I've enjoyed several of their memorable gatherings, either at table, marveling at Pari's endless parade of home-made Persian cuisine or taste-testing Kamal's more recent addition of brick oven pizzas with a variety of fresh, seasonal toppings, concocted on a Persian patio outside of the tasting room.

The Azari's ripe, dense wines are fruit forward and rich. To taste the Azari's French winemaker Nico Van Keirsbilck's (*San Francisco Chronicle* Wine Competition Gold Medal winning) 2009 Pinot Noir, is to taste the essence of northern California coast — a vibrant fusion of Pacific fog-infused mushrooms, fennel, tea and dark berries.

Kamal and Pari's 2008 Shiraz (which took a coveted silver the same 2013 San Francisco wine awards) is, by contrast, more of a smoky, supple wine with a silky finish and mouth feel, a medley of the same black tea, but with more of a dense violet and currant flavoring. I'm always keen to have a taste of the relatively few Petaluma-made syrah/shiraz wines, enlightened by the nuances of each neighborhood terroir, harvest date and, of course, each individual winemaker's guiding hand. Though located less than a mile as the crow flies from one another, the Azari's 15 acres of estate planted vines and the half-acre plantings in my backyard produce their own defining fruit.

The most enthralling of my visits to the Azari compound marked the celebration of Nowruz, first day of the spring equinox and the beginning of the year in the Persian calendar. Recognized by many civilizations in the Middle East, Central and South Asia (and increasingly here in the United States), the Norwuz tradition dates back 3,000 years. Persian Americans gather with friends and family at this special time for year for spring cleaning, sprucing up their wardrobes, feasting and visiting one another, over a 13-day festive period. Los Angeles boasts the largest Iranian population outside of Iran, with around half a million in its burgeoning community, today, though the San Francisco Bay Area has also proved a natural haven for many of the world's most highly cultured, displaced population.

Pari explained the relevance of her "Haft-Seen" table, beautifully decorated and laden with seven symbolic dishes and other items representing the seven angelic heralds of life-rebirth, health, happiness, prosperity, joy, patience, and beauty. Each item on the ceremonial table starts with the Persian letter "Seen."

The number seven has been sacred in Iran since the ancient times. Main items in "Haft-Seen" dishes are traditionally: *Somagh* (sumac) symbolizing the color of sunrise; *Serkeh* (vinegar) symbolizing age and patience; *Senjed* (dried fruit from lotus tree) symbolizing love; *Samanoo* (sweet pudding) symbolizing affluence; *Sabzeh* (sprouts): symbolizing rebirth; *Sib* (apple) symbolizing health and beauty; *Sir* (garlic) symbolizing medicine.

One of highlights of Nowruz is fire wherein celebrants jump over a bonfire to shake off the darkness of winter and welcome the lightness of spring. In Iran (and parts of Afghanistan and India), it is the custom to light bonfires in front of homes throughout the neighborhood and jump over them as the sun is setting.

This Persian ritual has been passed down since ancient Zoroastrian times. Though I didn't jump the roaring fire-pit on the tasting room patio and I wasn't audience to anyone else at the Azari's Norwuz gathering taking a leap, it was a welcome source of warmth and hospitality on a drizzly Saturday afternoon.

Here in Sonoma County, the Azaris and their guests had little to worry about when lighting festive New Year 2014 flames in a sturdy,

Persian New Year Haft Seen table, Azari Vineyards

protected fire pit on their tasting room patio, as much-awaited rain fell softly to mark the arrival of a lush, green, rustic spring panorama over rolling hills and vines.

Guests enjoyed traditional Norwuz buffet fare, mouthwatering array of delicious Persian dishes, teas and a special Nowruz tasting flight of estate wines.

Kamal and Pari's son, Kaveh, like so many of the region's youngest generation farming family members, has been recently drawn back into the fold, in his case, from a decade in consulting, mostly in Microsoft Technologies. Kaveh traveled all over the world, with stints in New York City, Europe and South America. He left behind the salary, benefits and prestige of a high tech career, but, also, more easily shed, long hours and irrational clients.

Not that running a family-owned winery and vineyard operations is by any means a walk-in-the-woods, yet Kaveh's readiness and realization of the quality of life he was missing out on reflects a growing trend in the region.

Young people are figuring out how to make their family farms more sustainable while at the same time, creating a work environment that offers an opportunity to love what they do. It's a win-win and a receptive food and wine market loves it.

Braised Sonoma County Lamb Shanks
6 trimmed lamb shanks
1/4 cup of olive oil
2 yellow onions, diced
2 celery stalks, diced
4 garlic cloves, minced
2 carrots, diced
1 cup syrah
1 cup diced tomatoes with juice
6 cups beef stock
4 teaspoons of minced rosemary and thyme
2 bay leaves
4 tablespoons of fresh parsley, minced
salt and pepper

Preheat oven to 400° F. Season meat with salt and pepper and brown in oil in a Dutch oven over a fairly high heat for around 10 minutes. Pour off fat and transfer meat to a plate. Add onions, celery, garlic and carrots to the Dutch oven and sauté for around eight minutes. Remove the Dutch oven from heat and add wine. Simmer, over medium-high heat while stirring for five minutes. Add tomatoes, stock, herbs and browned meat and bring to a boil. Cover Dutch oven and bake for two hours until meat falls off the bone. Skim fat off sauce, remove bay leaves and transfer meat to a deep platter. Blend vegetable stock until smooth. Serve over lamb shanks with a sprinkle of parsley.

Slow food aficionados are advised to stay on the beaten track during rainy season at Tara Firma Farms.

Chapter 8

don't fence me in

Nothing much beats being behind the wheel of my rambling old extreme mom mobile, an aging Chevy Suburban whose front license plate advertises my arrival, as I bump along the narrow, winding Spring Hill Road region of west Petaluma and out towards Two Rock, in the direction of the coast.

Chileno Valley Road, Marshall Road, Bodega Avenue, all equally captivating in their neighboring routes through tranquil beauty, but the craggy twists and turns of peaceful Spring Hill have a charm all of their own.

Late summer is pretty much as deserted as any other time of year out west into what is mostly dairy ranch country. Appealing for this very reason, as much for its scenic miles, cyclists cling to the smoother sections of the ramshackle road, content in its lack of motor traffic. I did pass one lone hiker on my most recent foray along Spring Hill Road — trundling along at a meandering foot pace, miles from anywhere and seemingly happy as someone surrounded by rolling pastureland and blue skies should be.

Belladonna lilies (*Amaryllis belladonna* or, rather, Naked Ladies if you prefer!) were in abundance that day, popping up unabashedly in long stretches of country roadsides as well as throughout town. These annual favorites amongst Sonoma County's easy-going gardeners are deer resistant, a prerequisite for survival in these parts.

My reason for this little road trip to Two Rock was to pay a first visit to Deborah Walton's sustainably farmed Canvas Ranch. Despite my many adventures into the rural west, I'd never quite managed to make it out to one of the occasional open days at Deborah and her husband Tim's bucolic ranch, positioned next door to the Coast Guard Training Center, just out of Two Rock, on Tomales Road.

I had first met Deborah back in the days of the *Petaluma Magazine's* quarterly publication editorial meetings, when a lively consortium of Sonoma County writers, photographers and lifestyle leaders in the region's burgeoning artisan food and farming community gathered to brainstorm future feature story ideas.

The husband and wife team were principals of their own advertising agency for two full decades, first in New York and later, in Sonoma County. Thirteen years ago the couple decamped the city of Santa Rosa for the blank canvas (Tim's an artist, so the name Canvas Ranch became doubly appropriate) of rural enterprise on 28 acres of what was, then, sprawling bare land.

The couple share a talent for wholesome positivity, purity of vision and savvy business sense: "We started our farming career with the mindset of not planting a seed or raising an animal without it having already been sold," said Deborah, whose skill and success in this arena earned her added kudos as a notable sustainable farming instructor at the Santa Rosa Junior College.

Luxurious cashmere goats were first on the scene at Canvas Ranch after Deborah discovered their elegant and entertaining merits on a farming fact-finding trip to Chianti, Italy in 2000, sourcing her first kid goats from Montana. It is the fine, soft, downy, winter undercoat of the goat that produces the fiber for cashmere.

Next came a flock of Olde English Babydoll Southdown sheep, a rare sighting in this part of the world. An early road trip to Washington State and Oregon for the first breeding pair proved fruitful indeed. Babydoll Southdown are smaller sheep than the norm, almost half the size of the standard American sheep and were endangered at the time. Deborah's eye for almost-forgotten treasure in the agricultural world has proved fortuitous, not just for her own farming endeavors.

Raised on the Sussex hills in Southern England, the Babydoll Southdown had to deal with a tough topography and had been on their way to becoming extinct due to their lack of edible meat.

It was interesting to learn that though Southdowns were actually the first sheep brought over to the United States; today's standard breed for the meat market bears no resemblance to the original, due to many decades of supersizing within the U.S. industry.

They looked to me like little teddy bears and were fairly timid, though perfectly happy to eat from my hand!

Deborah explained, over steaming mugs of tea at her kitchen table, how she worked closely with breeder Robert Mock in Washington State. Robert keeps the Olde English Babydoll Southdown Registry, maintaining a connection between sheep breeders who market the compact, exclusive Southdowns as nature's lawnmowers, fleece producers as well as good pets.

Over time, Deborah and Tim's flock has led to considerable success and renown for Canvas Ranch as a supplier of now hundreds of sheep leasing and sales for high-end vineyard weed control in wine country, starting with an initial contact at Cal Poly University, on California's central coast.

Next up was to be a lease agreement with the neighbors. Solar fields at the Coast Guard base make the use of pesticides and weed whackers, thankfully, impractical. Low grazing sheep are the ideal solution for keeping solar fields trimmed.

Sheep School in fall and Lamb Camp in spring bring students from around the country to Canvas Ranch, each year.

Five friendly barn cats call Canvas Ranch home. One particularly contented chap escorted Deborah and me around a tour of the property, purring loudly and curling himself around my ankles mid-step, no doubt in appreciation of a random spot of mid-week company.

Big, white and fluffy Maremma (Italian) livestock guardian dogs don't herd. They get along fine not just with sheep and goats, but the cats and chickens too. It's the flock-devastating coyotes and other west country predators that they're naturally wired to keep at bay.

These particular dogs lounge around amongst their flocks by day, but come nighttime, they switch to high protection alert. I learned from Deborah, who is as much a North American expert on the Maremma livestock guardian dog as she is a respected source on the merits of the cashmere goat, babydoll sheep and Ameraucana chicken.

A self-confessed research fanatic, this twinkly-blue-eyed, marketing-guru-turned-resilient-country-chick set out to create a manageable haven of family farming more in the style of what you'd expect to stumble across in the hills of Italy or France rather than the traditional dairy-lands of Sonoma County and west Marin. Regional farmer's market customers and restaurateurs love the Walton's extraordinary produce.

Deborah announced in the summer of 2014 that she was suspending her Canvas Ranch Community Supported Agriculture farm box subscription program. Customers who commit to a CSA agree to a specific delivery or pick up of fresh foods, typically on a weekly or monthly basis. This slow money concept is intended to educate the consumer and subsidize the cost of small-scale farming, providing farmers seed money to plan ahead. Deborah is one of the first in the area to have pulled the plug on an established CSA program, due to what she has outlined in regional media as the "bastardization" of farm boxes by non-sustainable, large operations jumping on the bandwagon and capitalizing on the purest form of the concept. The California State Assembly passed a bill in September 2013 allowing CSAs to source from multiple farms as long as they inform customers where the food comes from. All well and good if you have a penchant for papayas, but not at all what the farm box, in its purest form, was intended to be. And for farmers such as Deborah, now, more than ever, educating the organic consumer is an ongoing challenge.

Visits to Italy inspired Deborah's early days of ranch development from bare land to what is now a haven of dry-farmed beans and heirloom grains (such as rye, golden flax, farro, all now staging a comeback in the gourmet world), organic fruits and veggies and farm fresh eggs.

Clearly, lots of early experimentation was necessary to figure out what grew and what didn't in the soil and microclimate of Canvas Ranch. The farmers worked out simple, though ingenious ways to nurture several crops that had been previously considered a tough call out in Two Rock. It amazed me to hear that the couple manages the entire operation with the help of one full-time farm hand and one farmer's market assistant.

"We don't milk and we don't raise animals for meat," said Deborah. And though the couple keeps busy seven days a week, they still find time for outside interests and running a sweetly compact, on-site, single guest farm cottage retreat, close by professional artist Tim's spacious art studio.

Canvas Ranch is heavily dry farmed, without the use of water for many of its crops, planted in annual rotation. "The flavors are more intense," said Deborah "and we're all going to have to learn to dry farm this way in the future when the water runs out."

One of such dry-farmed beans grown at Canvas Ranch is the delightfully named Petaluma Gold Rush, apparently smuggled over to Sonoma County in the 1880s by early ranch pioneers from Europe. "It's a great bean," said Deborah, handing me a bag full for my next soup-making endeavor. It doesn't have to be soaked overnight, a couple of hours on simmer will do. I love the name and how evocative it is of the rustic nature of the historic Two Rock area.

A few miles east, grass-fed cattle at west Petaluma's Tara Firma Farms were up to their knees in emerald green grazing by early spring — much of it having sprouted at record pace during the heat of balmier days. The odd mud puddle from the last of the rains kept neighboring hogs in the glorious luxury they'd become accustomed to. Contented-looking cows and chickens romped in free-range seasonal splendor on hillsides overlooking rural I Street and San Antonio Road, a local's little trafficked back road short-cut for access on and off busy Highway 101.

As one of the best known biodynamic farms in the region, Tara Firma Farms follows a method of organic farming that was one of the first modern, holistic ecological farming methods to focus on the interrelationships of animals, soil and plants without the use of pesticides or artificial chemicals.

Contemporary though it may sound, biodynamic farming dates back to 1924 and seems to me, perfectly in keeping with the late Victorian farmstead that is the area's most talked-about biodynamic farm of today. Back in the 20s, German philosopher Rudolf Steiner lectured on organic agriculture by request of European farmers with shared concerns of degraded soil conditions and poor quality crops and livestock. No doubt he'd be thrilled to know that biodynamic farming is currently practiced in over 50 countries, integrating local breeds of farm animals with crop cultivation on Steiner's principles of astronomical sowing and planting schedule, organic care of the land and an emphasis on local distribution.

Walking across the courtyard at Tara Firma Farms a couple of days after one of the last major storms of the season, I'd been glad that for once, I'd managed to heed a farmer's sage advice ahead of time in donning a pair of sturdy and fairly sensible walking shoes In lieu of my everyday tendency towards an assorted range of impractical heels. Despite a two decade decoding of my European concept of appropriate footwear/gym-wear aside, I've yet to completely surrender my feet to the American ideal of the leisure shoe. Superficial though this may be to confess, I'm generally fairly spot on with figuring out a person's cultural heritage (at least by continent) from a pair of shoes. Footwear ranks up there with fresh foods in my book. Life's too short for ugly shoes!

Despite this stubborn predilection for inappropriate footwear in an otherwise country life, any idle notions of my tiptoeing through lush meadows of spring wildflowers in kitten heels, barefoot, strappy sandaled or anything other than in substantial wet weather footwear were clearly out of the question for a few more weeks. Rains had remained heavy, persistent and pervasive, creating a haven for the farm's hogs, flocks of clucking chickens and a magnificent head of 43 cattle, grazing contentedly in emerald-hued, hilltop pastures. It was the two-legged inhabitants of Tara Firma Farms, having trudged around in the mud for months, who were clearly most primed for a spot of long-awaited blue skies, sunshine and the promise of a return to dry land underfoot.

Bearing testament to the environmentally-friendly, community supported family-owned farm's wet-weather fashion code, I was encouraged by the sighting of a vignette of three or four pairs of stylish, colorful rain boots neatly lined up against the front door of the farm's compact, tidy HQ. I was surprised to see a light-colored wall-to-wall carpet inside, too, though further more evidence of the sort of classy, woman-run, agri-business enterprise in which it is always appropriate to remove one's muddy footwear before trudging indoors.

Farmer Tara Smith was on the phone as I padded in on a favored pair of beige and white argyle-socks for an informal update on the latest developments up the sleeve of one of the most forward-thinking and glamorous agronomists in the country. "Let's walk," she suggested, off the phone for a few minutes, ready to romp the well-trod tracks and trails of her sustainable empire of rustic acreage straddling the border of Marin County.

"My first and foremost goal was to educate the public in this region on the food system," explained Tara, who launched her farm in 2009 after complaining for years about abysmal standards in the heavily modified U.S. food supply. Both Tara and her husband Craig had spent over 15 years each in the trenches and upper echelons of the long term care industry, with remarkably scant knowledge of the food industry or farming.

"Basically, I've been encouraging people to stay away from anything made with government-owned products, for years. Our country's whole attitude to food still has to change," she said. It's a well-accepted irony that in this country of plenty, where American farmers are noted to be amongst the most productive in the world, it remains tragically ironic that grocery shopping for millions and millions of Americans living on a tight budget more often than not equates to the selection of foods that are the least nutritious. These are foods produced by the big ten percent of corporate factory farmers receiving billions of dollars from past farm bill subsidies.

Shockingly, as a direct result of the Great Recession, the number of Americans on food stamps has been estimated to have risen by more than 80% between the years of 2007 and 2013. The great food debate at this time is that many key agricultural reforms in a controversial new Farm Bill are being neglected. Wasteful subsidies for Big Ag continue, as politicians fight over drastic cuts of the nation's food program. With over 20% of American children living in poverty today, perpetual hunger, in such an otherwise privileged, wealthy country is a shameful reality.

According to the United States Department of Agriculture, the Ag Act of 2014 — Food, Farms and Jobs Bill claims its intentions to: "Create new opportunities for local and regional food systems, and grow the bio-based economy." Yet these lofty declarations of goals to provide a dependable safety net for America's family-owned farmer ranchers and growers are yet to be realized.

It is imperative in today's risky agricultural economy that small family farms be better supported by the USDA to farm well and in turn, provide fresh, healthy, affordable food for their communities.

Tara talked of the cost of our nation having turned a collective blind-eye to the many perils of Big-Ag, the fact that some form of cancer in the U.S. has skyrocketed in the past few years to one in two men and one in three women by age 65, that 72 percent of antibiotic use in the United States is on animals in factory farms, that the average American is 30 percent overweight. We talked about toxic pesticides, greenhouse gases and methane, water use and carbon footprint and the fact that she makes no apologies for the price of her farm's meat (expect to pay around $20 per pound for steak), given the vast sums of our tax money spent on a diabolically outdated food system.

The Farm Bill has cost American tax payers more than $168 billion over the past decade — with billions of dollars a year insuring almost all of the country's corn, soy beans, cotton and wheat crops. An average household pays approximately $500 a year in taxes and inflated food prices as a consequence.

Roland, Tara's boisterous two-year-old Blue Heeler cattle dog, leaped and bounded and barked at our shadows as his statuesque handler released the latch for an enthusiastic family of goats to join our impromptu parade. Our only other audience was a partially liberated female pig, who had by all accounts, ditched the roly-poly girls she'd been relegated to room with outdoors, a little higher up the hill. Tara stopped to scratch the pig's head and take a few minutes to figure out the reason for this unexpected rendezvous. A ranch dude in a cowboy hat approached on a muddy ATV and the two conferred. I watched the goats straddle his vehicle like a mobile mountain, securing a superior vantage point to peruse the lay of the land.

Pig breeds of Gloucester, Old Spot, Berkshire, Hampshire, Duroch and Tamsworth encourage a natural selection of healthy hogs and prevention of an overbreeding of one strain. Tara's pigs feast on a steady supply of grass in the pasture, during winter and spring. In the hot, dry summer months, they munch on kale and chard from the farm gardens, piles of unsalable greens from neighboring sustainable farms, organic, old fruits from Costco, stale bread from area food banks and a small amount of organic, GMO-free grain. It's a waste-not, want-not, pig's world at Tara Firma Farms.

This, as with many similar biodynamic farming operations around the country, is not a farm that worries about a nit-picking, pricey "organic" certification. Intensive, almost crippling, three-year-stipulations by the USDA make the certification prohibitively complicated and costly. Added expenses typically push the loaded price of organic along to the consumer. When sourcing local foods, I've learned it's more vital to look for transparency in farm operations.

I couldn't help but think of this as ideal fodder for a sort of James Herriot's *All Creatures Great and Small* meets San Francisco's bucolic, modern-day north Bay, only this time the main character is a tall, striking, highly articulate, American business woman possessing an enviable blend of good bone structure, steely-eyed approach to bio-dynamic enterprise, blessed common sense, determination and a deeply rooted accountability for the way that we are feeding our families.

I asked her if she'd been keeping a diary, though visions of a smash-hit, long-running TV series were flattened at the quick uptake of the fact that this farmer was quite rightly, despite a penchant for penning poetry, far more focused on the practicalities of the here and now, than responding to the media's wooing. "My blog," Tara said, "serves all sorts of purposes." Book publishers have started to come a' calling, but Tara has yet to find time.

Tara in her early fifties, is a poster girl for a sustainably farmed diet. Spearheading a sustainable, primarily community member-funded farm requires a grueling seven day working week commitment, days and nights and holidays on site, with miniscule windows of rare opportunity for even a partial day away from duties of the modern day farmer, master of crew, creatures, accounting, cutting-edge marketing, special events, education and social media maven.

Her goal is to raise animals in a stress free environment. No stress, no drugs, healthy meat. Public speaking has become a big part of her outreach and education to build increasing momentum and critical face-time with the outside world. As the most high profile spokesperson amongst several neighboring biodynamic farmers in the area, Tara Smith has more, much more in mind.

It's what I came out to the farm to find out. What's next for Tara Firma Farms? Now that her flagship farm is up and running with full-membership and profitability, Tara's primary goal is to filter this accomplishment into a dynamic non-profit organization that trains the country's future farmers in the bio-dynamic methods of Tara Firma Farms and theories of its role models, *Omnivore's Dilemma* author, and leading lights in U.S. food and farming revolution, Michael Pollan and Joel Salatin of Polyface Farms.

Tara explained how she planned to identify, establish and develop four or more training centers around the country to farm and educate with her proven method. Funded by the Tara Firma Farms Institute non-profit that she is currently in the laborious process of setting up, these four envisioned centers would ideally offer a diversity of settings for a variety of topographical conditions and climate.

"What would it take to train farmers from throughout the United States?" she asked, her inimitable sights set on securing future U.S. Farm Bill monies to boost non-profit funds, though continuing community fundraising efforts through farm membership has been supportive of her goals.

As she walked the green hillside terrain, she spoke passionately about how agricultural subsidies had all-but wiped out small family farms, enabled the perils of factory farming, high-fructose corn syrup, fast food, multiple-sodas-a-day and obesity.

Tara had eyed the expiration of the long overdue 2008 Farm Bill with shrewd attention to detail. Given the tight federal budget, there was little doubt in her mind that the old ways of funding outdated programs with vast agricultural subsidies have finally outlived an antiquated system originally developed to ease the after-effects of the first Great Depression.

According to Tara, what the historic Farm Bill did do was to pay the agricultural industry to grow cheap corn and soy, today's pillars of a catastrophic, standard American diet that has slowly infiltrated many westernized world cultures. Though left and right in politics appear largely in agreement that it is finally time for the "slush fund" of the Farm Bill to be given a good, long overdue shake-up, failure to pass a new farm bill until 2014, ironically, did little to ease what is, in the U.S. the world's highest rates of Type 2 Diabetes and obesity.

Introduced in 1933, President Franklin Delano Roosevelt's Agricultural Adjustment Act's commodity crop-specific price and income support programs was set up to assist farmers economically and to help feed the hungry. Legislation was intended to be renewed every five years or so. Though more than sensible at the time, when over 40% of Americans lived in rural areas, by 1995 to 2012 three-quarters of these desperately outdated government subsidies were being allocated to a mere 10% of the country's farms.

On a national scale, increased future funding for farming education might one day provide necessary incentives to attract up to 100,000 new U.S. farmers, a substantial amount and one that the country's Secretary of Agriculture, Tom Vilsak claims the country is in fact, going to need.

Good thing, then, that record numbers of young people under the age of 40 are reportedly being drawn to food culture careers in sustainable farming. If Tara Smith and her contemporaries around the country are heard and we, in turn take to buying more of our foods from local producers, so much more of our vital farmland will be saved from development as generations of future farmers establish their own viable, bio-dynamic enterprises.

At least, Tara explained, the United States must look to leveling the playing field for mid-sized farms to compete with major producers to become competitive in stocking local supermarkets with fresh food options. Never, in two decades of living and raising a family in Sonoma County, has my refrigerator, fruit bowl and pantry been stocked with such a variety and selection of local foods, wine and beer as it is today. It's heartening that this has become the norm for my young adult sons and proof that we're experiencing life in one of the core centers of an American food consumer awareness — one that is, it appears, gradually trickling into the country's mainstream in a far more palpable way than I might have envisaged a few years back.

And yet, reality and the refrigerator for my middle class family, is in vast contrast to many neighboring friends and families struggling to keep a roof over their heads and pay the bills, drowned under fiscal waters of the recession. For those working full-time jobs at minimum wage, around $15,000 a year, to support even the smallest household is nowhere near enough to source a fresh diet of locally produced food. Not unless that food is grown at home. In order for every-day people to put their diet as priority, biodynamic farmers such as Tara must be able to obtain a slice of the Farm Bill pie. Only when pricing is competitive will we see a significant change in the way that the community as a whole, eats.

Farmers of the future growing unsubsidized fruits, veggies and beans will, let us hope, eventually access some of the subsidization pie for their businesses so that the growing of healthy produce becomes far more of a widespread, demanded sustainable option and the recommended five servings of fruit and veggies a day becomes a standard and affordable reality.

Note to backyard chicken-keepers, I learned the pricey, organic chicken feed you've been shelling out for in the store is quite likely to be chock-full of chemical fortifiers. De-shelled and oxidized for as long as six years, even most organic brands of chicken and pig feed reportedly languish in silos both in the U.S. and frequently abroad, requiring substantial nutrient fortification. Basically, if you want your backyard henhouse eggs to be as wholesome as possible, then you have to take as much notice as to what goes into chicken feed as you do your own diet.

"Complete Feed is milled fresh-to-order from grains bought directly from organic Oregon producers," said Tara, explaining how soy-free is so vital, in that soy is not a grain that chickens can safely eat and has to be processed for them to be able to digest.

Similarly, she said, genetically modified corn is best kept out of animal feed, so as not to alter the flora of the digestive lining — protection from invasion of parasitic viral infections. Backyard chicken keepers in the area check in at the farm store at Tara Firma for the all-natural Cascade Feed for their own birds. "Ultimately, it's better for everyone, producing healthier, sweeter meat," said Tara.

Organic grains are only used as a supplement in Tara Firma Farms' chicken feed. Happy hens eat grass, bugs, worms, small rodents and greens from the farm's garden as well as other gardens in the area. Cows at Tara Firma graze on green, green grass. Never grain. In the hottest, driest months, alfalfa is laid down, but only when absolutely necessary.

California voters and lawmakers since decided, starting in 2015, that every single egg sold in the State must come from a hen that is able to stand up, lie down and extend its wings fully without touching another bird. Elsewhere in the country, lawmakers are not so keen on such a law to alleviate some of modern industrial farming's most deplorable conditions, arguing that such rules are in violation of the Constitutional commerce clause. Yet, California as the country's most populated state and biggest market, attracts eggs not only from within its state boundaries but from elsewhere around the country. In order for these new egg-production rules to be non-discriminatory, it's most likely that California will lead the way for a national and possibly global impact on the health and lives of hens and the quality of the eggs we eat.

Humane food producers such as Tara have long-since "pasture raised" chickens, on grass, under the clear, blue sky. Though "Free Range" certification labeling of poultry and eggs is a legal definition for chickens raised with access to the outside, Tara explained how there is no requirement for access to green pasture. Free range, on the other hand, has no legal definition in this country and no common standard. When shopping for chicken meat or eggs at Tara's farm store, I am rest assured that said hen had plenty of exercise, relaxation and low to no stress.

Come holiday season, each year Tara Firma Farms raises around 300 organic turkeys, free-range birds fed on cracked corn, wheat and flax seed, wilting veggies, fruit and field grasses. Though they are amongst the priciest turkeys around, at Thanksgiving, lines of dedicated customers bite the bullet for the best dark meat birds on the organic market.

I took the plunge and purchased one of these $100 plus birds for Christmas dinner. Despite my initial hesitation at the cost of such an undeniably decadent splurge, I had to admit, this extraordinarily, moist, flavorful bird was without a question of doubt, the most hands-down delicious turkey I'd ever tasted.

Of course, an increase in feed costs only adds to the farm's bottom line, though minimizing cost according to quality to the customer is key. "We're not out to gouge the market," said Tara. "Our intent is to be profitable, which we are — there's no need to raise prices any higher than they need to be. Fortunately, given Tara Firma Farms' location at the border of Sonoma County with affluent Marin: "We are barely keeping up with demand," she said.

Grass fed beef from Tara Firma Farms is slaughtered at the North Bay's only facility of its kind. Despite the growing demand for sustainably raised meats in the region, Petaluma-based Rancho Feeding Corporation, a weather beaten, rather shabby-looking long-standing enterprise on the outer edges of town, provided the sole slaughterhouse option for growing ranks of organic and biodynamic beef farmers from Sonoma and Marin Counties until the facility was shuttered, unceremoniously, by the USDA on February 9th, 2014.

Rancho Feeding Corporation was accused of circumventing inspection rules. An international recall of its entire 8.7 million pounds of beef slaughtered in the facility throughout 2013, has led to an investigation by the USDA, the agency's Inspector General and the U.S. Attorney's office. Thus followed a media frenzy with articles in the *New York Times* and the *Washington Post* applauding a "several" million dollar, federally-approved purchase of the facility by Marin Sun Farms, a Point-Reyes-located grass-fed, pasture-raised major player in the sustainable food movement.

Farmers such as Tara from around the region remained in limbo as to the financial outcome of having had all of their (100% untainted) beef from the previous year, recalled. The irony of the ordeal is that it took a scandal of this scale to reinvent the slaughterhouse wheel within the region.

Marin Sun Farms' planned increased range of services has expanded to include cut and wrap and distribution, where in the past, meat producers in the area had to transport slaughtered beef to San Francisco and back. The new owner's model is much changed from the previous. Marin Sun Farms does not deal in the non-producing animal processing market that had previously supplied major fast food companies, focusing on the region's private-label custom meat processing, instead. Ranchers in the area who do sell livestock to the commodity market are left with no alternative but to transport cattle to California's Central Valley. Interesting times indeed.

Around the same time, as fate will so often have it, downtown Petaluma warmly welcomed the much-anticipated return of a traditional neighborhood butcher shop. Thistle Meats, in its smartly outfitted space on Petaluma Boulevard in the heart of restaurant row, hit the ground running in 2014 with its whole animal butchery philosophy, serving the community with locally raised beef, lamb, goat, pork, rabbit and poultry from farms and ranches, owners Molly Best and Lisa Mickley Modica hand pick.

Meanwhile, in March and April of 2014, hot on the heels of the slaughterhouse scandal, four USDA visits were made to Tara Firma Farms in two months. According to Tara, the agents were polite but didn't agree with one another, in terms of variance of how the inspectors interpret regulation: "They had absolutely no idea about rotational grazing, raising animals on pasture, not using drugs or vaccines," the candid farmer informed farm box subscribers. These bastions of American farming who claim to be the gold standard in: "Providing leadership on food, agriculture, natural resources, rural development, nutrition, and related issues based on sound public policy, the best available science, and efficient management," had, according to Tara, never heard of Joel Salatin, or Michael Pollan and his *Omnivore's Dilemma* nor topics about repairing soil through natural means. "I respect what they know but I am shocked about what they don't know," said the farmer.

The next couple of years will be pivotal for Tara Firma Farms as, despite the lack of leadership from the USDA, a fast changing climate in the country's attitude towards farming and food continues to take hold amongst the people. Tara, I feel, is certainly the one to watch both in this region and farther afield.

She is not alone in her ground-breaking farming techniques. More and more of the region's farms have turned over to biodynamic, if not organic over the past few years, diversifying production to meet the modern demands of a growing marketplace for natural, local fruits, vegetables, meats, cheese and dairy products.

Green String Farm is situated across town from Tara Firma Farms, straddling the eastern edge of Petaluma's Old Adobe Road, heading out towards the neighboring city of Sonoma. It's my favorite place in which to pull over when headed out of town for a spot of partly al fresco shopping that, happily, bears no resemblance at all to the supermarket experience.

This is a one-stop farmer's market-style experience that keeps on expanding as the popular farm has added olive and other oils, grains and butter, grass-fed meats into the mix of small mountains of the sorts of heritage fresh fruits and vegetables your grandparents might have grown in a backyard garden.

The folks at Green String Farm and Institute wisely believe that our land is our greatest asset, doing everything they can to nurture and protect it in a method of sustainable farming that not only protects the environment but promotes a self nourishing ecosystem.

What I find refreshing in a frequently complex and confusing world of rules and regulations, is that, also shying away from the "organic" certification minefield, the Green String method instead meets its own extremely high standards for environment care, utilizing compost teas in place of pesticides and chemicals, naturally brewed, water-based formulas that provide nutrients and deter insects. Formulas are made from mixtures of molasses, rock dust, fish emulsion, microbes and a variety of natural ingredients that keep plants content and bugs away.

Sheep graze the farm to keep weeds at bay, and soil amendments incorporate renewable resources such as crushed volcanic rock and oyster shell. Naturally mined sulfur tackles any mildew issues. Bay area sustainable legend and educator, Bobby Cannard co-founded

Green String Farm in 2003, along with partner Fred Cline of Cline Cellars and Jacuzzi Family Vineyards.

In contrast to trail-blazing relative newcomer across town, Tara, as a core member of the sustainable food movement's development in northern California, Bobby has been farming sustainably for over 30 years. As one of the select few early small-production suppliers for his friend Alice Water's groundbreaking California Cuisine across the Bay at Chez Panisse, his 140-acre Green String Farm (50 to 60 acres of which are cultivated) responded to a boom in public demand by adding the farm shop to the east Petaluma property in 2006.

Farm fresh eggs, honey and tomato sauce
on the well-stocked shelves of Green String Farm Store.

This charming, ramshackle store is part of a sensory package in shopping for fruits, produce, fresh milled whole wheat flour, bulk olive oil and grape seed oil, farm fresh eggs, organic butters, cheeses, tomato sauces and grass fed beef direct from the source.

Flavorful, nutritious, fresh and smelling precisely as it's supposed to, outstanding seasonal produce piles up in full glory on sturdy stands under a basic lean-to, with paper bags available for those who forget to bring their own. I've found the quality of fruits and veggies at Green String, as with Tara Firma Farm's produce, to be utterly unbeatable by grocery store standards. Most of it doesn't even much resemble the store-bought stuff.

Simon and Garfunkel and many more albums of old standards are stacked beside a 70s style record player inside this congenial little farm store. It's the sort of place where standing in line at the cash register is more of a pleasure than an inconvenience. Young mothers wander around with baskets as toddlers in sunhats are unable to resist their spot of hand-selecting the ripest, most appealing, best of the day's colorful bounty.

Blue-jeaned, tank-topped, robust farming interns, who tend to be long-haired, tan and if male, mostly bearded, cruise aisles of outdoor produce, emanating an approachable, knowledgeable-vibe garnered from the venerable Green String Institute internship program. Ask one of these earnest young farmers what to do with the season's specific bounty and recipes abound.

Green String Institute was designed by Bobby and Fred in response to Bobby's conviction that factory farms have rampantly corrupted conventional farming methods in order to fit organic certification and ship around the world, the spirit of "organic" agriculture having become redundant.

The Green String Farming method effectively refreshes the more restrictive spirit of "organic" agriculture under a new, broader umbrella, one that better fits the real needs of small production farmers raising grass-fed animals and produce for a local market, with an overall focus on full respect for the environment and the planet.

Bobby teaches the majority of weekday afternoon lessons for these carefully selected interns, leaving no stone unturned on the practical aspects of natural process farming.

This naturally competitive internship program provides valuable hands-on opportunities for future farmers to train in sustainable farming. Eight interns join the Green String family for three-month periods, living, learning, working, and playing on this enterprising acreage.

Fledgling farmers help out in the fields, in the store and on special, seasonal projects, building a breadth of experience from being involved in all aspects of farm work, including site maintenance and carpentry, colorful and entertaining newsletters.

Agronomist Bob Shaffer lectures at the Green String Institute on soil science, enabling interns to build a solid foundation of knowledge on soil-dwelling microbes, compost, minerals and the relationship of plants with soil.

Small business strategies are taught by heads of departments at Cline and Jacuzzi, designed to educate and inform interns interested in launching their own farm or business Receiving a stipend of around $50 each week, Green String Farm interns share a four-bedroom house on the farm, with a provision of the farm's fresh seasonal fruits and veggies, staples such as grains, beans, rice, flour, sugar and a modest supply of eggs, meat and olive oil produced on the property.

Barn dances, pie-eating contests and rousing, rustic gatherings bring the community together at Green String, forging the type of memories the future farmers of enlightened America will come to hold dear as they step out to toil their own soil.

Virginia Silacci's Beef Stew
Hometown Favorite Recipes
by the Petaluma Young Homemakers

3 slices of bacon, cut in small pieces
4 tablespoons of flour
1 teaspoon of salt
1/2 a teaspoon of pepper
2 pounds of boneless beef round, cut into 1-inch cubes
1 large onion, chopped
1 clove of garlic, minced
1 8 ounce can of tomato sauce
beef broth
1 cup of dry red wine
1 bay leaf
pinch of leaf thyme
2 carrots, chopped
2 celery stalks, chopped
2 potatoes, chopped
8 mushrooms, sliced

Cook bacon until crisp. Drain and reserve fat from the bacon
and the bacon itself. Combine flour, salt and pepper in a bowl,
coat beef in flour mixture. Brown beef in bacon fat in a Dutch
oven. Add onion and garlic and cook for three minutes.
Add tomato sauce, broth, wine, bay leaf and thyme.
Cover, lower heat and simmer for one and a half hours.
Add carrots, celery, potatoes and mushrooms, uncover
and cook until meat and vegetables are tender.

Storm clouds carry a promise of precipitation
over rustic Chileno Valley.

Chapter 9

bring on the rain

According to the *Practical Winery and Vineyard Journal:* "How much irrigation water is required to grow quality wine grapes depends upon site, the stage of vine growth, row spacing, size of the vine's canopy, and amount of rainfall occurring during the growing season."

The Petaluma Gap's winegrowing region is characterized by warm days and cool nights. High temperatures occur for a few days each growing season. Most areas have fog lasting late into the morning.

Adobe soils in the area have a heavy clay density holding more water than sandy-type soils, retaining moisture and draining slowly. When the sun does come out, adobe clay soil hardens fast. As most of rainfall takes place during the dormant phase of growing season, supplemental irrigation of vineyard land is often necessary during summer months. The big questions for grape growers in the region are when to start watering and how much?

Researchers at U.C. Davis have spent years studying formulas for vineyard irrigation, given that there are so many variables.

During the final months of my writing this book, California was in seriously bad shape, water wise. Drought conditions were broadly feared to be taking on near-Biblical ramifications on vineyards, dairies, farms and breweries, Sonoma County being one of the thirstiest and subsequently parched counties in the State. When the first, long-hoped-for storms hit in February, ag production's perilous position eased a tad, with more, well-received rainfall in March and April further remedying an otherwise major drought.

While the rest of the country froze its socks off all winter and spring, farmers in this neck of the woods were in a state of panic. For grape growers, 2013 and 2012 had seen back-to-back bumper, record-breaking harvests. With dwindling water resources being held in reserve, waterways and reservoirs still below capacity, growers around the region were getting ready to hold back on water usage, normally tapped into in winter to prevent frost and in summer to irrigate the vines. When vines are not watered in cold snaps, vines are vulnerable to freeze and the crop shrinks dramatically.

A smaller harvest, in the bigger scheme of things, at least from the humble hobby grape grower's perspective, would not be the end of the world. Timo and I were thankful that we were not trying to make a living from our vineyard and wine production, like many of our friends and neighbors with small, estate vineyards. With extra wine in the barrel from the previous two years' harvests, we had little qualm in opting for a drastically water-reduced growing season. Syrah likes a little stress every now and again. A smaller, more intense crop should, we hope, bring about a unique vintage.

But for most farmers in the area, the water shortage crisis proved crippling, cost-wise. Sonoma and Marin counties are coastal counties and they don't benefit from the Sierra snowpack melt-off that is such a boon to the population in the rest of the state. Reliant on rivers and reservoirs, it is imperative as we face future rainfall shortage in the region that we keep on working to conserve and also to improve our rainfall capture methods. Ranchers throughout the area were forced to sell premium dairy cows for beef in the early months of 2014, given the increased costs of laying down purchased hay in dry pastures. Cows drink 35 to 40 gallons of water a day; not surprising then, that the State of California dedicates around 80 percent of its water to agriculture.

When we talk about our water footprint, changing the way we plant and eat makes a significant environmental impact, not just locally, but globally. Think of how much factory-use water we'd save across the country if we were all to plant a few (not too many, just enough for our own use) drought-resistant herbs and veggies with short growing seasons in raised beds or containers in our backyards, on balconies, porches and rooftops. Timo has long insisted on positioning a big, old bucket in our shower during warmer months specifically for the watering of our herb garden, conveniently positioned, a few feet out into the yard from our ground floor master bedroom and bathroom.

Toting buckets of cold shower water around is one thing, but the real biggie on my mind has been further reducing the amount of meat we eat as a family.

Meat-Free-Mondays and Fridays are a fixture at my kitchen table and have been now for years. Oldest son, Rocco, declared himself fully meat-free, not surprisingly, when he made the transition from Santa Rosa Junior College to study at the University of California, Berkeley. He was fortunate to live in the excellent cooperative housing system, with its finely-tuned and sustainably-stocked, 17 industrial-sized kitchens, learning to cook for large groups of hungry young people, vegetarianism being the norm.

Whenever Rocco is home to visit, we focus family meals on a mostly meat-free menu. His choice has helped us expand our repertoire, attitude and awareness towards the amount of meat we do eat. Paying attention to the water crisis before us, educated us further.

New York Times Op Ed contributor, Texas State University Professor of History, James McWilliams, pointed out in an article on the 2014 California drought and slaughterhouse scandal, titled: "Meat Makes the Planet Thirsty," that if we were to change our diet to replace half of the animal products we eat with legumes, nuts and tubers, we'd each reduce our own food-related water footprint by 30 percent. By eating meat-free, that same water footprint would be reduced by almost 60 percent.

Beef, according to the *Journal of Ecosystems*, requires around four million gallons of water per ton of meat produced. If that's not enough to think twice when meal planning for the week, I don't know what is. I think of my mother-in-law's traditional southern Italian, balanced meal rotation. Red meat on a Sunday, fish on Friday and very little meat in between.

I am a red meat eater. I'm not suggesting that we do away with dairy farming or beef production in the region, but awareness of environmental responsibility poses yet another enormous argument for streamlining our reliance on cattle.

Mother Jones Magazine brought it to the nation's attention in early 2014 that seeing as the state of California produces close to half the fruits and veggies grown in the United States, there's no time like drought time, to take notice of how much water it actually takes to grow many of our most popular grocery store picks. Almonds, broccoli, table grapes, lettuce, strawberries, tomatoes and walnuts were each exposed by the magazine as being unexpectedly water intensive. Tuck a tomato plant into your backyard patch of a veggie garden and know that each, individual tomato will suck up over three gallons of water by the time you've plucked one from the vine. Bucket in the shower? It's a start. Do we really need ten tomato plants per season? Better one or two.

Bovine beauties feast on forage and field crops amidst ancient rock formations on the road from Petaluma to Point Reyes.

Sustainable farmers in drought-hit Sonoma and Marin counties have talked openly about their concerns over escalating costs of alfalfa hay as emergency cattle feed, laid down at enormous cost over parched pastures. According to Professor McWilliams in his *NYT* Op-Ed and extensively reported by BBC World, California growers of alfalfa, a crop that guzzles more water than any other in the state, ship this protein rich animal feed, plastic wrapped in vast quantities to China, in effect, exporting somewhere in the region of 100 billion of gallons of the state's precious water resources each year to the Asian, meat-hungry market.

"A hundred billion gallons of water per year is being exported in the form of alfalfa from California," argues Professor Robert Glennon from Arizona College of Law, as quoted on the BBC. This vast amount is enough for a year's supply for a million families.

When rainfall lacks in Sonoma and Marin counties, the deer population dwindles. In turn, coyotes and mountain lions move in closer to the edge of towns. It's not unusual during dry periods to spot a coyote casually drinking from my backyard water fountain, a hundred feet from the kitchen door. A couple of times a year I've spotted a mountain lion on the horizon on the hilltop behind the vines. Deer fencing hasn't kept the coyote out, but as yet, the mountain lions, fortunately for us, have kept their distance.

Further showers in March and April, following those long, dry months of an extended drought, brought relief to all living creatures in the oak forests, hills and valleys around my home. From my writer's desk, with windows open after the storms had saturated the vineyard in my view, a cacophony of bird sounds from dawn until dusk chorused a celebratory sound track to the thirsty earth's relief. Taking time to listen for a good few, uninterrupted minutes, I would detect a frequent orchestral arrangement amongst the blossoming vines, tall, slim cypress archways, our olive orchard and the great oaks beyond.

A chirping, highly communicative quail family would make its morning perambulation, unhampered by our cats, Marley and Phoebe, taking short flight to tightrope walk a favored trellis, half covered with flowering wisteria.

Hummingbirds, in an array of astonishing hues, returned to make their magnificent moves, flapping their wings 200 times a second, hovering over nectar and darting from plant to plant. American crows, western scrub jays, bushtits and titmice, wrens, and western bluebirds make the vineyard and woods behind it home. My favorite late winter visitor is the American robin, larger than his British brother, who never fails to delight me with a sighting when back in the UK. Sparrows, dark-eyed juncos, orioles and finches rediscovered their spot in Eden, after the rains.

Turkey vultures hover on occasion of some small rodent having expired amidst the narrow pathways between the vines. A red-tailed hawk sits sentry on a vine post at dusk. Later, the western screech owl, barn owl and sometimes, master of them all, the great horned owl twit-twoos and swoops in the first darkness of late evening.

Mrs F. H. Atwater's Sunshine Cake
from the Collection of C. Edward Mannon,
Petaluma Cookbook 1915, Petaluma History Room

Take one cup of sugar,
one half cup of butter,
one cup and a half of flour,
one teaspoon of baking powder
and the yolks of five eggs.

Beat whites of eggs until stiff and dry, adding sugar gradually.
Add yolks of eggs (beaten until thick and lemon colored).
Cut and fold in flour mixed and sifted with baking powder.
Bake fifty minutes in greased loaf pan in a moderate oven.

*Symbolizing farm life, historic redwood barns dating back
over a century are dotted around Sonoma and Marin counties.*

Chapter 10

baby's got her blue jeans on

Today's farm-to-fork ethos has sparked a renaissance in an old fraternal order known as The California Grange. Founded in 1892, the Petaluma Grange was disbanded in 1974 and re-born by slow food devotees on both sides of the farm fence, in 2011. Its mission was and still is to foster local farmers' efforts to create a sustainable and resilient food and ag system in the area.

Modern day Petaluma Grange members include ranchers, gardeners, food literacy advocates, organic farmers, local produce purveyors who gather on the fourth Monday of the month at the Petaluma Seed Bank.

As family farms declined throughout the region in the second half of the last century, membership had seriously dwindled by the 1970s. New membership of the organization, which to this day abides by an eclectic range of symbolic Civil-War-era ceremonies, has tended towards a younger, more motivated generation of farming family members and supporters.

The *Pacific Rural Press* reported on April 16th, 1892 on the launch of the first Petaluma Grange, a scenario happily much altered by its equal opportunity 2011 redo. "Wanted," wrote one A.P. Martin, County Deputy, "a score or more of bright, active, sensible farmers' wives, daughters and sweethearts to help organize a Grange in Petaluma... It is preeminently a social order. Do not imagine that it is a dull, uninteresting meeting, where cows, cabbage and cultivation are the only subjects discussed.

"On the contrary, a Grange can be made one of the brightest and most interesting of assemblings. The range of subjects coming before you is almost limitless, embracing the home, the school, care of flowers and fruits and all the diversified industries and amusements peculiar to a farmer's life."

Whereas, back in 1892, the Petaluma Grange instructed the farming community (albeit, predominantly, then, wives, daughters and sweethearts) how to make home "brighter and happier" and "how to lift up your calling," today's Grange members, many of whom are women farmers in their own right, are focused on strengthening their platform for food policy changes and other "meaty" matters.

The *Pacific Rural Press* report is surely one of the most outlandish in terms of patronizing the hard-working women of the land, though its intentions were likely not a whole lot different to the sorts of how-to-improve features that still pop up in today's glossy women's magazines: "The homes on too many farms are like prisons to the female members therein." Harsh? There's more: "By constantly doing the same thing daily and yearly, without change of recreation, in the same old treadmill style, their natures become narrowed and cramped, failing to develop into that full fruition that the creation intended." But wait... "When they meet weekly in the Grange their horizons are broadened, their thoughts are lifted up to the better and nobler things of life."

A life of cows, cabbage, cultivation and more is thankfully not such an isolating affair in today's farming age. Social media and a modern take on groups such as the Grange make for a broader umbrella under which to share the trials, tribulations and future intentions of a life on the land.

Farming today in the region takes on all shapes and forms in a community's interest in growing its own.

Neighbors, Ed and Mindy are homestead fish farmers of sorts — located a 10 minute walk from my house. Their property is one in which a river runs through. Only there is no river in that part of town. If you and I were to wander down the couple's secluded driveway, set back off one of the main roads heading west out of Petaluma and step into the unimposing front yard of their small, meticulously restored farmhouse we'd likely both be fooled that a river does, indeed run through. Not only does the downward path of this narrow, meandering brook make its sweetly melodious way down hill to the fully reconstructed front porch, the illusion, at least on first impression, is that this otherwise modest 1916 home straddles a vast pond beneath its footings.

Ed is a master craftsman, I've seen his careful and creative work on other historic home kitchen and bathroom remodels. Years spent in India lent Ed and Mindy (a hospice nurse) a shared eye for color, an appreciation of time, movement and making something that both matters and will stand the test of age. Both take equal pride in this bubble of intrigue being gently burst as first-time visitors figure out the man-made study of a natural stream.

The tranquil scene of a fully stocked trout pond was, according to the couple, created by osmosis at the foot of their creative babbling brook — that pools under the reconfigured deck-like porch, an invisible barrier sealing the lower framework of the one-story house from the watery reach of this curious aquatic feature.

"While I was digging a French drain around the house to alleviate a seasonal propensity for flooding, I discovered solid rock," said Ed, during my first visit to the property one dewy spring morning.

"After completing the construction of the drain to prevent water pooling under the house, I'd built a trench for what I'd envisioned as a tiny water feature, a nuance to play with under the deck," Ed explained. "My brother-in-law, an avid fly fisherman decided at that point that we must have a rainbow trout pond on the property."

Ed and Mindy had fallen for the place, originally an old milking barn on what had been just under an acre of early dairy land, during an exhaustive house hunt for an affordable country fixer within walking distance to downtown. Having met while living and working in an international community in south east India, the couple had moved to Petaluma from San Francisco.

Shielded from the outside world and passing traffic noise by mature screenings of bushes and fruit trees planted over time by the old home's generations past, the whimsical waterway was carved into a drought-tolerant landscape of native plantings, rocks and contemplative outdoor seating spots.

An obstreperous resident bullfrog made his home in the reeds and grasses around the pond, I was happy to hear him proudly stake his claim to the waterway, apparently quite content with its suitability for his particular needs.

I learned that one dozen Pacific Northwest Fingerling rainbow trout from Mount St. Helens (which is located in Skamania County, Washington) are introduced one at a time in order for them to reach maturity in the lily pond under the porch. This precise amount of fish has been proven, over time to thrive in the filter-pumped, vector-controlled water, swimming around alongside several large, contented goldfish.

Ed and Mindy breakfast and read the Sunday newspapers on their porch. Evenings with wine and cheese are the second best time of day spent keeping one eye on the food source of such a sublime spot. "Whenever a special occasion arises, our favorite 'Blue Trout' French recipe is called for," said Ed. "One single fish is caught, killed, cleaned, seasoned and poached on the spot, all within five minutes. The fish turns a shade of faded blue jeans and is extremely tasty."

Timo and I were invited to experience this in a subsequent gathering at Ed and Mindy's, exactly as he'd described, the following summer. It proved to be one of the most unique, memorable dinners and certainly one of the most satisfying.

Rock excavated for the pond had been utilized elsewhere on Ed and Mindy's property, including the building of a rustic wall to portion off several enchanting garden rooms designed for growing produce, reading, conversation and meditation (under an old and portly curly willow tree).

"We grow figs, prune plums, Asian pears, peaches, apples, persimmons and all sorts of vegetables," said Mindy, a former lay midwife (during her years in India).

Faded wallpaper, outdated kitchen and bathroom fixtures and flooring were torn out of Ed and Mindy's home interior over time to reveal a classic west Petaluma country-meets eco-friendly, light-filled homestead. Subtle hues and salvaged wood reflect the canopy of foliage and water inside this tranquil, much loved home.

I'm not at liberty to reveal Ed and Mindy's secret recipe, but I will share a spot of my own research into the strict traditions of a French Country Blue Trout. In accordance with the French culinary bible *Larousse Gastronomique:* "for this dish, the trout must not only be absolutely fresh but actually alive. Ten minutes before serving, take them out of the water and dispatch on them a blow to the head; empty and clean them."

Following this rather abrupt demise, the newly-deceased trout is plunged into a boiling pot of court bouillon (carrots, sliced onions, bouquet garni, vinegar and wine, that has been simmered for 40 minutes with four liters water) and poached for seven or eight minutes until that magic moment when the skin turns the anticipated vibrant shade of blue.

I would consider a platter of French Country Blue Trout something that is highly unlikely to grace a dinner table in my neck of the woods anywhere other than at Ed and Mindy's place.

Over the county border into nearby coastal west Marin, one of the former vice presidents of the Petaluma Gap Winegrower's Alliance, rancher Mark Pasternak frequently pops up in the national news, despite the remote location of his rambling Devil's Gulch Ranch.

Kim Severson in her *New York Times'* 2010 "Don't Tell the Kids" article on a slow-food rabbit killing seminar that took place behind a restaurant in Brooklyn the previous year outlined how: "Chefs searching for local, fresh rabbit can't always find enough. In the Bay Area, cooks wait for a call from Mark Pasternak of Devil's Gulch Ranch in Marin County. Along with his wife, a rabbit veterinarian named Myriam Kaplan-Pasternak, he raises the most coveted rabbits in northern California.

"They are such believers in the economic and health benefits of eating rabbit," wrote Severson "that they travel regularly to Haiti to teach families to raise rabbits on foraged food."

In fact, the Pasternaks and their two daughters had just arrived in Haiti to further the work of the family's rabbit-farming non-profit foundation, when the devastating 2010 earthquake hit. The Pasternaks had not long returned from aiding survivors of the massive quake when I first visited Devil's Gulch.

Driving by pristine dairy land from Petaluma into west Marin, weaving around a mirror-still, then full-to-the-brim Nicasio reservoir and along an emerald hued, tree-flanked, one-track lane to the Pasternak's enchanted place was a scene of beauty in harsh contrast to thoughts of the ruined island of Haiti.

Higher butterfat levels in the region's sheep milk produce robust and nutty-flavored farmstead cheeses from lush pasture land that has been given a new lease on life by progressive dairy ranchers.

Mark started raising rabbits on his rambling 75-acre ranch in the late 2000s, by special request of his French mother-in-law. After the rabbit enterprise was underway, she'd invited a French chef to dinner at the home of her bearded, maverick winegrower of a son-in-law and word soon spread like proverbial wildfire to Bay Area cooks. It wasn't long before the wiry, unpretentious rancher was selling rabbit to the likes of the Napa Valley's lauded French Laundry.

Devil's Gulch Ranch is what I would call a diversified family farm nestled off the beaten track in the outer depths of the tiny hamlet of Nicasio, within a hair's breadth of the borders of the Petaluma Gap micro region.

The Pasternaks grow Pinot and Gewürztraminer wine grapes and asparagus as well as raising rabbits, pigs, sheep, and quail for retail customers and direct sales to an impressive roll-call of high-quality restaurants. Sustainable, humane agricultural practices and organic farming are important to this most eccentric and passionate of the region's farmers, who is not at all keen on requests to ship rabbits out of state, or anywhere for that matter, adhering rigidly to consideration of the carbon footprint as well as the care of his animals.

It's not only the gastronomic elite who clamor for a taste of Devil's Gulch. A well-established summer day camp at the ranch focuses on connecting children from around the region with nature and farming, so as to give them a chance to experience a range of ranch duties, life skills, campfires, cool waters of a private pond — remote rural life first hand.

Devil's Gulch is surrounded by the natural beauty of the Golden Gate Recreation Area and Samuel P. Taylor State Park. In Mark's words: "Our world is filled with forests, creeks, meadows and abundant wildlife. Children who visit the ranch are able to fully connect with nature through primitive and ancestral crafts and skills, animal care, gardening, free play and other fun outdoor activities."

Many youngsters have passed through the Pasternak's summer program, drinking in the country life and taking with them the principles of healthy and wholesome living.

Should the world's food and water source become more scarce, as predicted, in their lifetime, kids like this will have had a significant head start as they become adults and a generation tasked with finding solutions to feed the world.

Rabbit Stew

From *Household Science in Rural Schools, 1918*

If beef and mutton are not commonly used and
are not readily obtainable, but rabbit can be secured,
substitute rabbit for beef in the stew.
After the rabbit has been thoroughly cleaned,
cut up in eight pieces (four leg and four body pieces),
season, and dredge with flour, brown in the fat,
and proceed as with beef stew.

*Counting sheep. California Artisan Cheese Festival goers
tour Weirauch Farm and Dairy.*

Chapter 11

mammas do(n't) let your babies grow up to be cowgirls

Cowgirl Creamery's Sue Conley likens the area's current artisan cheese making boom to that of the American "Food Revolution" of the 1980s, when a wave of culinary enlightenment made a massive impact on middle class food culture, with restaurants and home cooks enthusiastically refocused on the bounty and benefits of unprocessed whole foods, fresh and hearty flavors.

Though making only a handful of its own (outstanding) cheeses (mind you, 3,000 pounds of it a week), Point Reyes/Petaluma-based Cowgirl Creamery actually represents over 60 prized artisan cheese makers from the best cheese making regions of the U.S. and Europe and is the country's most respected distributor for small-scale, premium quality produce.

California artisan cheese visionaries and pioneers, former D.C. residents, Sue and business partner Peggy Smith (who is newly elected president of the American Cheese Society) were on site to welcome myself and fellow farm tour participants from the annual California Artisan Cheese Festival during a visit to their Petaluma warehouse district production facility. Much to the delight of cheese aficionados, industry insiders, foodies and hobby cheese makers from all over the world, the California Artisan Cheese world's most unassuming celebrity duo spoke about the current renaissance in the state's rapidly expanding farmstead cheese industry. It was fun to be on board for a couple of the Cheese Festival's back road tours and illuminating to see the region through the eyes of visitors.

So rapid is the growth of artisan and farmstead cheese making (the difference being whether or not the cheese maker actually has his or her own dairy herd), experts such as tour leader Ellie Rilla (Community Development Adviser for University of California Agriculture and Natural Resources) predict that over the next decade, 90 to 100% of regional dairies will have converted to organic methods.

"The movement is spreading like wildfire," said tour leader, Ellie, co-author of *Farmstead and Artisan Cheeses, A Guide to Building a Business*. "Animals are more healthy than they have ever been," she said.

Happy, healthy herds make for extraordinary artisan cheeses, as I'd discovered during Farm Tour C, one of four options of a fleet of luxury mini-bus routes stopping in for a closer look at a compelling variety of cheese making operations from area start-ups to established giants in this new American Artisan Cheese Revolution.

"We've been so happy with what's been happening in this region," Sue told her visitors, equally delighted by the successful development of the Petaluma-located Artisan Cheese Festival and its showcasing of the area that Ellie frequently dubbed the "Normandy of the North."

Whilst launching their own original creamery in a converted barn in Point Reyes, back in 1997, the Cowgirls, who met as college friends back east, considered this prime, pristine coastal area with its rich, dairy farming heritage, ideal for the development of a revolutionary allegiance. By looking closely at the past and considering the wave of the future in farming, they had shared more than an early innovator's hunch that they were on the right business and ethical track.

"Families throughout the area were thinking they might have to give up their dairies after generations had ranched in the region," explained Sue. In fact, family-owned dairy operations were closing at an alarming rate at the time that Ellie put on an initial 1998 Artisan Cheese making and organic farming seminar at the Creamery in Point Reyes.

"When we saw them — the dairy farming mainstays in the community, leaders in the agricultural industry such as Straus Family Creamery thinking about doing something as renegade as transitioning to organic practices and cheese making, we knew we were doing something really significant," said Sue.

Twenty eight producers in rural west Marin and southern Sonoma County were artisan cheese making in the region by spring of 2012, up from the original four in existence in the region around the turn of the millennium: "People are being brought back to the farms with enthusiasm," said Sue. By 2014, that number had risen to 30.

Peggy said that early adaptors, Straus and the Giacomini family (Point Reyes Farmstead Cheese Company), were: "Very bold and innovative, everyone was watching them to see what they did."

In fact, it would not be too long before Peggy herself followed suit in a broader leadership role. As president of dynamic Marin Organic, a non-profit organization created in 2001, Peggy and fellow visionaries in the region have completely transformed an initial map of scattered, rural dots that represented isolated farmers and food producers into a thriving, inter-connected local, organic food system.

This vibrant, hyper-local market, nurtured within a rich ecosystem that teems with wildlife, stands as a powerful role model of collaboration and strength in numbers, showing what can happen when a community comes together to promote health and wellness through the protection of its fertile soil, clean water and air.

Certified organic acreage in Marin County has increased from 400 to 20,000 acres since 2001. Thanks to the remarkable work of this literal grass-roots organization, a countywide ban prohibits planting of genetically modified crops; a school lunch program has been developed and carefully implemented to provide 10,000 children each week, locally produced, nutritious foods and farmers markets, stores and restaurants throughout the region are stocked with Marin Organic's products.

Ellie explained how: "the old dairies are being fixed up again as the next generation of farmers are looking at sheep and goats in place of cows. The sky's the limit for sheep and goat milk at this time," she said.

A model example of how intertwined the artisan food movement is throughout the region, former Marketing Director of Cowgirl Creamery, actor, writer and "Dairy Heiress" in her own right — Vivien Straus led that particular tour at the Creamery's Petaluma facility, bringing cheese-loving guests full circle with recounts of her family's west Marin dairy heritage, interspersed with techniques of the Cowgirl's distinctive, rock star status cheese making process.

Fresh organic milk from Straus Family Creamery characterises Cowgirl Creamery's first and ever-popular trademark elegant triple cream cheese, Mt Tam.

Vivien spoke of the history of dairies in and around the west Marin peninsula since the 1850s and of the steep price of quality butter made in the area during the Gold Rush.

Federal milk price setting is an on-going threat to surviving U.S. dairy ranches, as more and more disappear across the country each year. The development of the Marin Agricultural Land Trust in the early 1970s was the initial factor leading to a transition toward organic farming methods that enabled California ranchers to participate in organic milk price setting, which, according to Vivien, has produced a more stable scenario in which small dairy operations are able to thrive.

The first cheese to have been made out at the Cowgirl Creamery in Point Reyes was the company's old-fashioned clabbered cottage variety. More popular today than ever, the freshness of this distinctive cottage cheese makes for an exclusivity that is reserved for the Bay Area market. This, as well as Cowgirl's Wagon Wheel "everyday" cheese, and several other of the Creamery's cult cheeses are still made with Straus milks and creams.

Though it was a decadent move, I did succumb to temptation and grate a pricey portion of the Cowgirl's Wagon Wheel at home, later that day, concocting a sublimely rich and creamy, homemade mac and cheese that would vanish from its baking dish, not to any great surprise, in one, swift, family-sized swoop.

This pit-stop to visit the Cowgirls certainly had set the scene, though it had been the second port-of-call on the day's tour, first being the picturesque Weirauch Farm & Creamery, located across town in the grassy east Petaluma foothills of Sonoma Mountain.

Go ahead and pronounce it "Why-Rock" and hopefully you'll remember to give this husband and wife farmstead cheese maker team with an unusual name your support the next time you're shopping a farmer's market in the area, or online to check out Weirauch Farm & Creamery members' cheese club.

Eighteen months into production at the time of my visit, a selection of lively, ambrosial organic cows' milk cheeses were lined up neatly on a Farmer's Market table on-site, to taste. Ruddy faced from winter and spring months out of doors for much of the day, Carleen and Joel had cut their teeth with year-round production of cows' milk cheeses, bolstering their seasonal sheep product, made in a portable, state-of-the-art cheese making facility converted from a mobile classroom unit. The young couple rent land for their enterprise and so building a permanent structure did not make sense financially.

"We can be gypsies, moving around if we want to," explained Joel. According to Ellie Rilla, such a sound and strong business plan is every bit as critical for newbie cheese makers as the physicality of a steady and secure milk supply source.

Still, the Weirauchs are not beginners in this business of farmstead, artisan cheese making. Carleen grew up in the area, raising backyard animals and Joel learned to make cheese in France. Their sustainable farming practice has garnered them considerable praise from fellow herders who describe the couple as being exceptionally good stewards of the land and a highly conscientious, caring shepherd and shepherdess with 99 newborn lambs joining the flock that spring.

I learned that sheep have a five-month gestation period; so, after a two month birthing season, just five months of milk a year provides for the farm's small-production sheep cheese making operation. Twelve sheep at a time are milked in the farm's portable milking shed (with cooling room). Though the couple used to milk by hand, a small-scale commercial, stainless steel, vacuum pump milking system represented the latest business investment. Since Carleen hand carries milk cans back to the cheese making room, smaller, five-gallon cans are optimal.

The couple raises mixed breed sheep, high milkers mixed with a hardy local breed, primarily East Friesian and Lacaune. Milking season starts in April and the farm's cheese club membership had built to such an extent that it's feasible to expect that small scale new releases might very well be entirely snapped up by an eager, online niche-market following, not unlike the best in boutique winery club-only sales.

A flurry of dollar bills emerged from pockets and backpacks of tour participants during a sampling of the couple's initial cow's milk cheese line in a sense that having wandered the green pastures of this impassioned enterprise and touched the heads of the herd, the artisan cheese world has found its niche at home on the kitchen table.

Oohs and aahs were attributed freely to the farm's soft, spreadable Doubloon, an aged, raw Carabiner, aged Tomme and a raw, washed Peau de Pêche. One little, bottle-fed, baby goat named Eileen followed us around the farm throughout the visit, bleating for Carleen's attention and delighting the crowd with the granting of copious free cuddles. I wouldn't want to be quite so chummy with the rest of the herd, but as we walked amongst the grazing mother goats and litters of suckling kids, these mellow, contented dairy animals didn't so much as bat an eyelid.

The third and final farm visit of the day's tour was an early afternoon foray out west to the small hamlet of Two Rock and into the working organic ranch and Victorian farmhouse home of dairy farmers and Two Rock Valley Raw Goat Cheese makers, Don and Bonnie DeBernardi.

Bonnie is the sort of immaculately groomed, unflustered, traditional farming matriarch of the region who represents a reassuring stereotype of countrified calm and efficiency. There is most definitely a look and a lot of it has to do with a proud European heritage mixed with wrangler style — mom-jeans, sensible shoes, embroidered sweatshirts, coiffed hair and always, those impeccably polished nails.

A hardworking homesteader with a large extended family and a herd of over 50 goats, Bonnie's goat milk dairy enterprise was developed in what had been intended as a tiny sideline in the midst of a long established 700-cow dairy farm.

Goats, some two dozen of whom were born in the two weeks prior to our visit (four that very morning), were clearly Bonnie's pride and joy, second only to the couple's own grown kids and grandkids. In fact, she told us that it was as a surprise for her two now teenage grandsons that Bonnie had first introduced a couple of Nubian goats into the fold.

With 37 gallons of fresh, organic goat milk currently on hand every other day, Bonnie's first generation Swiss-Italian husband steps into his secondary farming role to employ the same style of traditional cheese making skills as his relatives still do in the Alps.

Thirty-seven milking goats, one well-contained billy goat, plus all of the newborns tottering around the barn stalls were a hit with the visiting cheese lovers. Bonnie was clearly the one in charge of the herd and its twice-daily milking routine (she'd stopped milking by hand when the brood of does reached into the 30s). Four goats are milked at a time, with regular shifts undertaken by the couple's grandsons. "I do it my way," she explained, staunchly waiting six months longer than typical to breed her goats — after they have reach 18 months old.

Likely the "littlest cheese factory in Calfornia" — Don DeBernardi's utilitarian cheese making facility consists, quite delightfully, of nothing more than several meticulously converted shipping containers, positioned between the house and the milking shed.

After modifying his dairy to organic and expanding his dairy cow herd several years ago, the call of cheese making came at a time in his career when Don found he quite enjoyed the gentle, calming routine of shutting himself away in his self-designed, small-scale cheese making unit, radio on.

And after a couple years of experimenting with different styles, Don's organic goat cheese is proving popular with specialty cheese lovers around the region looking to taste the distinctive terroir amidst more than a passing nod to the cheesemaker's heritage.

Tour members from Chicago, New York and cities across the country were easily charmed by the couple's warm and genuine hospitality. A generous sampling of raw, young and aged goat cheeses, paired with an assortment of local wines, were served indoors at the DeBernardi's extended dining table in the comfort of a large, airy and traditional farm kitchen.

I have attended tastings all over wine country for a wide variety of foods and wines, yet not so often inside the private confines of the proprietor's own home. I munched away at the selection of cheeses while perusing the family's framed photo collection, proudly displayed on a dresser by the table. Hospitality of this type is rarely forgotten. The DeBernardis' opening their home to a small group of strangers represented the true spirit of farmstead cheesemaking. This won't always be the case, as popularity calls. A Two Rock Valley Goat Cheese tasting room is in the cards for the future, positioned for maximum impact a little ways across busy Valley Ford Road, linking Petaluma to the coast. In the meantime, Don continues to sell his cheeses in person at farmer's markets throughout the region, directly to customers across the country by phone order, as well as in the Petaluma Market and several specialty cheese departments in stores around Sonoma County.

Day two of the following year's Artisan Cheese Festival and my assignment for Saturday morning was *Seminar 16 - A Tale of Two Milksheds: Tasting the Cheese of Tomales Bay and Driftless (Wisconsin) with the Cowgirls.*

The Cowgirl's Peggy and Sue might well be considered as artisan cheese world elite, but you'd be hard pushed to find a more grounded, generous and inspiring pair of über-professionals within the local and global cheese scene. Though accessible and approachable, fun-loving and friendly, they are two of the busiest people in the American cheese movement. And so the chance to take a pew and hear them speak in person, once again was simply too good to miss.

I hadn't bargained on cheese pairing with wines at 9:30 am in the morning, I do try, at least, to pace myself, but over an hour and a half, the spread that was set before me, proved the perfect breakfast treat. Pinot noir and reisling poured were sourced from Handley Cellars, in Sonoma County's Anderson Valley.

When tasting cheese with wine, these are two varietals that tend to compliment cheese best. Syrah is good too, but I've learned that it's a good rule of thumb stay away from most other red wines for cheese pairings, unless fortified, such as port or sherry.

Now I know not to confuse the taste buds with too much, too soon. When reaching for a slice of cheese to sample with a wine, take a bite of cheese first, let it reach the roof and sides of your mouth before eating. Try the wine, then try both together. Crackers and breads will add to the dynamics, try cheese first without.

The Cowgirls taste cheese once a week, a whole lot of cheese. Yet still they prove the most impassioned in their on-going, generous educating of cheese aficionados, new cheese makers and industry experts alike.

Seminar-goers from around the country had arrived with their assemblage of Starbucks coffee-cups-to-go, but I didn't spot too much sipping of that more typical Saturday morning standard, given the mouthwatering and rarified display set before each attendee. When in wine country and all that.

We learned that when cheese makers operate in a cluster, most naturally collaborate with one another and with other farm goods producers in the area, consolidating shipping and sharing tables at farmers markets. By calling attention to their region, cheese makers are sharing the personality, geography and flavor uniqueness of their part of the world.

By tasting and studying eight artisan cheeses (a Bohemian Blue Cheese from Hidden Springs in the Driftless Milkshed was a bonus taste at the end) from two different regions of the United States, the Milkshed concept within cheese making emerges as similar to that of varying wine appellations.

I discovered that it simply would not be possible to replicate an artisan cheese recipe by making the same style cheese in Driftless, Wisconsin as one that had been aged naturally in the Pacific oceanic environment of Point Reyes. Terroir with cheese is every bit as evident as in wine. The grasses and spring flowers in pasture, the air the cows, goat and sheep breathe, the individual cheese maker's personal technique in touch of hand.

I'm more than familiar with Cowgirl Creamery cheeses, living and shopping in the heart of California artisan cheese country, so while I enjoyed the pairing experience of the company's outstanding Tomales Bay Milkshed cheeses, it was a lot of fun and super informative to compare and contrast local cheeses with the selections sourced from Driftless.

Inspired by her Basque sheepherding and cheesemaking heritage, Marcia Barinaga and her husband Corey Goodman purchased a farm in the rolling hills overlooking Tomales Bay. After attending a cheesemaking class in Vermont, they accompanied Marcia's dad on a trip to the Pyrenees to learn the secrets of cheesemaking from the Basque masters. At their ranch in west Marin, sheep graze on pasture all year long. Marcia's first cheese is Baserri, named for the ancient tile-roof huts in the Pyrenees where herders make milk in the traditional ways. Aged for at least 60 days and available only seasonally, Baserri was a rich, nutty stand-out amongst this extraordinary flight of cheeses.

A California Cheese Trail app is available for download for free for anyone interested in touring the Sonoma/Marin Cheese Trail. Visit http://cheesetrail.org/.

Despite the buzz surrounding the new artisan cheese makers of Sonoma and Marin Counties, a deep-rooted history long since exists in the area in the handmade cheese arena. Grandfather of the artisan cheese producers is historic Marin French Cheese Company. Locally known simply as The Cheese Factory and a much loved institution in the region for its picnic and barbecue spots and a picturesque duck pond (set amongst the pastures of west Marin), this iconic little factory sits along Red Hill Road on the way to Point Reyes National Seashore, around nine miles west of Petaluma.

The Marin French Cheese Company began its production of artisan cheese in this location in 1865. It is, in fact, the oldest continually operating cheese factory in the United States. Jefferson A. Thompson had launched a California fresh cheese concept during the thriving Gold Rush era's demanding San Francisco market. Returning miners flooded the city, creating a mad dash for a limited production of dairy goods. Thompson made a mint in marketing his fresh, California-made cheese to saloons where it was typically served on the bar as a welcomed alternative to the standard pickled egg.

Thompson's cheeses were delivered by horse-drawn wagon to the Petaluma River and shipped down stream by *The Steamer Gold* paddleboat across the bay to Yerba Buena, as San Francisco was initially called. By the 1900s, his family had expanded operations, having now organized the business as one of California's first small corporations. The Marin French Cheese Company maintained its early farmstead roots for the first 65 years by milking herds on its 700 acre land and expanding its selection of fresh cheeses with the addition of Neufchatel and cream cheese, also beginning to produce cheeses designed for aging. Over a century of artisan-crafted Camembert, Brie, Schloss and other soft-ripened cheeses represents the original California production of European styled soft-ripened cheese. Whenever I'm driving out on the back roads into Marin County or out to the National Seashore in Point Reyes, I make a habit of stopping into the Cheese Factory store to see whatever bargain of the day will bring my way in its still hugely popular soft cheese production.

During the Great Depression, Marin French Cheese made a monumental decision to support struggling dairy farming neighbors by focusing all of its efforts on local cheese production. All of the company's milk was purchased from its neighbors, from that point, as it still is, to this day.

Though some 40 different styles and varieties of Marin French cheese are sold around the world today, it is reassuring to know that each cheese is hand made, slowly, one cheese at a time, aged in the original hand-dug cellar, weighed and packaged by hand as it has been for the past century and a half.

Visit the Marin French Cheese Company on any given day and it's clear that the country's oldest cheese making operation remains in capable hands. The company's heritage and authenticity have been fastidiously maintained by its most recent owner, since 2011, a family-owned French company, Rians (also known as Laiteries H. Triballat), proprietor of 15 creameries in the U.S. and Europe, including Sonoma County's artisan goat cheese producer, Laura Chenel's Chevre.

The 146-year-old Marin French Cheese Company was sold to its French competitors after the death of its last owner, Jim Boyce, a major player in international cheese competitions.

Journeymen/apprentice traditions have been passed down through generations of cheesemakers since 1865, with many dedicated Marin and Sonoma County-based employees having worked on location at the production facility for decades.

One of the more unorthodox routes into the region's artisan cheese making farmstead micro-industry has to be attributed to a particularly ambitious, organic food-loving husband and wife team, entrepreneurs, former software engineer, Craig Ramini and his architect wife and business partner, Audrey Hitchcock.

Though not uncommon for Silicon Valley dynamos to take an about turn when finding solace and beauty away from technology proves a significant pull, Craig and Audrey took an extra leap of faith in launching California's first buffalo milk mozzarella production enterprise, located seemingly in the middle of nowhere, a little ways inland from the coastal farming community of Tomales.

It was a warm Saturday afternoon in June that I visited the Ramini's remote ranch, having allowed myself leisurely time for a meandering drive through farm lanes lined with the region's familiar groves of towering, 200 feet eucalyptus trees, their waxy blue leaves and grayish bark that shreds off, amidst bushes of flowering elderflower, in thin, lengthy strips.

Eucalyptus are most prevalent in the area, planted along rural roads from the 1870s through the 1950s, when it was finally deduced that these beautiful native Australian and Tasmanian behemoths were not the transplanted treasure trove that over 100 ardent promoters starting in the Gold Rush, thought they would be. Second only in size to California's native Coastal Sequoia, the largely Blue Gum varietal of the eucalyptus was intended for use in the state's booming early fuel and timber industries, as well as for medicinal use, oils and pulp.

Deforestation was a big issue from the mid 1800s; in fact, a Tree Culture Act in 1868 encouraged people in the area to plant trees, especially as windbreaks and by roadsides. The Blue Gum spreads if water is present, especially in foggy climates, hence the eucalyptus thriving in these parts despite proving not to be the best for lumber and, as non-native, changing the landscape forever. Controversial cutting down of well-traveled groves remains a major issue.

If the Australian eucalyptus has made itself at home, so much so, that roadside groves have been a part of the picture since the first homesteaders planted windbreaks around their Victorian farmhouses, it appears that the spectacle of river buffalo (native to Egypt and Italy) and swamp buffalo (South East Asia) grazing beyond the Blue Gum groves is not as much an oddity as it would first appear.

There was no question that I'd arrived at the ranch when I drove past a fenced pasture of stocky black, horned water buffalo going about their grass eating business oblivious to the rare passer by.

I had arranged to tag along on a tour with a group of motorcycle-riding tech-workers from the South Bay, several well-heeled older women in expensive western hats (who had been deep in conversation over a sophisticated al-fresco, pre-tour picnic they'd whipped out of a large basket, complete with tablecloth and small, glass wine tumblers) and a pleasant couple from the East Bay. The motorcyclists were all men, one of whom was reunited with his girlfriend, who had driven her compact, two-seater sports car separately from the South Bay, following what she'd described as a "little fall" off her own motorcycle in her driveway the week before.

It transpired that the two, back-pack-toting twenty-year-old French girls who managed to unfold limbs, sleeping bags and tents from within the tiny vehicle, she had picked up hitchhiking on the other side of the Golden Gate Bridge. Alex and Marion were headed north, past Eureka to Arcata on the Humboldt Bay. The glamorous woman with the biker guys offered to pay for them to take the tour. I'm quite sure the lure of a sample taste of freshly made buffalo mozzarella with sliced tomatoes, basil and olive oil had much to do with the two foreign students agreeing on such a substantial (and random) detour.

Audrey, dressed in ripped Levi's, western boots, a fetching, blue gingham shirt and pony-tailed blonde hair neatly tucked under prerequisite straw western hat, was our host for the afternoon. She and Craig, she explained, take it in turns to milk the herd, though the actual cheesemaking, the formation of perfectly soft, exquisite tasting balls of buffalo mozzarella that sell between $30 and $35 a pound requires both of their rapt attention.

After turning 50, her husband, Audrey said, had a mid-life revelation that the happiest times in his life had been spent with large animals in the picture. With an Italian sister-in-law on the east coast asking why it wasn't possible to buy American-made, true buffalo mozzarella in this modern day and age, a light bulb turned on and an entrepreneurial project like no other in the area, was born.

The Raminis met in their native Boston area, in the early 1990s. He had a "big, slobbery" St. Bernard dog and she had cats. Audrey's masters in architecture matched Craig's economics degree in terms of career success, though Craig spent the last 18 years of his business life in stockbroking to Silicon Valley start-ups searching for what was missing.

"Making a boat load of money was not the point," said a refreshingly candid Audrey. "For 18 years, he'd say: 'I have another great idea' but nothing that I would ever say 'Oh yes' to."

In 2009 they both lost their jobs. "Craig took a year to read, think, read and read some more. He turned our dining room into his thought room," she said. He filled out hundreds of little post-it notes. After a year, the five most important post-it notes narrowed the field.

"He wanted to be an entrepreneur," said Audrey. "He wanted to work outdoors, with animals, in a unique way, involving food." It was the couple's sister-in-law's passing observation at having to purchase imported buffalo mozzarella that caused the connection to occur. That was in August. By November, the Raminis owned five water buffalo.

Water buffalo are not related to the bison (American buffalo). In addition to being notoriously stubborn and suspicious, water buffalo have extremely low lactation levels, producing a mere 15 pounds of milk (less than two gallons) each day in comparison to the average dairy cow, with a general production in excess of three times that daily volume.

Ramini buffalo curd that must be closely watched for seven hours, as per the recipe of Sicilian mozzarella masters has, over its four year fledgling enterprise, ignited a whirlwind of interest in the food world, whetting the appetite of A-List chefs throughout the Bay Area and beyond, as they clamor to visit this emboldened micro-creamery on its 25-acre endeavor.

Craig and Audrey purchased their first five pregnant female water buffalos from a dairy in southern California, followed by four more sourced from a breeder in Arkansas. Since Mad Cow disease, buffalo, as with cattle in general, are not imported into the country from anywhere overseas, making the sourcing of water buffalo a big challenge. "A few other U.S. companies were dispanding," said Audrey. "We talked them into breeding for us, first."

Buffalo are best viewed from behind the fence at Ramini Ranch.

Now going into its fifth year, the couple's highly technical and sensitive farmstead operation, much of which was trial and error to start off with, is mostly in the black, depending upon how much milk production on any given week. Two or three more lactating females would tip the scale to where the Raminis would like production to be.

Audrey explained how they are strictly "no kill" (except for seriously wounded or the rare mercy situation), with seven male buffalo having been born on the ranch and adopted out to "forever homes" on private ranches, sanctuaries and occasionally, a zoo. Seeing as buffalo live for up to 25 years, I decided not to opt to adopt one for the backyard, but I did offer to find the French girls a place to stay in Petaluma, for that night.

"For us, it is about passion, perfectionism and growing the business slowly, doing it right and doing it the way that no one would imagine you would attempt to do it," said Audrey. She explained how she had continued to work full time in architecture for the first year or so, to pay the bills.

"It was a huge learning curve," she said. From the basics of ranching, to putting up electric fences on an historic former dairy ranch that they rent, to the milking of beasts who would really rather not be milked at all, life on the Ramini Ranch took years to settle into the much-sought-after agri-business it is today. "It took time to go out into the pasture and embrace them and get them to milk," said Audrey, regaling a wide-eyed crowd with tales of frequently having been thrown six feet when she inadvertently ducked her head to pick up a pail.

An expanding herd of 40 buffalo was mostly born on the ranch. Audrey referred to the likes of lactating mothers, Madonna, Shirley, Sinead, Cyndi and Bette as her "girls" and their offspring as her "babies." Dusty is the superstar of the lactating moms. She has been known to produce up to 30 pounds of milk a day. Her son, Sting, is set to stay on the ranch as a stud bull given his mother's disposition and milking prowess. "There's a hierarchy between them," said Audrey, recounting how the mothers and their babies are highly protective and motivated by their post-milking reunions in pasture. "They have genuine emotions," she said.

I was pleased to see the milking shed had been given a complete, shining overhaul from what Audrey had described as a formerly derelict state, with lots of natural light. The couple had studied the methods of Temple Grandin, livestock consultant, author, autistic activist and doctor of animal science at Colorado State University. They carefully constructed metal stalls in the milking shed for the buffalo to enter, comfortably and with dignity, in single file. Daily porcelain white milk production typically ranges between nine and 18 pounds each per top-producing free range, grass fed female.

During the ranch's first year of milk production, back in 2012, the Raminis realized a mere 500 pounds of their prized, new, fist-sized buffalo mozzarella balls. By the end of 2013, production had risen to some 3,500 pounds. It took an entire year to finesse the actual cheesemaking to a fine art. "We threw away cheese for 12 months," said Audrey, who designed the compact creamery, attached to the milking shed, on the other side of a breezeway, to suit their specific needs and capacity. "At first it was tough and leathery." Though Craig had studied mozzarella cheesemaking in Canada and Australia, the nuances and subtleties of their own herd makes the cheese unique. "Milk is only released when the buffalo has a release of oxytocin, the trust hormone," explained Audrey. Nurturing her animals is paramount. "Allowing them to feel safe and comfortable is our top priority," she said. "We're not doing this to get rich."

The gregarious blonde lady who had passed the two French girls into my care persisted with a line of questioning as to the organic status of the ranch. Audrey had outlined, as with many other sustainable farming enterprises featured in these pages, how organic status is so often prohibitive to the success of small-scale new operations. "If it comes to saving the life of a baby buffalo through the use of antibiotics, then, yes, I will take that option," she said.

As for the use of highly nutritious oats as a protein treat in the milking shed, the heavily Botox enhanced (among, I'd wager a guess, several more beautifying procedures) visitor continued to impart her position on genetically modified grains, berating the startled rancher with a tirade on oats. Audrey didn't seem to think the oats were genetically modified, but wasn't fully prepared for the onslaught.

I took note and studied up on my return. According to *Modern Farmer*, oats are the least likely U.S. grain to be genetically modifed given that there simply has not been enough money in research messing with the humble, hearty, awesome-for-us-and-buffalo, oat. This struck me as such a paradox. Finding myself amidst a heated debate with a woman who looked alarmingly like one of the women in the well-heeled picnic group, who'd clearly made considerable investment in the altering and improving of her physical appearance, taking almighty umbrage to the use of oats. I'm not saying you shouldn't shoot Botox into your brows and, at the same time, eat a healthy diet, but let's get our facts right before we go on the war field on farm tours, especially if we look like we've rolled off another production line of sorts.

Discerning chefs who know their patrons will pay for a silky smooth slice of such a delicacy receive deliveries in covered plastic bins. In Petaluma, Rosso's Pizzeria and Mozzarella Bar takes weekly delivery of Ramini buffalo products, as do several upmarket grocery stores and pizzeria's in Marin County and San Francisco.

I left Ramini Ranch a little late for a dinner date back in Petaluma. The two French girls were about to get to know Sonoma County for an unanticipated 24-hour stint. I didn't get to leave with anything for the teenagers at home other than some rather unexpected company! My son, Luc, home from university for the summer, rallied a fluent French-speaking childhood friend for showing our guests around town.

Rivetti Mountain Ricotta
1 gallon whole milk
1 quart buttermilk (or buffalo milk if you can get it)
cheesecloth

Heat milk and buttermilk in a non-reactive saucepan to 180°F., stirring as it heats. Remove from heat and leave to sit for half an hour while curds form.

Line a colander with a couple of layers of cheesecloth set over a bowl and pour in the mixture. Allow the ricotta to drain a couple of hours. Store in the refrigerator in an airtight container.

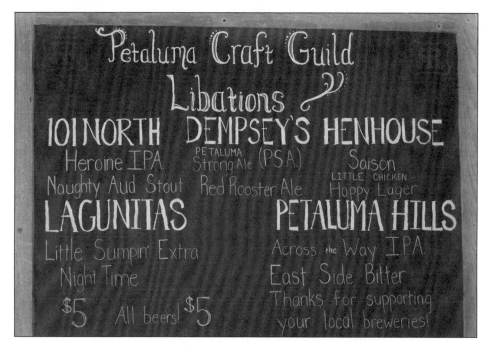

Petaluma Craft Guild, formed in the fall of 2013, is a collection of brewers, distillers and vintners who believe in sustainability through community involvement and philanthropy.

Chapter 12

big ole brew

Anyone thinking that the artisan beverage industry here at the gateway to wine country is focused solely on the grape, would be barking up the wrong vine. Craft and micro beer making has increased in astonishing leaps and bounds over the past few years. It has made an indelible impact within a community that feels a common ownership in the level of integrity ingrained in local ale production.

Still escalating, over 2,100 breweries currently operate across the country. This number now exceeds the historic benchmark set back in the beer-swilling days of America circa 1887. A rise in the popularity of ale is clearly not a phenomenon peculiar to beer-loving Petaluma.

The National Brewers Association released figures halfway through the still dawdling economy of 2012 indicating that dollar sales of craft beer had increased by a significant 14% of that year, a direct response to a buoyant demand from beer-passionate Americans.

On the subject of which of these breweries make it to cult status: "What makes breweries special is the communities they create," tweeted Petaluma's HenHouse Brewing Company's Collin McDonnell. "If you look at the most successful small breweries, they know this."

Collin and partners Shane Goepel and Scott Goyne took lead since launching their uncompromisingly small operation in 2011, from neighboring beer-making, indie-guru golden boys over at Lagunitas Brewery (located in an unassuming, hidden gem of a locale in the midst of an industrial park in east Petaluma).

Cranking out two beers in barrels at a time in what Collin, Shane and Scott describe as: "the work of our hands, hearts and brains in a fearless pursuit of crafting new and interesting kinds of delicious," their unadulterated love of beer, people and Petaluma fosters a strong sense of community in a increasingly competitive market, distinguishing craft beers from big brewery products by appealing to local bars, restaurants, taverns and independently owned and operated markets.

Collin smartly believes that: "the best breweries make great beer and great community. What's better than good beer and good people?" I have to agree.

Thomas Keller of Napa Valley's The French Laundry, did not take long to convince. According to HenHouse's staff, owners and head kettle scrubbing trio, a sample of their handcrafted Oyster Stout, made with crushed oyster shells and transported by a friend of a friend, made it over to the discerning folks at The French Laundry within the brewery's first year of production.

In keeping with The French Laundry's daily quest to piqué sensation of the palate through a series of surprising taste experiences, HenHouse's curious stout hit the mark to make it onto this most auspicious of Bay Area, if not iconic American restaurant's menu.

Holding down their day jobs, Collin, Shane and Scott made their first oatmeal stout home brew several years ago. "We've all been involved with the production and fermentation of delicious products for many years," Shane explained at a private, pre-launch of party of HenHouse ales I'd attended at Susan's farmhouse home.

Their collective experience included work with numerous professional breweries in northern California, as well as winemaking, kombucha (sparkling, fermented tea) production, medicinal and aromatic plant extract production and consultation within the local and global organic farming industries. "When all that experience came together and the three of us started brewing together two years ago, we realized the results were too good to keep to ourselves," said Shane.

The trio produces 60 gallons at a time of fruity, sturdy farmhouse style Saison, Belgian style Golden Ale as well as two varieties of Oyster Ale, the stout (or Porter ale) that appeared on The French Laundry beer menu, with crushed oyster shells; and a second that features a whole, local oyster thrown into the batch. Not uncommon in New Zealand and the UK over the past century, Oyster Stout first became popularized as nourishing stout and milk stout, following World War II.

No longer the small microbrewery it started out as, back in west Marin very briefly in 1983 (and now one of the top 10 craft breweries in the United States), Lagunitas Brewing Company is poised on the precipice of growing into one of the top five craft brewers in the country by the end of this decade.

The fact that Lagunitas will never be small again has forever altered its status amongst the quirkiest of small, quality ale making operations with near-cult-like local following, but that doesn't mean the community has been left feeling like it's been given any slight notion of the cold shoulder.

For Lagunitas continues to involve itself in community affairs and fundraising philanthropy to an extent that has rarely ever been seen on a public platform within Petaluma and surrounding area.

Its personality-packed flagship 800,000 barrel brew house, offices, factory store and beer garden, located in an unassuming, east Petalumas industrial district has replicated its exact winning style in a newly launched 600k barrel space on a movie soundstage complex in Chicago. This second brewery brings a large pour of northern California's craft beer movement to owner Tony Magee's native Chicago.

True to form as to how things are increasingly done here in low-key Petaluma, the media world was abuzz with big beer news in the spring of 2012 when Tony made his expansion plan announcement to the world, in a series of signature 140 character Tweets. Eschewing outmoded press conferences, media releases and press kits, the announcement to ease an escalating carbon footprint of truckloads of brews heading east, hit the industry with maximum impact and minimal fuss.

Where the guys at HenHouse brew two barrels at a time, Lagunitas' Petaluma operation brews over 160,000 barrels a year. Local euphemism for the Lagunitas' stronger and lighter ales is NightTime and DayTime and aficionados have long-since embraced the company's mantra to love what you love and know what you love. Ask any beer-drinking Petaluman what his or her favorite is amongst the Lagunitas regular and seasonal line up and you'll hear a compelling case for whatever floats their personal boat.

It's the dry, witty, original repartee and graphics of bold labeling that undoubtedly seals the deal for die-hard Lagunitas loyalists. Take the popular Under Cover Investigation Shut Down ale, immortalizing a 2005 Saint Patrick's Day police shut down of the brewery (referred to in-house as the St. Paddy's Day Massacre).

After an eight-week undercover investigation during regular Thursday night tastings in an eclectic, guitar-filled function room at the Lagunitas facility, frustrated police had failed to make an inroad into alleged under-the-table marijuana sale cash transactions. Eventually, police settled for arresting a few folks for possession and shutting the place down for a 20-day period, conveniently timed during scheduled renovation work in the production facility.

The not-so-subtle Under Cover Investigation Shut Down Ale was later released to continual acclaim. Moderately hoppy and well balanced, Lagunitas IPA (India Pale Ale) is the company's flagship beer, with its Czech-style pils another big hitter on the craft beer market. Other ales on the regular roster at Lagunitas are: its Hop Stoopid (American Imperial IPA) Ale; a bigger, hoppier and higher alcohol content Maximus IPA and a distinctive American Strong Ale, fondly known as Brown Shugga. Imperial Red is a variation on the original Lagunitas Red brewed during the company's first year in Tony's garage in the original west Marin hamlet that gave its name to the company. It was his Dogtown Pale Ale, brewed in the garage alongside a stout called Bugtown, bearing the first labeling of the Lagunitas doggie mascot inspired, legend has it by "Petey" in the movie, *The Little Rascals*. Named after another small, coastal hamlet in west Marin, not far from Bolinas, Dogtown Pale Ale went on to win the California State Fair in 1996, instantly branding the Lagunitas bulldog/terrier mix as a global thinking, local drinking man's staunch best friend.

Tony, now in his fifties, had studied music and composition as a boy and such was his respect as he grew up for the prolific rock icon, Frank Zappa, a limited edition beers series launched in 2006 through 2008, following the fortieth anniversary of Zappa's first album, *Freak Out*. According to *All About Beer Magazine*, the initial 8,000 case run of Freak Out Ale was bumped up to 15,000 cases each of Kill Ugly Radio, Lumpy Gravy and We're Only In It For the Money.

The series came to an early end after Gail Zappa reportedly took serious umbrage to Tony's donation of some of the commemorative series of beer for a memorial concert for one of Zappa's former band-mates, drummer Jimmy Carl Black. It apparently transpired that the drummer, who had died in 2008, had been estranged from Frank Zappa and his estate. Such was the end of Tony's vision to compose in beer form each of Zappa's whopping 40 album legacy, though undoubtedly causing the limited run of five original releases to become more valuable than they otherwise would have been amongst a receptive customer base of beer lovers and rock fans alike.

Hugely popular in Petaluma beer circles and elsewhere is the craft brewers' Little Sumpin' Sumpin' Ale and its big sister Little Sumpin' Wild.

Wilco Tango Foxtrot is another rather ironic winner, coming into bubbly being to mark the failure of an economic recovery following the country's epic market bust. 2009 Correction Ale was to have been followed by a 2010 Correction Ale, already in the pipeline, but was pipped at the post by a seemingly more appropriately named WTF. Add to the line-up a Bavarian Deppelweizen, The Hairy Eyeball, a Lucky 12 ale and an Olde Gnarly Wine.

As its label suggests, Lagunitas Day Time Ale serves for everyday situations when, in the company's words: "sometimes you want a beer, then you realize how much crap you need to do before you call it a day." A deep amber, double American, Imperial Cappuccino Stout appeals to the late afternoon, caffeine-tolerant, real ale, peanut-eating post-work crowd, gathered at the big, old bar that sits under cover beyond the alfresco Lagunitas beer garden.

The fall 2013 Federal Government Shutdown's disagreement over spending shuttered most federal agencies as well as the country's national parks. The Treasury Department's Alcohol and Tobacco Tax and Trade Bureau (TTB) was one of the agencies impacted, temporarily curtailing efforts by Lagunitas Brewery to produce a new seasonal ale in a larger, 32 ounce bottle size.

Owner, McGee told the *Petaluma Argus Courier* that the company was waiting on labels for its new "Lagunitas Sucks" bumper bottles: "but since certain parts of the Treasury are shut down, the phone just says it's closed. There is no response," McGee was quoted.

Buzz around town is the evolution of a brewery district, a hub being developed at the north end of Petaluma, with Lagunitas as head honcho and anchor. Veteran home brewer J.J. Jay's "Pico-brewery" — Petaluma Hills Brewing about to open a small tasting room nearby. Likewise, nearby 101 North Brewing launched its pint-sized IPA operation in the fall of 2012 under the leadership of three beer loving brothers, Joe, Jake and Joel Johnson and the trio's pal John Lilienthal.

After my first visit to the inner mechanisms of the Lagunitas micro-brewery production plant along with several dozen, fellow goggle-protected Artisan Cheese Festival-goers, I shuttled on over to the Sheraton Hotel in the Petaluma Marina, to partake in my the one and only beermakers dinner I've ever been invited to. I've been to plenty of winemakers' dinners in my time, including those that Timo and I have routinely rustled up each harvest season, at home. The idea of pairing beer with cheese-themed dishes struck me as a refreshing change from the standard wine and cheese fare and one that ought to be easy enough for people to attempt to replicate at home.

Beer and cheese lovers mingled and munched on miniature pizza wedges, hot from the hotel's sizzling wood burning oven, as kitchen crew under the chef's keen eye busily plated up five distinct and delicious courses to highlight a wide variety of regional cheese and Lagunitas beer pairings.

Charcuterie — salumi (mortadella, salami and prosciutto) — and Marin French Brie was paired with Wilco Tango Foxtrot, American Brown Ale.

A Lardon Lyonnaise salad was elegantly composed of finely shredded brussels sprouts covered by a creamy poached egg, La Bodega Sherry vinaigrette and Cypress Grove fresh chevre. Ingeniously, this perky salad course was paired with the brewery's super-popular crispy wheat and pale malt flavored, big round and juicy hop-finished "Little Sumpin' Sumpin.'"

Next course (breathe in, breathe out, drink a glass of water!) was a little bitty roasted quail with creamy Oregon truffle polenta, pomegranate pan jus and Cowgirl Creamery Wagon Wheel cheese, paired with a spicy, dank and roasty, newly-re-introduced Imperial Red.

The spectacle increased with each new, infallible small plate delivery, including a fifth course consisting of melt-in-the-mouth braised veal osso bucco with a wild mushroom risotto and favorite of mine, Giacomini's Farmstead Point Reyes Blue paired with a Lagunitas rich, malty, coppered Censored Ale.

If that wasn't quite enough, along came a scrumptious, individual pear tarte tatin for dessert, complete with salted caramel drizzle and a side of Bellwether Farm's buttery, Jersey milk-flavored Carmody cheese, coupled with a knock-your-socks-off caramel and rich toffee-flavored barley Olde Gnarly Wine.

What a cool and contemporary dinner party idea to try for yourself at home. Beer and cheese aficionados will unite on this one. If you happen to love both, what could be better?

Petaluma Imperial Stout Chocolate Cupcakes

Inspired by chocolate Guinness cupcakes, a long-time holiday hit in the Rivetti household, my latest, locavore version adds a rich and smoky depth, made with Lagunitas Brewery's highly roasted malted barley Imperial Stout. Makes 24.

1/2 22-ounce bomber bottle of Lagunitas Imperial Stout
1 1/2 sticks of melted, unsalted organic butter
1 tablespoon of vanilla extract
3 large, farm fresh eggs
3/4 cup organic sour cream
3/4 cup unsweetened cocoa

2 1/2 cups of sugar
2 cups all-purpose flour
1 1/2 teaspoon of baking soda
for frosting
18 ounce package of organic cream cheese
1 cup organic heavy cream
1 1/2 pounds confectioner's sugar
dark chocolate for grating

Preheat oven to 350°F. Combine stout, melted butter and vanilla. Beat in eggs and sour cream, gradually. In a separate bowl, whisk cocoa, sugar, flour and baking soda. Thoroughly mix dry ingredients into the wet. Line cupcake pans with paper liners. Divide mixture evenly. Bake for 25 minutes. Cool.

For frosting, beat cream cheese, heavy cream and confectioner's sugar until smooth. Spread on cooled cupcakes. Grate a dark chocolate sprinkling on top.

*The National Heirloom Expo at the Sonoma County Fairgrounds
in Santa Rosa, attracts crowds of more than 10,000 people each September.*

Chapter 13

wildwood flower

Barack Obama, arugula appreciation poster boy (as first reported in the *Chicago Tribune*, during his campaign for Presidency in September 2007) would, no doubt, approve of the wild and voluptuous, volunteer arugula (otherwise known as rocket) patch that reappears each April in my herb garden.

Dominic, my youngest son, planted a packet of wild arugula seeds, purchased from a newly-opened Baker Creek Heirloom Seed Bank in downtown Petaluma, several years ago. Neither he, nor I had any idea that this would be one of the most value for money investments in terms of the pungent, nutritious, green gift that keeps on giving. Dom, or I, depending who is on salad duty, alternate the daily arugula harvest, just enough for the evening's meal. Peppery, rich in vitamin C and potassium, grown as an edible herb in the Mediterranean region of the world since Roman times, and by now, in my yard, substantial in leaf size, a few quick trims of the burgeoning patch is all it takes for sufficient dinner greens.

When twenty-first-century heritage seed pioneers Jeremiath (Jere) and Emilee Gettle opened a west coast storefront for their established Baker Creek Heirloom Seed Company (headquartered in the Ozark Hills of Mansfield Missouri), in Petaluma, back in 2007, this quiet, yet intriguingly dynamic pair of young homesteaders hand picked a lofty, austere, early Sonoma County Bank building. Since the 1920s, this cavernous structure has managed to withstand the test of time on the corner of two of the historic downtown Petaluma's busiest thoroughfares, Petaluma Boulevard and Washington Street.

Gettle's Baker Creek Seed catalog has long since been darling of magazine moguls, Oprah and Martha Stewart. The aptly named Petaluma Seed Bank garnered almost immediate national, regional and local media attention as a mecca for natural food enthusiasts, gardeners, shoppers, agri-tourists and unsuspecting wine country visitors fortunate to have stopped for a bite to eat and a browse around Petaluma's downtown, stretching their legs en-route through the bustling gateway to Sonoma County.

With a staggering 1,300 plus varieties of heirloom seeds in stock on library-style wooden shelving in the spacious, marble floored Seed Bank, locals and visitors alike found themselves quite suddenly awash in the country's largest selection of meticulously preserved nineteenth-century seed varietals, not just from the U.S. but sourced and saved from many Asian and European heritage vegetable, flower and herb seeds as well.

The Gettles came to town with a magnetic, impeccably timed intent to further their already massive impact in the States in the promotion of the vital importance of preserving the country's agricultural and culinary heritage with the exchange of seeds, thoughts and ideas, handed down from generation to generation.

In their boycott of all genetically modified seeds, the Gettles were amongst the first in the area to have a public platform for the mass rejection of seeds and products of all gene altering food manufacturers.

Non-hybrid, non-GMO, non-treated and non-patented, Seed Bank customers' purchases were frequently the first point of awareness for many of the company's west coast customers as to the impact of genetically modified crops on the future global food supply. The fact that the Seed Bank sailed into town to such applause spoke volumes. If ever there was a more appropriate moment to reawaken dormant back yard gardening instincts, this was the one.

Described in the *New York Times* as: "The Evangelists for Heirloom Vegetables," anyone who has ever met the generally overall-clad Seventh Day Adventist (hence the store being closed on Saturdays, Sabbath for the 16 million strong worldwide Protestant Christian denomination that evolved in the U.S. in the mid nineteenth-century) Jere Gettle at one of his Seed Bank's many educational events would tell you that this is clearly not a guy with a hidden agenda behind what has been oft-reported as a near meteoric business success.

For what we have here is a business that branched out west in the midst of the country's massive economic crisis (into a former bank building, no less) — a well calculated case of being in exactly the right place at the right time as an entrepreneur with gentle giant potential to share the bounty of his specific lifestyle brand.

Jere grew up in Montana where his parents' appreciation for growing their own apparently rubbed off. As their homesteading experiments took the family on the road to pursue pastures new, their son learned to read largely through the pages of seed catalogues. By the time he was a teenager, he had rustled up his own 70 plus varietals of heirloom seeds, fitting the criteria of having not been mass cultivated for more than 50 years. He'd printed 550 copies of his first 12-page catalog in 1997, aged just 17. Baker Creek Heirloom Seeds was officially born, physically evolving over the next decade or so in headquarters of a replica pioneer village, complete with bakery, store, gristmill and barn, on his father's 176-acre Angus cattle farm.

Today's bumper 196-page annual Baker Creek Heirloom Seed color catalog mails to more than 310,000 gardeners across the country, featuring seeds such as the Cherokee Purple Tomato, an old Native American variety, producing denser, more complex flavors and 50% more vitamins and minerals than modern varietals.

The Gettles also produce a nationally distributed *Heirloom Garden Magazine* and several recent books on the subject that has captured the imagination of locavores, chefs and gardeners keen to preserve the fruits, vegetables and herbs they remember from their childhoods.

I vividly remember the first time that I stepped into The Seed Bank. I'd never seen anything like it. Cool, quiet, more of a library than a garden store, I half expected a Jack and the Beanstalk experience — magic afoot in the alchemy of growing something truly awesome from one tiny seed.

Over the past five years The Seed Bank has become a major player in Sonoma County's heritage food movement. No longer are we skeptical of an entity so organic taking up so much square footage in a boutique shopping district. In fact, we're delighted that it brings so many people to town.

Now working towards its fourth year, a three-day National Heirloom Expo, drawing crowds in excess of 10,000 people to the Sonoma County Fairgrounds, in Santa Rosa, each September, was also the brainchild of Jere Gettle.

A rostrum of nationally and internationally renowned speakers, including activists, authors and seed experts has gathered around what is most likely the largest exhibit of heirloom produce in the world. Spearheaded by a 12-foot squash and pumpkin pyramid, submissions represented many different states.

Elaine and I came away laden with honey, soaps and all sorts of heirloom planting ideas after a late afternoon browse of the exposition sales hall during a visit to the Annual Heirloom Expo, quite a mind-boggling first-time experience for us both.

Of course, nowhere does this fertile and unblemished by chemical invasion exist without a natural drawback (or two or three). For one, an infamous odor permeates the air throughout the city of Petaluma and outlaying areas at certain times of the year, more than a bit disconcerting to newcomers and visitors, and known to locals, charmingly, as "eau de Petaluma."

Imagine something not unlike a giant cowpat infusing the air. It's actually the agricultural industry at large, spreading manure in fields that surround the city. It generally only lasts a couple days at a time and it's very much a reminder that we do in fact, live in the country.

Poison oak on the other hand, is far more of a pain to live with. It is the plague of my household. With an oak forest behind the back fence being a frequent wonderland of exploration for my two cats, Marley and his half sister, Phoebe, even without a regular romp along the poison oak-laden wooded trails, this oily, invisible enemy infiltrates at multiple times a year. It makes its way into the house and onto the skin of its inhabitants, spreading its suffering for two to three weeks at a time.

Fortunately, for my family, no one is too horrendously allergic, though irritating, red rashes in between the fingers and toes, behind the ears, or just about everywhere you really don't want inflamed, is bad enough even without having to haul in the use of steroids.

Then there's allergy season. For a hay fever sufferer such as myself, I'd take a dose of eau de Petaluma every day over an extended spring season of pretty intense respiratory distress. It is my greatest price to pay for living in this patch of rural paradise.

There really is only one thing worse for a hay fever sufferer than an involuntary inhalation of a mountainous abundance of airborne noxious tree, grass and weed pollen and that is actually being the one behind a preventative weed whacking contraption, electric or otherwise.

Take it from me, the notorious Sonoma County allergy season represents the epitome of a hellish, skin crawling, eye-itching, asthma-inducing two-month nightmare, the flip-side of living in a place where everything grows like weeds. A daily intake of honey from the farmer's market has helped build up quite a bit of immunity, but only if I remember to take a teaspoon full each day, every day.

By the end of May, green, tall grass on hills surrounding the vineyards and farmland on the outer edges of Petaluma are at their most verdant. Left to bake as dried-out, dusty brush land, it is vital that overgrown hillsides are razed to the ground before the heat of summer and chance of fires set in.

Each spring, shortly after Easter, an apparition of wonder and relief manifests itself along the sloping ridges of the dehydrated, grass-covered hillside areas close to my home. Herds of goats return to these grassy vistas for targeted grazing — a smart, green, regional enterprise of a savvy young husband and wife team who've brought the natural back into vegetation management.

Ray and Virginia of North-West Sonoma County Russian River-based Billy's Mini Farm Goat Grazing Services, and now, other providers in the area, are in demand on farm as well as municipal and private land in the Petaluma area as well as throughout northern California, supplying electric solar-powered fencing to keep their non-stop, weed-munching workforce focused on one patch of land at a time. With no need to dispose of any debris and no need for noisy, machinery or harsh chemicals, land clearing permits are no longer required, saving landowners of grassy expanse both time and money.

This young family travels around the region with goats in tow, herding Australian shepherd dogs and a house trailer. The couple's small child romps the hillsides alongside her mom and I often spot them out for a walk when they're in Petaluma, newest puppy on a leash, the happy little girl a delight in her pink cotton sundress with pigtails and a pair of pint-sized rain boots.

*Goats and sheep and other of nature's woolly whackers
are in big demand come spring time in Sonoma and Marin counties.*

On one such occasional stroll, I learned that Virginia grew up in Sonoma County with an agricultural background, not unlike so many of her Sonoma County contemporaries, but it was while she working as a health club manager that she developed the idea of a more natural way to combat the fire-hazardous dried grass issues threatening so much of her native north.

Goats love weeds, grasses and brush in equal measures. It is a fact that greedy goats will happily snap off and eat acres of flower heads, picking off leaves and leaving bare stock in their wake, conveniently preventing vegetation from going to seed, photosynthesizing and building a perpetuating root system.

"I was pregnant and wanted to figure out a way to work and stay home with my child at the same time," said Virginia, in passing during dog walking one May morning.

"It all started with Billy, who we adopted as a baby because his mother didn't produce enough milk, so we crate-raised him in our home and then decided that Billy needed a family," she said. "He was way too big to be in our home so we then bought a pygmy mommy and baby who became his sister and mother. One day our neighbor said hey do you rent your goats out for grazing and the rest was history."

Neighbors take great delight in sharing the news of the goats' annual (and on alternate-years, sheep) return. It struck me, walking back home after meeting Virginia and her daughter, that people like her and her family, stewards of the environment, are the embodiment of this region. It is those who best know and love the land and its limitations, who have transitioned it through the ravages of a post-industrialized America, these most contemporary of countrified folk, who call us back whenever we've been away.

Pinpointing a narrow, tree-lined driveway leading into rural west Petaluma's secluded Wetmore Lane is a lesson in careful observation. For it is easy for the eye to wander towards one pleasing pastoral distraction after another, winding one's way along the charming twists and turns of rambling Chileno Valley Road.

Home to an eclectic community of creative, individual homesteaders and those who enjoy a life lived somewhat off the beaten path of the Valley's ranch-lined route out west, one-track, unpaved Wetmore Lane weaves its way around a number of vintage farmhouses to culminate at new frontierswoman Peggy Shafer's innovative and organic Chinese Medicinal Herb Farm.

There, situated amidst an unassuming 10-acre parcel, Peggy's compact two-and-a-half acre primary medicinal herb fields, demonstration gardens, small Chinese fruit orchard, shade structure, green house and drying shed collectively represent the most diversified Chinese herb farm in the United States. Certified by Marin Organic, the farm serves a highly specific niche market of Chinese herbalists, acupuncturists, Oriental medicine scholars, botanists and fellow professional growers across the country.

Chinese herbs have been used in northern California since the Gold Rush days. Over 222,000 Chinese came to the U.S. between 1850 and 1882 in search of better economic conditions, the majority attracted by employment, albeit brutal hard labor in the heat, dirt and dust of the Mother Lode. Several hundred Chinese were living and working in Sonoma County by the 1870s and though anti-immigrant pressure from white settlers led to many Chinese fleeing the area after a decade or more, small Chinatowns were established for those who stayed, in Petaluma, Santa Rosa and Sebastopol. The practice of Chinese medicine has continued to thrive.

Peggy is an expert on worldwide issues of the international herb trade. She teaches workshops on the cultivation of Chinese herbs. A widely respected horticulturalist and founding member of the American Medicinal Herb Consortium, secretary of the Sonoma County Herb Exchange and nationwide speaker, you might expect to meet someone considerably less modest and self contained.

I'd visited Peggy on the recommendation of my friend Gail, a fellow Brit and artist, located a few houses down from Peggy's farm.

The idea of a regional medicine farms fits perfectly with the conscious effort to eat local foods. Peggy's experimental farm grows no large numbers of any specific Chinese herbs.

With China currently undertaking what Peggy describes as "a good job of sinking itself with poor quality of mass-exported herbs," this mild-mannered guru of U.S. domestic medicinal herb generation has championed the cause of developing demonstration gardens here in the Petaluma area for the increased study of trialing crops for an emerging American market.

"It is widely recognized that it is a good thing to grow herbs here so that over harvested and rare, endangered Eastern herbs are not imported and subsequently made sparse," said Peggy.

I was surprised to learn, that given the similarity of latitudes between North America and China, most bioregions of the United States are able to produce over 150 species of Chinese medicinal herbs, giving a distinctive local character to the quality of individual grower's plant medicine.

"The best Western herbs go directly to Europe, while Eastern herbs stay in China," said Peggy. "Until now, the U.S. has been at the bottom of the barrel for quality Chinese herbs."

Peggy imparted that clean, pure, fresh herbs and foods grown in a healthy ecosystem such as that of her Chinese Medicinal Herb Farm are the very foundation of real wealth. When payment for fresh herbs and produce goes directly to the farmer within the community, all of that money is retained locally while at the same time keeping ecological farmers like Peggy fully entrenched on their land.

Peggy's comprehensive 2011 book, *The Chinese Medicinal Herb Farm: The Cultivator's Guide to Small-Scale Organic Herb Production,* is the first guide to present detailed information on how to produce high-quality efficacious herbs in all climates of the United States, incorporating historical connectedness of ancient practitioners.

A Wild Stinging Nettle Tea

Stinging nettle weed is prolific in and around Petaluma during allergy season. It inhibits the body's ability to produce histamine. If you're brave enough to make your own basic stinging nettle tea, be sure to protect your hands and arms with gloves, while handling the fresh leaves. It's a good idea to look for younger, smaller plants with potent leaves that are easier to snip. Boil water and add leaves. Infuse for 10 minutes to thoroughly remove sting. Discard leaves before drinking no more than a cup a day. Check with your doctor before drinking nettle tea to avoid potential interactions with other medications.

A series of eleven owl boxes are positioned between the high ridges of west Petaluma's Victoria neighborhood and the rolling hills of Helen Putnam Regional Park.

Chapter 14

walking after midnight

Wild Wing Company of southern Sonoma County was busy digging the sun-hardened dirt on the hills of West Petaluma throughout the summer months, sinking a series of eleven barn owl box poles into the ground for a new flight path, as part of a progressive effort to avoid the poison paradigm in dealing with vermin control.

The Victoria Housing Association neighborhood, in which I live, grow grapes and write, dates back to the early 1990s and enjoys a bucolic setting on the western-most reach of city-limits. Positioned between the high ridge hillside housing the city's west side water tower and spectacular rolling hills and trails of 216-acre Helen Putnam Regional Park, neighbors enjoy all of the benefits of country life just a 15-minute walk from the community's historic downtown.

Naturally, part and parcel of backing onto acres of glorious, open space is dealing with the fact that vermin are equally keen on this as an ideal habitat. Norway brown rats, black rats, pocket gophers, voles and field mice are the primary perpetrators when it comes to home and yard invasion in this neighborhood.

After much deliberation, the Homeowners Association and its Petaluma property management company came to the conclusion that a long term investment in brown owl boxes was not only the most cost effective way to keep vermin at bay, but by far the most environmentally friendly, natural way to control unwanted critters from the hillside sanctuary, close to homes.

Wild Wing Company's John Schuster is one of the world's leading experts on bio-diversity habitats for American kestrels, barn owls, bluebirds, screech owls, tree swallows, violet-green swallows, and wood ducks. And he just so happens to base his business in Petaluma's neighboring Cotati.

With his reputation in wine country (and internationally) as the go-to-guy for his American-made, state-of-the-art owl boxes, John's Wild Wing partnership with the Victoria neighborhood represents his two-decade-old company's largest single project in the Petaluma area.

From his wealth of experience implementing successful, high profile vermin control projects in a variety of locations around the world, John took considerable pleasure in surveying and strategizing the perfect plan for this particular, green initiative, close to home.

I'm not sure what I was thinking the day that I met with John to take a look at the project, but my wedge heeled sandals were a silly choice for clambering up the parched and slippery hillside for a closer peek at owl boxes positioned 100 yards apart in a carefully devised flight path that incorporates the whole of the housing association's domestic territory. Practicality is not always my thing —especially, as I've already mentioned, when it comes to shoes.

"We know more today than ever before about the barn owl and others," said John, mid-hike, as we traversed the hill (he in cowboy boots, me in my sandals) up to one of the centrally positioned owl boxes, perched on a steel pole, cemented into the earth. I learned that it's a common mistake for people to mount owl boxes in trees. "The owl is an open space predator," explained John. "It is our goal to get owls into these boxes to breed."

Position boxes in a clear, open flight corridor, with openings all facing the eastward moonlight and the owls will come. Hide a box away in a tree and the big-winged beauties probably won't ever find it.

Though barn owls love evergreen, especially the live oak, eucalyptus, redwood, palm and cypress trees prolific in this area, rainy season interferes with their nesting in natural habitat. Boxes were positioned in an ideal hunting path to provide them what amounts to a dream-home environment for owls.

"Barn owls hunt a mile and a half in all directions," said John. "At least one or two families will inhabit each of these 11 boxes, breeding within the first six months of moving in."

One of the most skilled hunters of rodents in North America, the importance of the barn owl in California is gaining ground as landscape companies and homeowners continue to look toward more environmentally friendly methods of keeping vermin under control.

According to John, just one single barn owl will eat on the average of 155 gophers per year. With 48 barn owls in an area the size of the Victoria neighborhood, some 7,440 gophers alone will be gobbled over a 12-month period. "I'm calculating that there will be between 1,600 and 3,000 rodent kills per box per year," he said. Times that by 11 and that's as many as 33,000 rats, mice, gophers, voles and field mice fewer to nest in the garage!

Barn owls don't eat ground squirrels. And more good news for snake-fearing residents is that the fewer the vermin available, the less likely rattlesnakes are to favor this as suitable habitat.

"When push comes to shove, barn owls will hunt in the day," said John. Keep your eyes out for activity if you're in the neighborhood, especially at night.

Another benefit of mounting an owl box on a metal pole is to protect the owl's habitat from mammals, raccoon, possum and the elusive ring tailed cat, all of whom are able to climb this slippery structure.

Boxes are cleaned out on an annual basis. "The barn owl is a true raptor," explained John. "It kills with its talons, crushing its prey, swallowing it whole and then regurgitating it. After it's done, it's ready to eat again." Compared to the slow digestion process of a snake, the barn owl's proclivity to ingest is by far the most productive.

Wild Wing's approach to eliminate rodents naturally in avoidance of what John coins the "poison paradigm" is an age-old practice that has been used throughout history, all over the world.

Controversial rodenticides used in more recent years on a widespread basis to rid homes and businesses of rats and mice has been linked to all sorts of horrendous health problems in humans and pets. John's website offers a wealth of information on barn owl programs for any habitat from the backyard home to farms and vineyards, industrial grounds and regional parks.

John trained with the California Division of Forestry Ecology Corps in the early '70s, taking a significant diversion in his career path in the form of a professional musical detour, performing all over the country as a singer, guitarist and harmonica player, opening concerts and guest recording on albums for the likes of Bob Dylan, Al Green, The Cars, Chris Isaak, The Neville Brothers, Van Morrison, and Huey Lewis and the News.

Following his heart back to conservation, he founded Wild Wing in the early 1990s and has never looked back. Describing his vocation as a labor of love, John hopes to bring educational tours to the Petaluma hillside to promote a passion for barn owls amongst school aged children and area residents of all ages.

"I'm hoping that the young people who live in this neighborhood, as well as homeowners, will take an interest in keeping an eye on the owl boxes and taking pride in what we're doing for the environment."

We made it back down the hill, John and I, with me in my silly sandals and (with a sturdy arm offered wordlessly, without a spot of judgment), I never slipped once.

Ahead of the game on the fright-night theme, a pre-Halloween gathering at a pop-up, west Petaluma country Cackling Coven Café certainly was a sight to behold. I had agreed to test the waters as one of the more recent members of the Ladies of the Long Table dinner group mentioned earlier on in the book.

In my mind, the bevy of broomsticks, pointed hats, local ghost stories and an outrageous spread of spooky-looking, locavore's "finger' food" was just enough to shake up any spirits lurking along those lonely country lanes. And of course, how could I resist?

Farm fresh eggs had been hardboiled and transformed into eyeball appetizers alongside a handmade loaf of mummy-shaped bread, split and stuffed with slimy spinach dip. Squash from backyards all across town popped up in a range of blood-curdling pot-luck dishes, but my favorite had to be a platter of tendon-wrapped elf knees with reduced Kraken blood (bacon-wrapped scallops in bbq sauce).

Just as much fun for grown-ups as the trick-or-treat tots, Halloween in Petaluma has long since been a very big deal, in large part due to the city's well preserved historic homes that provide the picture-perfect backdrop to haunted goings-on.

Ingenious friend, Lawrence, aka Captain Jack, has captured the imaginations of today's generation of Petalumans with his annual Cavity Cove pirate-themed transformation of his Spanish-style home in the heart of the city's heritage home neighborhood.

I never experienced anything close to this growing up in the UK, though I do recall as a teenager, being "dared" to run around the Abbey graveyard in my hometown after dark, holding my breath up and down a ruined, ancient stone stairway that led to nowhere. Quite who was supposed to appear I forget, fortunately the paranormal failed to make an entrance.

A tribute to the late newspaper columnist Bill Soberanes, founder of the World Wrist Wrestling Championship and host of an annual Harry Houdini Séance, held at secret locations around Sonoma County from 1964 to 2002.

Spooking ourselves silly at the Cackling Coven Café brought to mind the late *Petaluma Argus Courier*, self-named "peopleologist" columnist Bill Soberanes' and his Harry Houdini Séances that were held once a year from 1964 through 2002, in a variety of secret locations around the county.

Bill had put Petaluma on the map as founder of the World Wrist Wrestling Championships and spent the majority of his adult life pottering around Petaluma and beyond, armed with his camera, amassing an estimated 45,000 photos of himself with other people, some of them ordinary, everyday folk, other times, celebrities (including Frank Sinatra), senators and presidents (Teddy Kennedy, Richard Nixon, Ronald Regan), sports figures, even a gangster or two.

Just so that no one would be in any doubt as to his prolific social skills, Bill's business card read: "Unique Trademark: Columnist Soberanes has been photographed with more famous, infamous, usual and unusual people than anyone in the world. Home base — *Argus-Courier, Petaluma.*"

An old fashioned newspaperman through and through, "Mr. Petaluma" never missed a deadline, with his column appearing in every single issue of the *Argus* from June 2, 1954, until two days after his death, at aged 81 in 2003.

Interestingly enough, Bill never learned to drive, though he had no problem traveling the world with his Wrist Wrestling Championships. He was extremely proud of his heritage.

His maternal grandfather had been a pioneer Petaluma cattleman, Thomas Caulfield and he was also a descendant of General Mariano Vallejo on his father's side.

Thirteen people were invited to Bill's annual Harry Houdini Séance, grasping hands for 13 minutes at the stroke of midnight each Halloween spanning four decades in an attempt to raise the spirit of Houdini.

Although Houdini was never reported to have ever appeared, the infamous gatherings went on to inspire a movie — The Annual Harry Houdini Séances, which aired at downtown Petaluma's movie theater for the first time in November 2012.

I found the perfect recipe for a spirited Halloween gathering in the Petaluma Museum's archived *Break Bread Together*, a pre-1970s fundraiser booklet of the Petaluma United Church of Christ.

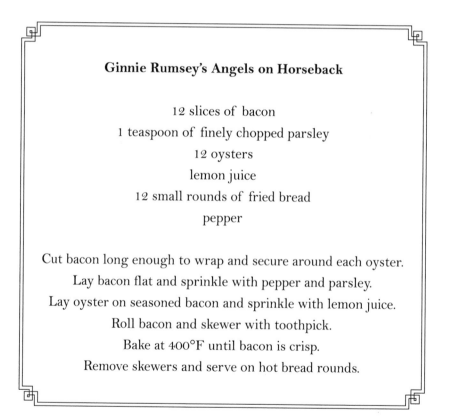

Ginnie Rumsey's Angels on Horseback

12 slices of bacon
1 teaspoon of finely chopped parsley
12 oysters
lemon juice
12 small rounds of fried bread
pepper

Cut bacon long enough to wrap and secure around each oyster.
Lay bacon flat and sprinkle with pepper and parsley.
Lay oyster on seasoned bacon and sprinkle with lemon juice.
Roll bacon and skewer with toothpick.
Bake at 400°F until bacon is crisp.
Remove skewers and serve on hot bread rounds.

McEvoy Ranch in all its scenic splendor. Some 18,000 olive trees, and 25 acres of vineyard populate this 550-acre hill country property between Petaluma and Nicasio in west Marin.

Chapter 15

all the gold in California

November at McEvoy Ranch, on Petaluma's scenic Red Hill Road, pinpoints northern California's premier olive harvest season. The region's celebrated organic, extra virgin olive oil producer mills the season's exquisitely rich and peppery Tuscan-style oil. And it's time once again for neighboring growers and backyard farmers such as myself, having picked and gathered fruit to congregate for the much-anticipated annual community mill.

Luxuriant, complex aroma and flavor detectable in the mere slightest drop of McEvoy's oil is lauded amongst discerning olive oil aficionado as being every bit as good as the top quality oils milled in the Italian countryside. California's premium oil has, in fact, fast become some of the finest in the world.

It is all about the fruit. Six distinctive, Tuscan varietals combine in true artisan style to produce complex and award-winning, blended "nuovo" California oil with the required mild and savory bitterness that is at the same time reminiscent of the old country and bringing something fresh and new by way of terroir, to the international olive oil scene.

The champion McEvoy extra-virgin olive oil blend consists of 75 percent Frantoio, 20 percent peppery Leccino, and five percent of a soft, balanced mix of Pendolino, Maurino, Leccio Del Corno and Coratino olives. Structure, flavor and color are all important factors in top-notch olive oil production, hence the practice of milling a combination of distinctive Tuscan varietals together. The olives, some strong, some sweet, grow side by side in groves and unlike in winemaking, don't require the meticulous measuring as does the vintners blending process.

Two Sunday morning community milling sessions each November beckon a civilized barrage of small-scale olive growers from far and wide.

Backyard olive farmers from Lake County, Napa, Marin and Sonoma counties congregate from the break of dawn, as mist rolls off the treetops in the orchard and a sound of friendly banter fills the air. Bearing five gallon buckets brimming with healthy, pest-free, strictly Tuscan varietals, olive farmers are typically a friendly lot.

Waiting my turn in line as a first-timer, with a meager couple of five-gallon buckets of Frantoio, Leccino and Pendolino from my backyard, it didn't take much time to feel at home, swept up in the excitement and convivial spirit of the community mill atmosphere.

It takes a lot of patience to embark upon an olive oil endeavor, with Tuscan varietal trees taking typically six to seven years to bear fruit. By the time our trees bore sufficient, first-class fruit to harvest and mill, we experienced what a major undertaking it is each fall to physically hand pick a good year's bountiful produce. Hot on the heels of a grape harvest, this is no small task.

Providing plentiful moral support, longtime friend and olive aficionado Teela stood behind me in line.

"Didn't I tell you it was your year for the first harvest?" the multi-generation Petaluman asked, whilst eyeing my neighbors' vast haul laid out in a variety of eclectic wicker baskets, boxes, barrels and tubs. Our previous year's crops hadn't come to much.

"It's magical," she said, dashing off to grab a steaming hot cup of coffee and a freshly baked pastry.

A steady stream of sturdy Volvo wagons and dusty, aging wine country SUVs flowed gently along the crunchy gravel driveway from D Street extension, through the large, olive-wreath-clad cast iron gates of the ranch and toward the mill.

As the olive-growing populace continued to build, cheerful small-talk entertained while waiting my turn to present the family's haul to sweater-clad ranch staff. An imposing woman in her late sixties diverted attention from the line, deftly straddling the back of a pick-up truck to unload an impressive 80-gallon haul of Tuscan fruit from her home in neighboring Napa Valley.

By the time it was my turn for the fruit to be weighed and inspected, I'd figured out that it was actually entirely feasible to produce a one gallon bottle of prized extra-virgin olive oil from a single olive stone.

The fellow behind shared how he had thrown a particularly fruitful party in his Santa Rosa home a decade ago. An unsuspecting guest had spit out an olive stone over the deck and into the steepest elevation of the backyard beyond. After renting a three-sided, rather precarious ladder, the lucky homeowner nowadays looks forward to a day-long Pendolino olive harvest enterprise ahead of him each fall.

Nan Tucker McEvoy was one of the first visionaries to bring what was officially designated as a "new crop" to the wine country region of Sonoma/Napa and Marin Counties. In fact, back in the mid 1990s, the powers that be were, at the time, reportedly considering her relatively modest initial mission to be doomed. Clearly the idea of the first Tuscan fruit tree-lined transformation of a 550-acre hill country property nestled between Nicasio in west Marin and Petaluma was a reach for those stuck in the region's agricultural past.

San Francisco socialite, *Chronicle Newspaper* heiress, Peace Corps volunteer and reporter, Nan purchased the sprawling, former dairy ranch property in 1990 for a reported $3 million, with a simple and very specific desire to spend quality weekends and vacation time with her grandchildren, as she had, with her own grandparents as a young child, fully intending to take time out to enjoy the rural beauty of northern California in a playful retreat.

Little did she know at the time what was in store for the former dairy farm. Nan's zoning options for making the most of this stunning agricultural-zoned hillside property were to reintroduce cattle, or grow fruit. After touring Italy with a group of fellow affluent Americans from the Bay Area, she and another entrepreneur from the region, Ed Stolman, struck upon the idea of introducing olive trees for high quality oil production in Marin and Sonoma Counties. As renegade, new oil makers in the region, Nan initially imported 1,000 Tuscan seedlings; Ed, for his own enterprise, a further thousand.

Today, some 80 acres of 18,000 olive trees, fruit orchards, an abundance of flower and organic vegetable gardens, as well as 25 more recently planted acres of vineyard have transformed Nan 's ranch into a veritable wonderland, a whimsical estate spectacularly visible by car or road bike from steep, scenic and winding Petaluma Road, weaving and climbing through west Marin county from Point Reyes Station across the Sonoma county border and into Petaluma.

Breathtakingly beautiful in its maturity, Nan's vision for producing premium grade organic oil blankets the hilly, V-shaped property with a mature canopy of silvery green. Her only child, son Nion McEvoy is partner in the olive oil enterprise.

Fifteen semi-visible and secluded buildings include a remodel of an original Victorian farmhouse, now used for staff yoga parties and events, Nan's art-filled, private 5,000-square-foot family home (built in 1990), a playful swimming pool set inside a pond, guest house, hot house and ornate Chinese Pavilion, inspired by Nan's tours of Chinese gardens in Shanghai. Last, but certainly not least, the stylish and spacious commercial milling facility, completes the estate with its Italian frantoio machine, used to crush the olives and extract oil amidst the traditional washing, grinding, mixing, separation and stocking process.

Ranch offices and a seasonal showroom (opened during tours and special events) blend into this storied land with optimum low impact on views.

Nine Mediterranean grape varietals have since been planted in tight rows, of pinot noir, syrah, montepulciano, grenache, viognier, mourvedre, Alicante bouschet, refosco and barbera. A winemaking team on the ranch works closely with advice from growers and winemakers amongst the tight-knit community. Dr. Maurizio Castelli, agronomist and oenologist hailing from Pistoia, played a major part in the birth and development of McEvoy's extraordinary extra virgin olive oil. One of Italy's leading and most respected experts on olive oil and wine, Maurizio visits the ranch several times each year to consult and to celebrate each new harvest. And there is even a body-care line enriched with the property's bounty.

County officials who had pooh-poohed Nan's initial plans, were later (reportedly), most sufficiently humbled and first to issue an apology, not long after it became clear to all within the region that Nan had in fact, been well ahead of the curve in timing her olive products with the market.

The *Wall Street Journal* featured domestic olive oils as the new American Gold Rush, in a 2013 report. The article cited studies from U.C. Davis, that exposed two thirds of Mediterranean olive oils as being labeled extra-virgin, when in fact, they are anything but.

Extra virgin is only applicable if oils are extracted without the use of heat or chemicals and solely from the fruit of the olive tree itself. There must be no more than 0.8 percent free fatty acidity.

U.S.-produced olive oils are being held to a higher standard of transparency, with harvest location and date most often than not now visible on labels.

I met olive oil expert Alexandra Devarenne via email in my youngest son's lacrosse team snack-schedule trade. Chatting, later, in person on the bleachers at a weekend game against a rather bolshie team from a neighboring county, we'd discovered a common interest in artisan foods and wines. Alexandra is an international olive oil consultant and educator, based in Petaluma and one of the world's leading lights in campaigning for new, far more stringent standards for olive oil grading in the States.

The Berkeley-educated mother of two also happens to be a member of the advisory board of the new U.C. Davis Olive Oil Center at the Robert Mondavi Institute for Wine and Food Sciences and had participated in extensive research and surveys of the oil industries in California and around the globe. As a co-instructor of U.C. Davis' Sensory Evaluation of Olive Oil Course, Alexandra was about as good as it gets as a source for talking about the best of California extra virgin olive oils as well as how to avoid being hoodwinked in the grocery store by fraudulent imports.

It was on Alexandra's recommendation that I picked up a copy of Tom Mueller's revelatory book, *Extra Virginity*. That book and her brief, yet convincing bleacher stand summary of the woeful state of regulatory affairs on quality control of domestic and imported olive oil in the American market sent me packing in the direction of the promised land of the nearby lauded Olive Press.

Elaine and I made a date to visit the tasting room at the Olive Press, housed within the Jacuzzi Family Winery, on a balmy, late August morning. Just a fifteen-minute jaunt by car to Sonoma, it was a great excuse to take a field trip away from our respective writers' desks and laptops. Plus, I needed olive oil. Our small portion of house oil from the annual McEvoy community crush tends to

McEvoy Ranch annual community crush blends Tuscan olives from around the region. Frantoio, Leccino, Pendolino, Maurino, Leccio Del Corno and Coratino olives are blended together for the quintessential small-scale producers' extra virgin oil.

run out late spring and I'd been resorting to begging or bartering top-ups from former olive farmer, Teela and on occasion, a pricey bottle of McEvoy's boxed oil would, by default make its way into the grocery cart at the Petaluma Market.

The main reason why oils from producers such as McEvoy and The Olive Press might at first appear overpriced to the uninitiated, is in large part due to the price wars in the industry created by the pirates of the trade. These con-artists continue to pass off sub-quality oils as extra virgin for a fraction of the price of a true, organic, top-grade olive oil.

Standing before a row of equally attractive, pleasingly bottled and marketed olive oils in the grocery store, how many times have you boggled at the price variations, wondering how important Italian extra virgin could possibly be marked at a quarter of a price of an organic California grown oil, or less? Since my informative first chat with Alexandra, I now know to flip the bottle and read the small print, if it's even there at all.

What might be depicted as a wholesome draught of imported old world Tuscan amber might very well have originated in some other country altogether: Turkey, Tunisia, Morocco, Spain to name a few. After its arrival in Italy, consumers and authorities had, until fairly recently, little idea of the levels of adulteration taking place — the processing of carcinogenic, low-grade industrial fat at dangerously unhealthy heats to produce oils that have no bearing at all on the freshly crushed olive juices that they are passed off as.

The sad thing is that most consumers can't tell that this cheap, fake extra virgin oil they're slathering over their salads and cooking is nothing like the real deal. Extra virgin olive oils from McEvoy and the Olive Press are pungent and spicy, peppery, made from olives that thrive in the hot, dry heat of the region. Olive oils are as varied as wines, complex in identity according to varietal, elements, terroir. It was hard to know where to start at the tasting bar inside The Olive Press shop — delicate, medium, robust. Flavored oil and citrus crushed ranges of oils have become increasingly popular and practically begged to be sampled with small chunks of bread for dipping into teaspoon-sized disposable tasting cups.

Elaine, ever mindful and diligent, brought along her own empty, screw-top wine bottles to be filled at the bulk counter — an old world practice that is becoming increasingly in mode in urban olive oil bars around the country.

Olive oil, though popular throughout Eastern Mediterranean since Neolithic times, actually made its most significant debut in the western world after World War II. Tom Mueller wrote of Minnesota epidemiologist Ancel Keys' discovery of the dramatic contrast in incidences of coronary heart disease in hospitals in post-war Italy, Spain and on the Greek island of Crete, compared to escalating heart disease amongst considerably dietary-deprived Americans.

A subsequent seven-country study concluded that saturated fat was the culprit for raising cholesterol in the blood, clogging arteries, leading to heart attacks and stroke in countries such as the U.S. where most fat was derived from saturated meat and dairy products.

Following a convincing series of subsequent publications issued throughout the 1960s and 70s, a reduction of fat intake was widely recommended throughout the United States alongside a suggested core diet of an olive-oil infused Mediterranean-style regime of fruits and vegetables, bread, fish and pasta, moderate dairy products and wine. Right now, the fat reduction recommendation is under attack since it is widely accepted that factory-raised animal fat is the culprit, not fat itself.

Master oil maker and former partner (with Ed Stolman) in The Olive Press, Deborah Rogers lives and breathes this classic Mediterranean diet and lifestyle, having made her reputation milling olives from thousands of contracted acres around the region, in a 24-hour-a-day, frenzied four month crush season, visible for all through large, clear plexiglass windows in the tasting room, until winery owners Fred and Nancy Cline purchased The Olive Press in April of 2013.

According to the *Olive Oil Times:* "The story of California olive oil cannot be told without the recognition of Deborah Rogers. A trailblazer in the California olive oil industry, her contributions are far-reaching. Impeccably attentive to detail and passionately driven to produce only the highest quality extra virgin olive oil, Deborah Rogers (appropriately well-known as the Olive Queen) has earned the respect and admiration of this industry that she has worked so tirelessly to lift to its current position."

Deborah, one of the first female master olive oil millers in the U.S., developed her passion for the product from a love of cooking and gardening that was a natural response to growing up with a Polish grandmother who grew much of the family's food, cooking everything from scratch and wasted nothing.

With reputations as amongst the New World's leading ladies of extra virgin olive oil, Deborah and Alexandra continue to become increasingly politically active in the promotion of exemplary oils produced in Australia, New Zealand, the States and South America. These trail-blazing women have established themselves as major voices in the development of more exacting global standard requirements. And olives, like all agricultural "products" are subject to the flotsam and jetsam of environmental factors.

While Community Milling Days at McEvoy Ranch have, over the past decade, or so, typically enjoyed a steady increase each year in droves of small-scale olive growers, the annual regional pilgrimage to combine 2013 season olive hauls for a premium local blend posed a significant problem.

That year, for the first time since the olive oil production facility launched in the mid-1990s, those familiar, jolly lines of fresh-faced, convivial, small scale olive enthusiasts were decimated to a few, staunch growers who'd listened to the professionals and had taken precautions against an unprecedented fruit fly infestation.

"This year has seen the worst olive fruit fly infestation in Bay Area, if not entire California coastal history," Samantha Dorsey, Farming Manager for McEvoy Ranch told me during what would normally have been the busiest week of the year out at the ranch.

Samantha, who oversees the care and organic management of the olive orchard (as well as 25 acres of vineyards) at the ranch, is an expert in quality olive care and production, upholding the McEvoy family's philosophy towards its diverse and sustainable form of farming.

Hundreds of small scale olive growers (including several wineries) from as far away as Santa Barbara in the south, to Boonville in the north had reported 2013 crop infestation and decimation.

According to the University of California's Agriculture and Natural Resources department, the Olive Fruit Fly *(Bactrocera oleae)* continues to pose a severe economic threat for the state's olive oil industry. Samantha explained how any one individual fruit-bearing ornamental olive tree, untreated on a private property, is at risk of exacerbating the problem.

The first case of Olive Fruit Fly was recorded in California in October 1998 (a single female fly was captured in west Los Angeles). By the following fall, olive fruit flies had spread to seven additional counties.

"A number of extraordinarily detrimental factors have led to this year's scenario," Samantha explained. "This year's very mild summer failed to shut down Olive Fruit Fly production. Without extreme heat, they keep on reproducing."

Thousands of untended trees throughout the region served to provide ideal reproductive conditions. McEvoy's own 2013 estate-fruit harvest had, however, been exceptional: "We provide the perfect example of how to protect a crop through good, educated management," said Samantha.

Community crush-customers such as myself were advised to be thorough in pre-checking and disposing of all diseased fruits, easy to detect, as the Olive Fruit Fly leaves a distinctive, brown, pitted mass over each olive.

A simple method for controlling the Olive Fruit Fly is for property owners who have olive trees that are not harvested each fall to take action to prevent the fruit formation in the spring. A plant growth regulator or high-pressure water spray during bloom does the trick. Those such as myself, who do have hopes to harvest their olive fruit, are urged by neighboring growers to research basic sanitation practices for olive trees and consider using traps, bait sprays, or barrier films.

Basically, the more unprotected olive trees there are in the region, the greater the problem might well escalate. Un-harvested fruit left to hang tends to cause even more trouble each consecutive spring.

One west Petaluma neighbor told me he was considering removing his backyard fruit-bearing olive tree in light of this news. It sounds drastic, but this is something that might, at some stage in the near future, be deemed a necessity for the prevention of the olive fruit fly infestation worsening any further.

For a Petaluma-perspective, I talked with Teela (known locally as "The Olive Lady" for her years of experience in tending a medium-scale olive orchard, closer to town). Teela and Samantha were, at the time of my writing this book, in earnest discussions to develop an action plan for the provision of a Do-It-Yourself kit with instructions for ridding the immediate area of further invasions. These two experts have been seeking out a garden center in the area with whom to collaborate so that neighbors are able to access the correct materials to tackle this major problem.

Pantry Staple Spaghetti
with Chili, Garlic, California Olive Oil and Basil
14 ounce packet of spaghetti
3/4 cup of extra virgin California olive oil
3 garlic cloves, finely chopped
1 red chili, finely chopped
a large handful of basil, finely chopped
salt and parmesan cheese

Boil the spaghetti in lightly salted water until al dente. Heat oil in a heavy pan over low heat. Sauté garlic in the hot oil for a couple of minutes, stir with wooden spoon to prevent sticking. Add a couple of tablespoons of water to the garlic/oil mixture and add chili and basil. Continue to stir, over heat for a couple more minutes. Add cooked, drained pasta and toss before serving with a sprinkle of freshly grated Parmesan cheese. Serves four.

Della Fattoria Bakery's downtown Petaluma café.

Chapter 16

café on the corner

When it comes to cooking day after day, for motivation and purposes of staying power, I'd like to hang a variation of one of those widely popular "Keep Calm and Carry On" signs — one that says "Keep Calm and Cook On."

Keeping a fridge full of the best foods my budget can stretch to is the key to coming up with something or other appetizing and nutritious without the agony of constant meal planning. For me, cooking is a lot like writing. An idea pops into my head and if it feels good, a quick exploration of the kitchen cupboards more often than not provides the means to make a pretty decent, basic meal, even if it's not exactly what I first had in mind. The food we eat speaks volumes about where we live, especially if we pay attention to what's growing — locally, or better yet, in our back yards.

The American way of life doesn't lend itself to home meal making. Yet so many food-loving friends are obsessed with television cooking shows and celebrity chefs. Culinary artists are idealized in our culture and yet, so few people take the time to act on this inspiration and cook. I don't consider myself a great cook, but a willing and consistent one and I find that actually baking a batch of old-fashioned oatmeal raisin or chocolate chip cookies to be more beneficial to myself and the universe than my being glued to the TV screen wishing I were the Barefoot Contessa.

Having extolled the virtues of mostly home-cooked meals, eating out is a pleasure that I enjoy as much as the next person. When traveling elsewhere in the world (Italy being the preeminent exception) it is generally a challenge not to compare the quality and freshness of ingredients to the standard fare at my favorite neighborhood eateries at home in Sonoma County.

I'm not alone. Chances are, when I pull up a chair in the warehouse district's Petaluma Coffee Company, or at Aqus Café, at neighboring Foundry Wharf, it doesn't take more than a few minutes to find myself rubbing shoulders with someone with a terroirist's (no, not a terrorist's) in-depth knowledge and passion for what comes out of the ground in these fertile lands. In a coffee-crazed culture, why settle for the blandness of corporate chain shops, unless on the move and traveling?

I like to think of these independently owned and operated interpretations of democratic, social meeting spaces as the sorts of social hotspots of the early days of the eighteenth-century coffee houses in England and America. Tea and coffee are treated here with as much respect as wine. Coffee shops have had a significant impact on the cultural re-awakening of modern day Petaluma and are the gathering spots for foodies and artisan producers alike.

Independently-owned stalwarts such as personality-packed Petaluma Coffee Company, newer, urban-style Acre Coffee, in downtown Petaluma and the bustling community hub that is Aqus Café at Foundry Wharf make their own unique contributions in the fostering of discussion and debate, gossip, sharing of stories, ideas and entrepreneurial enterprise amongst the food movement movers and shakers, artists and writers, students, educators, politicians, moms and tots and freelancers looking for tabletop real estate for an hour or two while telecommuting around the country.

This brand of cultural reawakening has had a positive ripple effect on the revival of the food and farm movement in the Petaluma area as community members take the time to connect, in person, to share a growing, mutual awareness of the very real benefits of a solid, wholesome lifestyle so reflective of our sense of place.

Long-established Petaluma Coffee Company was, when I moved to Petaluma, housed in the location now known as Aqus Café at Foundry Wharf, an anchor in the mixed-use light industrial riverside warehouse district located by the river, on the corner of H and Second Street. Owners Sheila and Gardner Bride launched their small, retail coffee roastery back in 1989, using only the most carefully selected Arabica coffee beans, roasted in small batches of 10 to 20 pounds to fulfill order requests from cafes, delis, restaurants and wholesale clients across the city.

This haven of aromatic hospitality was within easy walking distance from my first Sonoma County address, a compact, cottage rental on the busy main thoroughfare through town. With its modern warehouse feel, sacks of coffee beans, casual seating and a European-style selection of fresh, baked goods, the Coffee Company was an easy magnet for English and Irish ex-pats and fellow immigrants from all over the world.

We made many of our first and some of our most enduring friendships with young families, several of whom were in a similar stage of transition to American life and culture. Our first born, Rocco, was a rambunctious toddler at the time, yet he, like most other young customers, would be blessedly content to stand and stare for half an hour at a time, cookie in hand, captivated by a model train running continuous loops on a track mounted on a deep ledge above the long espresso bar.

Trailblazers, Petaluma Coffee Company purchased a tea and tea accessories importing business ten years on and as business continued to boom in the custom order roasting arena, the coffee house part of the business was sold to a long time, trusted employee in 2001. Not surprisingly, after roasting operations moved down the street, customers could not resist the ambient lure of roasting coffee beans and an informal new base camp literally "popped up" with coffee still served today from a small cart, surrounded by piles of newspapers and old books.

The stalwart Coffee Company has retained and still attracts its own particular crowd, predominantly retirees and intellectuals, busy professionals who like to pop in and out without too much of a line for a bargain cup of quality coffee to go. The intimate Petaluma Coffee Company is about as far from the Starbucks model as a coffee aficionado might hope to stumble upon. Despite the community's passion for independents, I find it ironic that one of the busiest (mostly drive-through) Starbucks in the country is located on the corner of a small, non-descript strip mall on Lakeville Highway, en-route out of Petaluma, headed towards Sonoma/Napa/Vallejo.

Aqus Café at Foundry Wharf might, on first impression, appear as the sort of independently owned coffee shop you'd expect to find in any west coast city — peopled with students, artists and free-thinking sorts. Bright red sun umbrellas shade outdoor seating with cheerful planter boxes, brimming with bright flowers a welcome sight on a busy street corner.

Pull up a chair inside the café, sit awhile and take in an especially unique brand of energy that has made this small, independent café one of the region's most talked-about hot spots for modern social capital. Old and young, entrepreneurs and retirees, artists, musicians and chief instigators of dense community circles intermingle from the minute the doors swing open come early morning, through closing at night. This is a thrumming place where solid, person-to-person connections are made away from the chatter of today's social media networks.

Co-owners, English and Irish expats Lesley McCullaugh and business partner John Crowley specifically designed what was initially John's dream meeting space for a multigenerational tangle of grandparents, parents, teenagers and kids, a gathering spot for business, pleasure, breakfast, lunch and happy hour, conversation and live music.

Part social and cultural center, part café, part European-style pub, Lesley and John's café is the anchor of a thriving, mixed-use light industrial neighborhood that houses local food luminaries such as Three Twins Ice Cream and Sonoma Portworks. The Café counter is stocked with freshly baked pastries and pies from area bakeries, local beers and well-priced, premium wines by the glass from Petaluma and Sonoma County. Gluten-free, vegan and vegetarian crowds flock to Aqus for its multiple, fresh menu offerings. Lesley says the most popular menu item is the Michael Salad (named for her hubby) — smoked (nitrate-free Zoe's meats) chicken with organic mixed greens, spinach, dried cherries, pecans and Point Reyes blue cheese.

As a long-time regular, I'm sure to hit the jack-pot whatever hour of day I stop by in number of friends who happen to be taking time out for a brew. It is as close to a "local" — a favored neighborhood pub in the old country, as we could ask for.

Evening hours see the Café come into its own as an intimate event space, peopled by a growing Aqus Community of poetry and other writing group members, foreign language conversation, improv comedy sessions, trivia (with Lesley), open mic, science buzz, indie film festivals and a steady stream of live music performances.

Hands-on matriarch Lesley has an extensive career background in the restaurant business that dates back to her first job in her teens at the four-star Midland Hotel, Manchester. A Lancashire lass, through and through, despite over a quarter century of west coast American life, her brand of traditional, European training paired with a meticulous attention to table-bussing detail translates to a rare standard in coffee shop comfort and service.

John enjoys a widespread reputation throughout the south county for his range of innate social inclinations, derived most likely from serving pints in Ireland as a teen. His grandfather was a Dublin publican.

John describes the Café as: "A nice place to hang out," but anyone who frequents Aqus knows it as the java-infused multigenerational "utopian" bonding space that he had envisioned back in 2007.

His smartest move was bringing Lesley (and, behind the scenes, Michael, long time co-owner of popular Redwood Cafe in neighboring Cotati) on board as unsung hero of all of the day-to-day machinations of the running of this outstanding community hub.

Chief social instigator, champion connection maker and a regular celebrity in his art-filled Café, John, with his extrovert personality, was named as official Petaluma "Good Egg" for the city's 2014 Butter and Egg Days celebrations.

Together, John and Lesley have created a place where old and young, entrepreneurs and retirees, artists, musicians and rainmakers from a wide variety of community circles intermingle from dawn to dusk, connecting face to face, above and beyond the isolating chatter of social media networks.

I first met Lesley when her oldest son and mine discovered the common bond of their British moms, in kindergarten. Actually, she had singled me out in a lineup of novice parents after boldly sending Rocco to school for class photos in a houndstooth blazer. "No one other than an English mum would kit him out like that," she'd joked. Rocco called that first, pintsized jacket his "James Bond Blazer." He still dresses like the bit of a Brit he is.

I have Lesley to thank for 17 years of the most enduring, consistent of friendships. Generous, loyal and armed with an untarnished brand of caustic British humor, she has been there, as I hope I have for her, through life's ever exciting thick and thin and, invaluably, through those hazy, crazy, hands-on parenting years.

Walking from Aqus Café, past Petaluma Coffee Company, into downtown Petaluma, across the street from the historic McNear Saloon (named for one of the city's founding families), a distinctive corner spot commands my attention at the bustling crossroads of Petaluma Boulevard and Western Avenue. Here, one of the best chefs of Sonoma County rules the roost.

Stocky, raven-haired and indisputably "Chef" — Central Market's Tony Najiola personifies real slow food with his trademark fervor in the sourcing and serving of some of the most consistently fine regional dishes I have tasted anywhere in wine country or the greater Bay Area for that matter.

And people do travel from all around the region for Tony's signature brand of "Slow food, good served," that has earned him a coveted "Recommended" rating in the *Michelin Guide, San Francisco Bay Area and Wine Country Edition*, an Open Table Diners Award and numerous "Best Chef" readers-pick awards in a variety of Sonoma County media.

There's a brooding intensity in Tony's personality that I find reflected with gusto in his Mediterranean-style menu, sourced from the best and most sustainable, fresh, local ingredients, meat and fish the area has to offer. In fact, he's so serious about sourcing the sorts of quality natural produce and meats that his Sicilian farmer great grandfather would have considered fit for the family table, the robust chef/restaurant owner has, in recent years, expanded his vision to his small, three-acre Muleheart Farm, located at the edge of Petaluma. As homesteader, he raises pigs and grows vegetables for Central Market's hand picked seasonal specials.

The brick-walled Central Market with its high, urban-style ceilings, open kitchen and large, central Italian Mugnaini wood-fired brick oven was a dream come true for the New Orleans-raised chef. Prior to opening his own restaurant, he enjoyed an illustrious career of intensive cooking in New York City, San Francisco and until 2003, as Chef in Residence at Ravenswood Winery.

It was here in Sonoma County that Tony discovered the Mediterranean pull of his family heritage with unrivalled access to fresh bounty of the region and the handsome 1918 brick Maclay Building, has enjoyed a renaissance of its own as Central Market.

Through the recessionary years of the recent past, I found it reassuring to pass by Central Market at night, a beacon of taste and sustainability with its soft lights glowing, illuminating an ever-present, lively crowd of contented diners, foodies and farmers at table. Tony's flair and heart for bringing farm to fork have proved an enduring benchmark for what a truly great restaurant should be.

Half a block heading north from Central Market, on restaurant row, I'm taking a left across a pedestrian crossing towards the little landmark fountain in Helen Putnam Plaza, named after one of the city's most influential mothers (also a school teacher, principal, mayor and county supervisor).

Tucked away towards the back of this little square on the left, is Petaluma Pie Company, a tiny hole in the wall that brought filmmakers Lina Hoshino and Angelo Sacerdote back to their respective roots. Angelo's stints as a chef and produce buyer in New York led him to interview east coast purveyors with regards to the burgeoning awareness of genetic modification and he would eventually produce a 2002 documentary on the subject *"Fed Up! Genetic Engineering Industrial Agriculture and Sustainable Alternatives."*

Lina is also a filmmaker as well as a graphic designer, with a shared background in food. Educated at the Carnegie Mellon University, she was raised in a Japanese/Taiwanese family with a restaurant in New Jersey.

The couple, who are avid gardeners, opened the doors to their novel little Petaluma Pie Shop in December of 2010, handcrafting and baking sweet and savory pies, as well as soups and salads, daily. They incorporate organic and locally produced ingredients from farms in the vicinity as well as their own, abundant east Petaluma back yard. I like to pick up a hand-pie or two while strolling downtown's boutique district, such a treat to take home to the boys.

Hand-chalked blackboards cheerfully announce daily, seasonal and holiday specials and we'll spot lots of reminders written around the shop walls as to where the various fillings have come from. This is something that speaks to pie aficionados, the proprietors' freedom to select foods based on preferences for particular area producers. Local wines and beers are big with Petaluma Pie Shop regulars, and if you'd stop to eat a warm broccoli and cheese pot-pie with me at the counter, we might be persuaded to take home a triple berry pie for dessert.

Though most of downtown Petaluma's top dining spots occupy the city's older buildings, including popular newcomer Twisted 2 in the historic Landmart Building, one of my favorites, Water Street Bistro, is snuggled into a street-level, front corner location of a pale yellow, modern, commercial building straddling Western Avenue and Water Street, at the Petaluma River. It's here that we wait in line for an outdoor table for two to sit in the sunshine and feast on fresh crab and citrus salads with thickly sliced pieces of warm whole wheat bread.

Chef owner and intrepid baker, Stephanie Rastetter cooked alongside owner Daniel Patterson in the 1990s as a celebrated haute cuisine chef at his French Restaurant, Babette's in Sonoma. Stephanie selected this small, intimate new bistro location in which to launch her own rustic, French-neighborhood-inspired communal bistro, after Babette's closed, in 2000.

Bon-vivants, intellectuals, artists, software engineers, students, foodies and international visitors from around the world join familiar faces of daily regulars at outdoor seating at the patio corner of the cobblestoned Water Street, with its view of the Balshaw Pedestrian Bridge at the river's historic turning basin.

Stephanie's Frenchified, soul-food-orientated hand-written blackboard menu is inspired by the seasons and regional produce, with scrumptious sandwiches, soups and salads bolstered by a tantalizing array of house-baked fig tarts, quiche, croissants and crumbles, coffee, teas and wines by the glass.

Step inside and décor is simple and homey, an unpretentious, traditional French Provençal palette of lemony yellows, cool blues and warm reds. Always jazz playing away in the background. Friendly and efficient counter service operates on an honor system — pay as you leave as you're bound to be tempted by Stephanie's labor of love — a slice of tart or something sweet and flaky balanced on an abundant countertop that separates the tiny open kitchen from an indoor eating area that typically fills for breakfast with conversational groups and chef owners of neighboring restaurants.

Eating at the Water Street Bistro is the opposite of a fast food lunch. It's my family's favorite lunch spot, along with the Tea Room on Western Avenue a couple of blocks to the west.

Slap bang in the middle of bustling restaurant row on Petaluma Boulevard (the heart of the city), the intimate realm of Della Fattoria Bakery and Café beckons disciples of deliciousness from far and wide.

Infused with richly aged patinas and dignified elements of old European-style charm, this north bay destination café has a foodie following throughout the Bay Area. *Saveur Magazine* named Della one of the country's 20 great bread bakeries, back in May 2012.

Natural, organic food aficionados flock to this pioneering Sonoma County bakery and café, rubbing shoulders with the locals at a hand-crafted walnut community table.

Perhaps it is the familial warmth of this cozy café that proves the secret of its success. Owners and founders, the Weber clan, celebrates the very essence of effective business partnership in an enterprising and highly democratic "all hands on deck" approach to this one-of-a-kind culinary venture. Della Fattoria is housed in an old U.S. Bakery building (circa 1860). Baked goods have been in continual production in this location for over a century and a half and the ghosts of bakers past, I'd wager a bet, are contented by its current incarnation. Back when the building was first built, there were bakeries on every corner of downtown Petaluma. I've watched several traditional bakeries close up shop in the area over the past two decades. I never take a good bakery (including Bovine Bakery, on nearby Fourth Street) for granted.

Established after nine, long years of commercial bread braking at the Weber family's west Petaluma heritage ranch, the café was a natural evolution for matriarch, Kathleen her daughter and son, Aaron, now head chef.

Della's pastry chef arrives at the downtown café at the wee hour of 4am. In the peace and quiet of early morning, French style, fresh and crispy, buttery croissants are religiously recreated each new day to satisfy even the most serious of Francophiles.

The Webers don't worry about what other restaurants are doing in their midst. According to Kathleen: "My personal preference is to tend to my own knitting and maintain a completely original approach."

Ranch egg-rich breakfast and lunch times are big business at Della. The "Farmwich" — cucumber, eggplant, Swiss cheese, avocado, piquillo red peppers, romaine and tapenade on thick, doorstep wedges of Della Seeded Wheat Pullman is a favorite of mine. With one eye on a tray of chocolate eclairs in the glass front refrigerated cabinet come lunch time, I find nothing much better than taking time out with a loaded lunch time sandwich, perusing a few pages of the day's newspaper and indulging in a spot of people watching.

Saturday evening summer dinners out at the Weber family's private ranch on Skillman Lane typically produce a sell-out series, in which al-fresco diners are treated to a bounty of seasonal ranch specialties in a more intimate setting.

Kathleen is considered an accidental, although much lauded, baker. The family's original heirloom vegetable business was proving a bit of a financial challenge back in 1995, when she struck up the idea of building a bread oven on her back deck.

A friend of Aaron's, who helped construct the early oven, just happened to be a chef at the Sonoma Mission Inn, in Sonoma. Disgruntled with the quality of bread in the hotel restaurant, an alternative order was placed with this clearly capable and inventive home baker. The rest, as they say, is history, though the vegetable garden is back in full glory as a mainstay of the bakery and café's produce for its trademark soups, stews, salads and sandwiches.

Della's famous and my weakness, Rosemary-Meyer Lemon bread, a knockout at weekly farmers markets in Marin County and the San Francisco Ferry Plaza, are described by *Saveur Magazine* as: "salty, lemony, herbal, with a beautiful sheen to the well-structured crumb and a crust that bears beauty marks from the floor of the hearth it baked upon."

After several seasons of gazing online at tantalizing photos and delicious descriptions of Della's home patch dinners, calendar magic worked its wonders for seats at the last of the summer's line-up of Saturday late afternoon/early evening epicurean soirées out on the ranch.

A sensory explosion of seasonal goodness greeted me on arrival at the ranch where late afternoon mingling with fans from all over the Bay Area was already underway. Most of these folk, I learned, make it a priority to return each summer for the earthy pleasures of platter after platter of fire-grilled figs, perfectly cooked frittatas, cheeses, nuts and tasty tapenades and of course, huge, round loaves of ranch-baked breads filled with baked brie.

And that's just for starters. As the afternoon wound down for table seating, I wandered, with fellow diners, around the ranch, welcome to take a peek at the famous bread baking operation, meet the chickens, pet the family's numerous, friendly pooches.

Deep, family-style dishes of crisp fall salad with butternut squash passed from guest to guest, followed by toppling platters of grilled chicken and steak.

Coffee and desserts from the bakery were savored by the satiated crowd, as sunset and shadows drew in to close a quite extraordinary experience of Sonoma County food theater at its least pretentious and best.

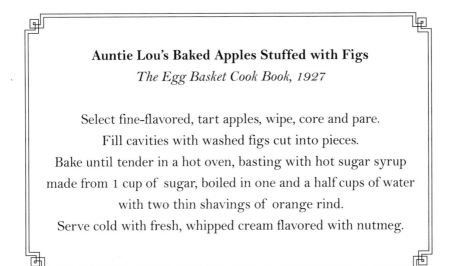

Auntie Lou's Baked Apples Stuffed with Figs
The Egg Basket Cook Book, 1927

Select fine-flavored, tart apples, wipe, core and pare.
Fill cavities with washed figs cut into pieces.
Bake until tender in a hot oven, basting with hot sugar syrup
made from 1 cup of sugar, boiled in one and a half cups of water
with two thin shavings of orange rind.
Serve cold with fresh, whipped cream flavored with nutmeg.

Visitors enjoy a 360 degree view and the natural tranquility of Tomales Bay from the lighted boat shack at the end of the pier at Nick's Cove. Mixed cocktails by candlelight are a specialty.

Chapter 17

the grand tour

Dinner at Sir and Star at the Olema Inn is a taste of some of the region's most lauded locavore cuisine. My first visit occurred just as temperatures in coastal west Marin and southern Sonoma County reached a record, freezing low.

Despite the early Sunday evening hour of six, Timo and I shared the road with little more than two or three other vehicles, in either direction, for the duration of the half-hour, 18-or-so mile, winding drive from west Petaluma, into the dark and quiet embrace of quirky, compact Olema. "Olema" — Miwok for coyote — is not far from the Point Reyes National Seashore's Bear Valley Vistors Center.

Holiday lights twinkled from a neighboring inn, a contrast to the subtly lit, subdued Sir and Star, formerly known as the Olema Inn, which was purchased in 2012 amongst considerable buzz in the foodie world, by the region's first farm-to-table chefs, Manka's Margaret Grade and Daniel DeLong.

Built at the crossroads of curvy, coastal Star Route One and Sir Francis Drake Highway (which follows the route of an original Pioneer pack trail from just west of the Richmond/San Rafael Bridge, to Point Reyes National Seashore), Sir and Star is aptly named for its location, an historic anchor in an iconic spot. Elizabethan explorer Sir Francis Drake claimed the Point Reyes seashore on which he landed his ship *The Golden Hinde* as "Nova Albion" — for England, in 1579.

A dark, cold, December evening made for a haunting backdrop to this particular dining destination.

Sir and Star tips its hat to Hitchcock's *The Birds*, with an abundance of ornithological (primarily black bird) taxidermy, indoors, but for me, its rather mysterious walk-up approach had a mild-mannered making of the scene at the start of the *Rocky Horror Picture Show* in which Janet and Brad wander into the bizarre residence of Dr. Frank-N-Furter after breaking down in an isolated area. I wasn't quite sure which door to walk into and once inside, whether to turn left or right. Inviting French music piped from behind a series of closed doors, all of which looked equally intriguing.

After finding our way to the roaring fire-lit foyer, replete with high backed, black Windsor chairs (my favorite) and a reception desk painted (according to a Remodelista.com report Benjamin Moore's Black Panther) to match exterior and all interior trim, I would have liked to have sat a while longer in this atmospheric reception area in order to let it all sink in. A huge and spectacular vase perched on top of the desk with enormous branches bearing persimmons and the last of the fall foliage softening the surprising welcome party of a solo Victorian china doll — one of the sort that, if you had sat there long enough, you'd swear was looking straight at you.

The main dining room, sparse, white and with the most beautiful hardwood floors and ceiling to match was set with simple, stunning table top arrangements of brown strips of butcher paper, black glazed Heath ceramic plates under a series of period sash windows (wear a jacket in winter).

Bolinas/West Marin locals and luminaries gathered in convivial groupings, no doubt toasting a spot of winter respite, bubbly being clearly de rigueur for Sunday supper amongst the organic farming set.

I had the good fortune to eat at Manka's Inverness Lodge once, if only once, and it was for my fourtieth birthday dinner, months before the restaurant in the lauded 1917 hunting lodge above the water in Inverness, burned down, back in 2006. The French Laundry's Thomas Keller ate his birthday dinner at Manka's, Prince Charles and Camilla supped while staying out there, too.

Margaret and Daniel were able to keep their one-of-a-kind retreat of rustic luxe in operation after the fire, but without its legendary restaurant. A gaping hole in the forager's feast had been evident in the area as the owner/manager/chefs took time to start a family and regroup.

According to an article in *Food and Wine Magazine*, this internationally-renowned and celebrated pair of culinary eclectics (who you are unlikely to meet in the dining room, just so-you-know) had their eye on the Olema Inn for some time before making the move to buy it and to take it to an entirely new dimension from "wedding cake white," cute B&B to the world-class wonder of all things fished, farmed, foraged, hunted and harvested at its back door.

The article quoted Daniel as describing he and his partner as being: "Like the fog, the dark, brooding coast."

Though wait staff was professional and impeccably turned out, as on a return visit six months later, though, a tad abrupt, perhaps a touch irritated in having to explain over and again a notoriously esoteric menu to a discerning and steady flow of ducks out of water, taste makers, or otherwise intrigued. Then again, given the exclusivity of Sir and Star hours — Wednesday through Sunday from 5pm to 9pm, by eight on a Sunday evening — we had picked last leg of the weekend rush.

Sir and Star proprietors are the sixth owners of the The Olema Inn, which opened in July 4, 1876, as a gathering place for loggers, ranchers and farmers. According to a report in the *San Francisco Chronicle:* "The property was part of a 9,000-acre land grant from Mexico to Raphael Garcia. His son, Felix, lost the inn as a gambling debt to John Nelson, who ran the stagecoach line to San Rafael. It stayed in the Nelson family for three generations."

Former owner, Jennifer Sulprizio was quoted in the article with regards to the property's reputation as being haunted. "It is a Nelson, in fact, who is the ghost." The United States Army had taken over the historic inn for a barracks during World War II, and according to reports, a deeply despondent Edgar Nelson, shot himself to death in the yard.

Jennifer and her husband Dana Sulprizio moved to her native Nova Scotia after selling the Inn to Margaret and Daniel. Though Jennifer was quoted as saying that she met the ghost once and he honored her plea not to scare her, the ghost of Edgar Nelson has reportedly made himself known to more than a few staff and guests over the years.

By all accounts, benevolent and non-threatening, I don't doubt a spirited presence within its four walls had some influence on the tone of the interior and exterior transformation of the Inn as a roadhouse.

Best and the whole point of the place is its hyper-local, whimsical, if not bewildering menu, one reminiscent of two decades of Manka's signature flair, enigmatic vision and obscure taste, yet perfectly suited to its new surrounds.

Timo and I restrained from overdoing it with our order, though here was a menu that made for considerable debate in which of so many outstanding dishes would make the cut in a dinner for two. I guess that's the appeal of the restaurant's Saturday night special Chef Menu, in which diners are encouraged to linger long over several small courses.

We weren't disappointed with our selection. A Duet of Salads for starters featured *"One of Peter's Pickled Fennel, Crimson Beets and Herbs and Another of Coastal Artichoke, Rocket and Radish."*

A second starter, we snuck in for good measure: *"Sir and Star's Bubble and Squeak Salad of Coastal Cabbage, Peter's Potatoes and Bacon, Crowned with a Coastal Duck Egg."*

Mains that made our mouths water most were: *"Last Seen Grazing On the Grasses of Roger Ranch, Goat, Times Two, Rack and Stew"* and: *"With a Deep Bow to Dave, Short Ribs of His Beef, With Cream Braised Coastal Cabbage."*

I did partake in a couple of must-mention sides: *"Finger Fries of Peter's Potatoes With a Dip of Stinging Nettle"* and *"Bolinas Broccoli at Its Very Best (oh yes)."*

Dessert is not what it's about at Sir and Star, although for those who simply must have a little something sweet: *"The Softly Served Bean of Local Dairy Cream Doused with a Housemade Concoction of Farmers' Market Bitter Almonds"* would, I'd say, hit the spot.

Hang a right at Olema from Sir and Star on Highway one and follow it north to Marshall for the oyster trail where more than three million Pacific (Hog Island Sweet Waters), Kumamoto and Atlantic oysters are harvested by Hog Island Oyster Company each year, along with mussels and Manila clams.

Oyster lovers must bear in mind that oysters and shellfish are to be kept refrigerated or stored on ice until time to eat, particularly during warmer summer months and so an outing to score oysters mustn't be made without an ice box (and ice) in tow. And as for the old adage from the pre-refrigeration period of the 1700s as to only eating oysters in the months with a letter R, its always wise to note that warm water months are not the ideal time to slurp oysters caught in the wild.

Oysters naturally spawn or reproduce as ocean temperatures rise and long time conservation practices have discouraged harvesting in the wild during the spawning seasons.

Today's strict water quality monitoring, sustainable practices and wet storage techniques actually have made it safe to eat farmed oysters and mollusks throughout the year and traffic from foodies in search of fresh oysters has rejuvenated this remote stretch of the coast. More often than not, finding a place to park is a bit of a challenge along Highway One on weekends.

One chap with city license plates on his SUV took a notion for oysters on Memorial Day and as I drove by on a coastal hiatus, the hapless hunter was on the side of the highway scratching his beard in wonderment at how he'd managed to tip his vehicle entirely onto its side in a hedge-lined ditch.

In its April 2013 issue, venerable *Travel and Leisure* listed Tomales Bay-side Marshall Store as one of the magazine's best seafood restaurants in the world. Over the past 136 years, this enduring institution has had many lives and two locations, beginning with its role as a general store with poolroom at the Marshall Train Depot, present day home of the Hog Island Oyster Company.

Current day owners of the Marshall store, Tod Friend (owner/ operator of Tomales Bay Oysters), his daughter Heidi and son-in-law Shannon Gregory and business partner Kim Labao famously now operate the facility as an oyster bar, serving the sort of splendid fare that makes the grade for a *Travel and Leisure* global top pick.

The magazine's preferred preparation of Tod's oysters is: "grilled, topped with the tangy, house-made barbecue sauce and served with buttery bread. Pair them with a bottle of crisp white wine (sold at the store) and views of bobbing boats."

Customers are treated to the bounty of the bay while overlooking the harbor. It is Australian-born and French-trained chef, Shannon who runs the kitchen of this charming little dockside shanty — wowing seafood and meat lovers alike with his outstanding menu, including previous owner Kathy's original, ever-popular, mouthwatering oyster Rockefeller dish.

But for a six month reprieve, a century long tradition at another mainstay of the area, Drakes Bay (formerly Johnson's) Oyster Company will likely have come to an end by the time this book is in print, following a late November 2012 controversial decision by U.S. Interior Secretary Ken Salazar to shut down this historic shellfish operation and return the estuary to the wild as the first designated, protected marine wilderness on the west coast.

The Ninth U.S. Circuit Court of Appeals in San Francisco granted its temporary reprieve after Drakes Bay Oyster Company challenged the Federal Government's refusal to renew its lease at the site of a proposed marine wilderness area. Raising serious legal questions, the historic company bought itself a six-month operational extension in 2013 hoping for a different judge to hear its appeal.

For thousands of years, long before Drakes Bay Oyster Company, Coast Miwok sourced shellfish as one of the native people's major, natural food wellspring.

Locals have been up in arms over the announcement to shutter the iconic oyster farm that is the last oyster cannery in California, employing some 30 experts in sustainable seafood handling and processing, in effect wiping out as many as 40% of the state's oyster supplies.

Social media has been ablaze with posts of outrage towards the National Park Service's decision to allow the permit for Drakes Bay Oyster Company to expire at the end of its current term. This ends an on-going ecological dispute over the future of Drakes Estero, homes to thousands of endangered birds and the coastline's largest seal colony, since Congress first had in mind to return it to its original wilderness state in the mid-1970s.

Yet many who were born and raised in the region, shellfish fans and farm supporters believe strongly that one of the world's most respected oyster businesses should be allowed to remain in the pristine waters of National Park Service land, alongside the 15 historic dairy farms and organic farms that are still in operation within the designated wilderness area.

"Are oysters really a danger to the wilderness?" asked one infuriated, longtime customer, calling the decision a travesty. Those who remembered Virginia Jensen's Beer Bar and Oyster Shack south of Tomales Bay on Highway One spoke of: "A small outpost of comfort and civility on the water's edge, until condemnation by the Park Service forced the Jensens out. Virginia was a Miwok, living where Miwoks have lived for thousands of years, yet somehow not genuine enough to be allowed to stay."

Influential others firmly disagree, including regional conservationists, such as the Sierra Club, the Wilderness Society and the Marin Audubon Society.

Rancher Kevin Lunny bought the shellfish business from Johnson Oyster Company in 2004, with full disclosure of the National Parks intent. It was Kevin who received the call from Secretary Salazar informing him of the department's decision not to renew the oyster operation's 40-year occupancy agreement. "Although we are somewhat shocked," Kevin was quoted in the *Marin Independent Journal* "we are considering all of our options."

One social media posting that gave me pause for thought asked those commenting on this impassioned thread to imagine the sacrifices made during the drive to save the coastal redwoods: "Someone has to care about the future."

Still, seven families live on the Drakes Bay Oyster Company property and would have been stripped not only their jobs but also their homes within 90 days of the November court ruling.

It's not over until it's over, but Kevin lost his apparent last ditch appeal in July, 2014 when the U.S. Supreme Court declined to hear his challenge to Interior Department orders, backed up by lower court judges, to shut down the oyster business on Drakes Estero.

"Ban bayside refineries, super tankers, container ships, nuclear submarines ... super pesticides, plastic, air pollution, roads to and from the wilderness," posed an articulate oyster farm supporter from Petaluma, pressing for a reversal of the Parks Service decision and protection of the history and diversity of the area's agricultural community. "Sadly and ironically, the park rangers and visitors to the wilderness will wreak more havoc on the scene than the oyster farmers," he said.

Not far from Drakes Bay Oysters is my favorite coastal/bay get-away, one that I'm able to escape to without going too far out of my comfort zone, (geographically or time-wise). It is here that I followed the call of the tidal waves that gently swirl round time-worn, stilted wooden footings of Ruthie's Cottage, overlooking the wilds of oyster-rich Hog Island, by the side of still staggeringly remote Tomales Bay.

Visitors to the area have been holing up for overnights at historic Nick's Cove on Pacific Coast Highway State Route One since hard-saving Slavic immigrants Nick and Frances Kojich converted a ramshackle herring curing plant into a restaurant, fisherman's depot and lodgings, back in 1931.

Construction of the highway that followed the contours of the east shore of Tomales Bay, coupled with the advent of the automobile (and the completion of the Golden Gate Bridge in 1937) opened up access to the largest, most unspoiled coastal bay on the California coast, a mecca for hunters, fishermen, sailors and nature lovers drawn to the pristine beauty and bounty of the bay's calm, relatively shallow waters, secluded coves and rich marine wildlife.

Pulling up at Nick's today, I'm able to easily envision turning the clocks back a few decades to arrive side by side with the sorts of classic American sports tourers that had been built for the pursuit of adventure and romance of the early open road.

In fact, the most photographed of Nick's Cove's original vintage roadside paraphernalia is probably the resort's own signature red truck, parked in a permanent pit-stop in the primo spot, out front. The fact that there's no cell phone coverage in this largely un-peopled outpost of coastal California makes a detour from modern pressures all the more compelling. Sunrise and sunsets are spectacularly beautiful over Tomales Bay. To say that this is an enchanting and naturally remote, rustic and romantic landmark is to be entirely accurate.

The view from Ruthie's Cottage conjures a rare and convincing vision of how the area must have appeared to its first inhabitants. For this was the coastal center of the richly bountiful territory of the Miwok. Who was Ruthie? And where does her story fit into the lore of this distinctive locale? Alfred Gibson and his wife Ruth purchased the place from the Kojich family, following that first, fabled, 40-year-run, back in 1973.

After her husband passed away, a widowed Ruth stayed on out at Nick's, for several years as sole proprietor of a place that is particularly isolated on winter nights. Determined to outwit any would-be opportunists, it is said that she took to sleeping in a different cottage each night.

Ruthie, whose well-protected property was eventually sold to restaurateur Pat Kuleto in 1999, lives on in the lending of her name to one of the most popular of the resorts 12 charming guest cottages, each with its own very distinct personality and appeal thanks to Kuleto's vision to carefully preserve the authenticity and character of each structure, paired with heritage coastal style and comfort factor inside and out.

While the relative remoteness of Nick's Cove is most of its appeal, staffing and running an operation an hour or more from San Francisco proved complex. New owners, a group of silent investors took the reins in 2011 and its reputation has grown along with the recovering economy and steady management.

*Named after one of Nick's Cove's early owners, Ruthie's Cottage,
with woodburning stove and waterfront deck is perched
on the edge of Tomales Bay.*

Inside Ruthie's, rest and relaxation beckons with the cheery sight of a pot-belly wood burning stove, thoughtfully pre-stacked with paper and logs. Walk through a back door off the bedroom opening onto a waterfront deck, overlooking an aquacultural haven. The only sights and sounds are those of wildfowl, your footsteps on bare wooden floorboards and the snap and crackle of the stove. Sometime, during the night, you'll awake to the idea of a dream, though it is, in fact, a gentle tide, swooshing beneath the stilts and pilings, to shore.

I've stayed in a couple of different cottages at Nick's at various points over the past decade, but a mid-winter weeknight at Ruthie's Cottage was my first visit since the Cove changed ownership for the last time, very quietly. I was keen to see how the return to a more localized approach might have influenced the atmosphere in a small, boutique resort that relies as much on its friends and neighbors in such a remote outpost, as the urban coastal escape crowd.

You're every bit as likely to be seated at a water view table next to the folks from nearby Bellwether Farms, Point Reyes Farmstead

Cheese Company, a weathered, long retired coastal cattle rancher, cool climate winemakers, oyster farmers, fishermen and women as a destination diner, or overnight guest seeking a spot of respite from San Francisco.

That's the beauty of the place and one that General Manager and Director of Operations, Petaluman, Dena Grunt, takes obvious pride in presenting with a greatly expanded locavore's menu, nicely depicted in the new addition of a hand-illustrated map of area suppliers on the menu.

An inspiring sampling of Nick's dinner menu took appropriate launch with a haul of outstanding Hog Island Oysters (harvested 200 yards from the table), eaten fresh from the half shell (enjoyed with a pairing of a well balanced, bone dry, mineral-slate scented Chateau du Cleray Muscadet 2009 from the wine list "Interesting Whites").

How we love a fresh haul of oysters from the picturesque inlet bay shores of neighboring west Marin but what would they be without a chilled, crisp cool-climate Sonoma coast chardonnay?

How does poached halibut with asparagus and pancetta sound? Every last morsel was as delicious as you'd hope it to be if you'd picked it out yourself, paired with buttery chardonnay, followed by fresh tuna over carrot reduction with chanterelle mushrooms (with a French oak barreled small production Belle Vallée Cellars 2008 Pinot Noir from the Willamette Valley, Oregon).

Topping these flawless tastes — a side of Rossotti Ranch grass-fed goat meatballs with melted leeks, a dribble of Very Dry Creek Estate olive oil and a pairing of Rancho Bodega's coolest of the cool climate medium-bodied reds, a robust 2008 syrah.

Smoked veal gnocchi with tomato preserves and cipollini mushrooms, Nick's Cove (Oakville) Merlot and a zesty salad covered all the bases, though I found just enough room left for sweets, in the form of chocolate torte with Three Twins Ice Cream, and poppy seed biscuits with a citrus twist.

The pastry chef's historic homage to the history of Nick's Cove combined with nostalgic memories of childhood inspired a classic American dessert menu, sparked with the freshest California seasonal ingredients. Kitchen and bar staff move on with unfortunate frequency, undoubtedly due to Nick's challenging work location and the lonesome drives on dark, winding country roads early morning and late at night. Still, Dena has brought about a strong, renewed bond between Nick's Cove and Petaluma and increasing numbers of its staff are making their home base in the small riverfront city, a great private balance for pairing with a professional life in one of the most stunning outposts of the region.

Just the ticket for an after dinner stroll through the mist is a visit to the pot-belly-stove-warmed boat shack at the end of the pier and back again, with thoughts of the next morning's in-room continental breakfast tray of warm, baked scones, muffins and a freshly brewed Petaluma Coffee & Tea Company roast already crossing my mind. Calories don't count on an overnight, at least when the food's as good and fresh and wholesome as this.

One of the best things about holing up for the night in the spirited style of one of Nick's Cove's Ralph Lauren-inspired fishing-shacks, is without a doubt, the added bonus of having no cell phone reception. No emails, no texts, no pesky Facebook perusing. In fact, the only things worth doing with an iPhone at Nick's Cove are snapping photos of the sunset, sunrise, scenery and playing tracks from iTunes via a handy, in-room docking station.

About 20 miles south, past miles of undeveloped beaches, protected lagoons, sand dunes and trails, a neighboring national seashore area hot spot for pilgrims of culinary elite is equally tucked away off the beaten trail.

Overlooking the Giacomini family's heritage dairy land that borders beautiful, remote Tomales Bay, The Fork is the sort of place you'd expect to find in a considerably more populated setting than in its actual, isolated, though splendid ideal.

One of the most popular items up for bid during a live auction portion of the annual glitzy, Petaluma Educational Foundation's fundraising gala BASH a couple of years ago came with the promise of crisp, linen aprons and rolled up sleeves for participation in a cooking class and luncheon at the Giacomini's renowned culinary center and cooking school.

Paired with goodie bags stuffed with cook's knives, custom, cotton kitchen towels, chopping boards, whisks and other goodies provided by the event's co-donors Nancy and Angie Leoni of downtown Petaluma's family-owned upscale culinary emporium iLeoni, a mild winter's weekday epicurean event was made memorably scrumptious in its pastoral setting out at the coveted Fork.

I had volunteered my services as assistant and head dishwasher to Mel. She had generously stepped up to donate her time and expertise as instructor for this particular fundraiser, along with her haul of several bulging box loads of delicious, organic ingredients, seasonings and oils donated by the local Whole Foods Market to add to the bounty of artisan-cheese-centric, coastal west Marin.

The Giacomini family, originally from the Swiss Alps border mountain region of northern Italy, has been farming in the region for over 100 years. Some 300 to 400 bovines thrive on the farm. The family's nationally acclaimed Point Reyes Farmstead Cheese has been in operation since the early 2000s and is run by the four Giacomini sisters. Matriarch and patriarch (the late) Dean and Bob Giacomini (who still runs dairy operations) purchased the farm in 1959, running their business as a milk-supplying dairy for 40 years.

The family, widely respected leaders in the U.S. organic dairy industry, recently installed a methane digester that converts all of the farm's methane gas, that unavoidable by-product of manure into useable energy. This energy powers the Giacomini's dairy and cheese plant operations. Additional cutting-edge technology has also been adopted to assist with waste management, water quality, pasture management, animal husbandry and the cheese making operation.

Dedicated to producing its fine and distinctive, organic cheeses, the family continues to focus on a closed-herd, with all cattle raised from birth and pasture-grazed in this bucolic setting. Flavors in the Farmstead's milk represent the climate and soils of this spectacular location, producing cheeses that are special and unique. My absolute favorite local cheese is the Giacomini's wonderfully creamy Toma, fashioned after traditional soft or semi-hard Italian cow cheese.

Teams of two amongst an intrepid party of ten local ladies, all movers-and-shakers within the community, took to their stations for our super chef's PEF Winter Cooking Party, "A Feast at the Fork." I wasn't about to pass up the opportunity to help out in this kitchen, with this particular ensemble, in equal part as an education supporter, friend and fan of the cook and equally keen to report on the tucked-away treasure that is the Fork .

With a flourish of team spirit, some serious chopping, rolling, whisking, broiling, pickling, cheese tasting and impeccable timing, a feast of plenty duly presented itself in the sun-drenched farm-style dining room, where class participants were able to fully enjoy the fruits of their collective labors.

We're talking melt-in-the-mouth eggplant rolls with ricotta and pesto, pickled carrots, pork tenderloin with olives, feta and mint, endive and watercress salad with kumquats and Point Reyes Blue Cheese, paired with a medley of fine, Sonoma County wines, followed by sublime Glazed Lemon Curd Cake served with Sonoma County roasters, Taylor Maid Coffee.

I'd been around Mel's earthy, epicurean escapades in many a country kitchen over the years, but had yet to see her in her element as captain of the crew in such an extraordinary team cooking facility. It was one of matriarch Dean Giacomini's last gatherings and several of the class participants were her longtime, close women friends, all stalwart education supporters in the region. Dean passed away at age 75 the following year. One of the grandmother of eight's greatest joys was known to have been with her four daughters in business with her and her husband of 54 years.

Heading inland, back home to Petaluma after every last plate and piece of silverware had been washed and put back in place, Mel and I had energy yet to marvel at this place we call home. Cattle-studded hills, rolling vineyards, Tomales Bay at low tide and bathed in glorious, late-afternoon sunshine. The food and the people and the fact that we find such spirited common-ground when gathered at the table had made for considerable labors of the day all the sweeter and more satisfying.

En route from the coast via Bodega Highway, one of several routes we took to ramble out west, where dairy farming is at its best.

I first met Kathy Tresch, matriarch of the Straus partner farm during an Apple Pie Orchard-to-Oven fall workshop produced by dynamic duo Mel (again) and Free Range Provisions and Eats and collaborative dinner party host, Suzanne a few weeks before Thanksgiving. A little slice of heaven on earth transformed a misty November Sunday morning, out at the family's rustic Two Rock Ranch, a few miles west of Petaluma, where Olympia's Apple Orchard is tucked away on the farthest reach of rolling Tresch Dairy land.

I couldn't help but feel that Kathy's enthusiasm coupled with Mel and Suzanne's sumptuously crafted workshop evoked the spirit of the area's early pioneer energy and resourcefulness. This was one of a series of meticulously envisioned Orchard-to-Oven workshops taking place out at the ranch, expertly blended with a modern sensibility for celebrating the land and its seasonal offerings, in one its tastiest of traditional American dishes, the apple pie.

Husband and wife team, Joe and Kathy typically work side by side along with their own adult children in the style of the staunchest homesteaders of this historic farming region, but it was Kathy who led the workshop series' apple picking expeditions off road, by tractor and trailer, into the enchanting realm of an heirloom orchard at harvest.

Olympia's apple orchard grows more than 50 heirloom varietals of apples including old favorites such as Jonathon (used in the workshops), Wickson, Kidds Orange Red, Cinnamon Spice, Fuji, Honeycrisp and Gravenstein. The orchard was named after the farm's first homesteader, Olympia Tresch, Kathy's husband Joe's grandmother.

Her maiden name was Olympia Nonella and Olympia's parents were part of the mass Swiss-Italian immigration at the turn of the twentieth-century. Their homeland had been Canton Ticino in Switzerland. "They first lived in Cayucas (a sleepy little California seaside town), then came to this ranch in 1905," said Kathy.

Olympia loved the land on which she was raised. She had often spoken to the family of her memories of the great 1906 earthquake, first thought to be epicentered in nearby Point Reyes that struck the Bay Area when she was a small girl. "Agriculture and her work ethic were very influential to her grandson, Joe, my husband," said Kathy, as we moved around the orchard, selecting apples for our pies. Olympia passed away on the ranch in her little house in her 90s, as it seems, has been the fortuitous trend amongst her contemporaries. "Our children are the fifth generation to live and farm here," said Kathy. The home ranch was originally 320 acres, nowadays spanning over 2,000 acres.

Kathy continues to plant more apples. Most recently she introduced Crown Prince Rudolph and several other rare, heirloom varieties that she sells at Sebastopol and Occidental farmers markets and at an honor stand at the gate to the farm.

Back at the ranch, after an apple picking expedition in an atmospheric, light grey drizzle, Mel led instructional, hands-on pie making activity stations out on a covered porch as a couple dozen workshop attendees ranging from ER nurses from San Francisco to a local grandfather and granddaughter duo, peeled apples and made pastry.

Everyone left with a pie. Even the most novice of pastry students departed with a big, brown box holding his or her picture-perfect apple pie to marvel over at home along with a copy of Mel's step-by-step reminder instructions for repeated pastry making prowess back in the real world.

Suzanne paired Cline Cellars' crisp and cheerful Rhone-style viognier as a quintessential Sonoma County white wine to compliment tastings of the workshop's signature apple pie, local cheeses and slices of homemade brick oven pizza.

Naturally, sample pie was paired with Straus organic vanilla ice cream. My first instinct in the ice cream aisle over at the Petaluma Market is, I have to say, to reach for Straus, though I'm partial to Petaluma organic artisan ice cream producers, Three Twin's Madagascar Vanilla, too. Clover's organic vanilla ice cream is just as good to serve with a homemade apple pie.

Diana Welch's Raw Apple Cake
Favorite Recipes of the St. James Ladies Guild, 1979

1 tablespoon of cinnamon

2 cups of flour

2 cups of sugar

1 teaspoon of salt

1 teaspoon of baking soda

1 teaspoon of nutmeg

4 cups of chopped local apples

1 cup of oil

1 cup of chopped nuts

2 eggs

Sift dry ingredients together. Peel and chop apples. Break eggs over apples. Add everything else, stir to blend and spread into a greased 9x13x2 inch pan. Bake for 45 minutes at 375°F degrees. Cool and top with sifted, powdered sugar.

Apple Muffins
*Business and Professional Women's Club
of Petaluma Cookbook 1937*

One pint (2 cups) of flour

1/2 teaspoon of salt

2 teaspoons of baking powder

1/4 cup of butter

1/2 cup of sugar

1 egg

1 cup of milk

1 cup of thinly sliced local apples

Mix it all together and bake in a quick oven.

Fiber art devotees flock to Valley Ford for its Wool Mill and Mercantile and a fledgling, annual Wool Festival.

Chapter 18

down on the farm

If ever I was doomed to roam one country lane endlessly for time eternal, I'm pretty sure I'd choose to wander the meandering curves of west Petaluma's Chileno Valley Road.

For each rambling homestead, ranch and farm tucked into the neighboring hills of the borderlands of Sonoma County and the golden-grassed folds and ancient Coast Miwok trails of west Marin would be worthy of my gentle haunting. Past, present, future, a place for all time.

A one-stop country holiday season shop for meeting a whole consortium of creative (and not at all ghostly) Chileno Valley neighbors takes place each late November, in the form of author Mimi Luebbermann's annual art fair at her enchanted 26 acre Windrush Farm.

A plethora of Sonoma County fine and fiber artists and crafters bask in the wintery afternoon's sunshine as art-lovers browse umbrella-shaded farmyard stalls, sipping wine, eating pizza from the farm's outdoor brick oven and I am left wondering why we haven't all moved out to the country and taken to the loom. I've picked out numerous handmade hats, gloves and socks and such over the past year as some of the best loved gifts for friends and family and I try not to miss this most pleasurable of holiday shopping experiences.

This non-profit Marin Agricultural Land Trust-registered farm welcomes scores of Bay Area children to Farm Camp come summertime. It is home to sheep, cows, goats, chickens, llamas, alpacas, cats and Greer, the farm dog. Mimi raises types of sheep — several flocks of small, soft Shetlands, Corriedale/Finn mixes and other breeds such as the eccentric-sounding California Variegated Mutant.

Mimi and fellow fiber artist Marlie de Swart started a yarn company called Local Pastures, in 2011, sourcing fiber from farmers and shepherds within a 150-mile radius of west Marin. Their yarns are of natural color, dye-free and mostly (except for the Shetland wool) soft and resilient blended wool and alpaca. Since then, the natural fiber movement has exploded in leaps and bounds in the sheep-rich region, in large part to the launch of Valley Ford Wool Mill and Mercantile, located at the two county border.

Fiber growers in the area (including alpaca and llama) process wool close to home, reducing carbon footprint, repurposing fiber that might have otherwise been discarded, providing shoppers with eco-friendly yarns, rugs, bedding, clothing and even insulation while boosting the economy all at the same time.

Educational tours and workshops at the mill continue to promote fiber arts and products to people interested in natural dye, felting, spinning, weaving, knitting and kitting their homes out with green products.

Meanwhile, back at Windrush Farms, author of twenty books on gardening and cooking, Mimi has long since taught fiber arts classes, including one for home-made holiday gifts, incorporating various techniques, from wet and dry (needle) felting to sewing to knitting, utilizing a range of new, re-used and re-purposed materials.

It was during my first visit to the farm's holiday art fair that I fell for the charms of the distinctive work of fiber artist Dan Tanner. I'd bought an Icelandic Lighthouse Keeper's cap from Dan as a Christmas gift for one of the boys and took his card so that I might visit him at his workshop in west Petaluma the following spring. Tucked away in a lush, forest-like enclosure off another winding, one-track lane, the prolific craftsman's passive solar home and studio literally hummed to the daily rhythm of the loom, the gentle clicking of knitting needles, the silent motion of a needle and thread. It had taken me longer than usual to find the place, despite my tendencies to leave home without a pre-planned route. Towering redwood trees encamped the property to such an extent as to render it completely private.

Dan, a retired scientist never makes the same piece of fiber art twice. Although it can take him months, even years to get hand-dyed colors just right on some of his more intricate projects, the self-taught, spinning/weaving, knitter-man's remarkable array of one-of-a-kind works-in-progress were not contained to the studio itself.

"The entire house was converted from an old chicken ranch," said Dan, talking me through the art-filled property's decade-long transformation as a labor of love for he and his wife.

Everywhere I looked in the white-walled, salvaged-wood-beamed one storey home, Dan and his wife's intricate woven fabrics adorned chairs and tabletops, appeared at every turn as decorative wall hangings and rugs.

Hand woven curtains hang from windows framing an outdoor scene of forest-like glen with lily pond and trickling waterfall.

"I'm addicted to the fiber arts," Dan joked. He was raised in "the woods" on a 200-acre family farm in Pennsylvania. "I find the city too confining," he said. Having utilized mostly native plants and trees on his property, he has created another type of farm in a more urban forest.

If what this lithe older man is doing is farming hats and scarves, socks, shirts, sweaters and skirts, tablemats, cushions, curtains and towels, one piece at a time, he finds himself in a tiny minority amongst the Western male.

"I'm quite accustomed to being amongst a sparse, half-dozen men in a crowd of a thousand knitting and weaving convention-goers," he said, attributing his first hands-on experience with yarn to a memorable unraveling and then arduous re-creation of an outdated sweater in college.

Although he was one of the first in the country to use early computers and programming for scientific work, Dan's wooded haven remains entirely free from the distractions of internet access. "If Carol or I need to look at a specific web site for some reason, we go to the library," he explained. Though the meticulous couple does keep detailed hard copy records of natural fiber dying processes and sampling of original design patterns, these blueprints are not intended for replication but rather more careful adaptation.

"It was a steep learning curve for me for several years," he explained. "Considering that humans have been mastering the art of weaving for many thousands of years, I tend to come to my own weaving work with a fresh approach and for a few hours at a time."

Captivated by what Dan described as a current "revolution in fiber" he experiments liberally with every conceivable mixture of materials utilized in creative blends such as llama wool with corn fiber and nylon, even soy silk from the left-overs of tofu.

Bags of fluffy sheep wool from early mentor Mimi's farm are stored under custom-built countertops in Dan's light-filled studio. Bolts of his hand woven fabrics sit neatly folded with needle and thread at the ready for gradual transformation into items of natural clothing.

"My knitting projects are sometimes simple but mostly tricky. I like to challenge myself with a double-knit, such as a two-sided sock," he said.

Aromas of freshly baked bread wafted along the walkway in the heart of the house, filling Dan's studio with a sense of timeless tranquility where all is right in the world. If this was retirement, it felt good. "Bread is the only thing that I can bake," he confessed, unfolding his latest fiber craft creation and settling down for a session in diversion from domestic life's many distractions. "I'm devoted," he said. "It's a fact."

Communal Thanksgiving in the charming red barn in Chileno Valley, on Wetmore Lane had taken considerable strategic planning, especially in the sorting out of sufficient lighting and heat for a semi-outdoor festive gathering and efficiently heated dinner under the rafters for five families.

We were around 20 in number, pitching in to put together a traditional menu commencing with a more unconventional al fresco aperitif of mulled wine and toffee apples heated over a camping stove. Tables were decorated with grape vines, pumpkins and foraged fall foliage. A variety of delicious dessert options, some gluten-free, followed the turkey dinner and a safely-contained campfire set the stage for after-dark drinks and story telling.

Woolen sweaters, hats, mittens and boots were the order of the day, though it had threatened, it didn't rain and was not a bit muddy underfoot. After dining decadently and at length, at vine-laden trestle tables under the flickering overhead lights of the barn, the party divided for recreational options of a long afternoon walk down country lanes or sketching in Gail's bright, little art studio housed in one portion of the barn behind she and her husband, Michael's late-Victorian ranch home.

It is the colors of that Thanksgiving that most stay in my mind — earth hues of crimson and gold, deep green, aged woody-brown, darkest red and orange. This timeless tableau was without a single artificial element to throw off the autumnal palette.

Heating a barn in the cold weather months is a bit of a perilous task and so we'd decided ahead of time to come prepared, dressed in multiple layers as is so often the way to cope with changing elements on a November day in Sonoma and Marin counties.

Hundreds of Gail's canvases are stored in carefully curated spaces throughout the barn, adding to its allure as a creative haven for a communal holiday feast.

I cherish the memory of that particular Thanksgiving for its spontaneity, simplicity and spirit of camaraderie amidst fellow settlers from far away places, gathered to share a common bond in celebration of the lives we had each carved out in the United States.

We remembered, with more humility than perhaps is present in plusher surrounds, the pioneering spirits not just of the men and women who set sail for America nearly four centuries past, but of those early settlers in that exact Chileno Valley spot.

The United States, land that I do call home, has welcomed people from every country, every religion over the centuries. I speak for most other immigrants I know when I say that Thanksgiving is not about the trimmings, the travel or the sometimes maddening family dynamics, it's about an awareness of belonging, of sharing and of being grateful.

Pumpkin pie, apple and pear, pecan, apple-cranberry ... I worked long and hard to master the art of homemade pie baking for the holidays after discovering the joys of pie dish shopping, soon after arriving in the States. I remember my first visit to Nation's burger and pie shop, an institution still, on Webster Street in Alameda, while still figuring my way around the unfamiliar culture into which I'd plunged. It was here that I sampled my first taste of such all-American delights as banana cream pie, chocolate cream and custard pies, not to mention the super-sized shakes, burgers and fries that I thought might have satiated an entire family back in the UK.

Slicing into one of my homemade apple pies a few years ago, during a visit from England, my equally astonished dad could not contain the urge to inform fellow dinner guests that he had never, in his life, set eyes on a pie so huge.

Pies, like most any other edible offering, tend to be significantly more modest in size, pretty much anywhere outside of the States. Something as simple as American pie is the perfect example of our abundance mentality here in the States — though it appears so extreme to Europeans. I don't think my dad meant to criticize his good fortune at securing a generous slice. On the contrary, he's always had a sweet tooth, one that my non-sweet eating mother has long attempted but not succeeded to temper.

Gail and Michael, in whose red barn we'd spent that most memorable of Thanksgivings, offered up their barn and pasture as backdrop for a mini-music festival for friends in August under the dappled canopy of a massive old oak tree.

Not Woodstock, but Wetstock — at least that was my mantle for the first gathering of its kind, for several years. And the name stuck.

As responsible party hosts and conservationists, these dearest friends of mine are highly sensitive to the narrow, shared farm lanes and delicate conditions of parched pastures surrounding a secluded property. Keeping crowd control to a manageable amount was key to this under-the radar-gathering of familiar Petaluma faces and brave new souls game to follow cryptic directions for a first time out into the secluded western hills.

Not Woodstock but Wetstock, this private, mini-music festival
for friends takes place under the canopy of a majestic, old oak tree.

Highlight of Wetstock, Brit band, The Hoovers' exuberant and still rocking ex-pats Bill Sell and Paul Whiting's ska-folk-style band of veteran Anglo and American musicians played their hearts out in an extended set on a tiny outdoor temporary stage constructed under the tree. Back in the day, The Hoovers toured with the likes of British bands Madness, Squeeze, The Police, Level 42 and, in the States, Chris Isaak. Their propensity to churn out great songs and performances around the Bay Area has led to several successful recent record releases.

Food and wine was as much a priority at Wetstock as the music and I can't think of a potluck gathering that has produced more impressive spread of fresh, local, late summer dishes (along with wonderful wines and local beers).

Virginia Mason's Easy Pie Crust

Favorite Hometown Recipes,
Petaluma People Services

3 cups of flour
1 teaspoon of salt
1 1/4 cups of butter
1 egg
1 teaspoon of distilled, white vinegar

Blend flour, salt and butter with a pastry cutter
to the size of small peas.
Mix one beaten egg with one teaspoon of vinegar
and five teaspoons of cold water.
Mix it all together with a fork.
Stir in circular motion until dough leaves the side of the bowl.
Chill. Makes more than enough for two double piecrusts.

Little Red Bench number two. Its predecessor collapsed under the elements and the cumulative weight of gifted bounty from friends and neighbors.

Chapter 19

mama sang a song

Pre-industrial Americans preserved mounds of fresh fruits and vegetables in seasons of abundance in preparation for the lean winter months and times of inevitable strife and scarcity to come.

If the mention of the age-old domestic art of preserving and canning conjures images of robust ranch wives rolling up their apron sleeves and batting down the hatches for a week of serious kitchen-counter labor, think again.

Something is stirring in the quiet confines of streamlined modern American kitchens. All sorts of quirky, elegant, inventive and sometimes utterly unexpected culinary combinations are coming together in a delicious new wave of nostalgic home canning operations.

This retro-chic revival of preserving backyard and local produce is as much about the polka-dot apron as it is the call for good, honest, high-fructose-free slow food. It is as fine and fun to give as it is to receive.

And according to today's top domestic divas and stylists, vintage hostess (and canning guest) aprons are back in style and action! Whether we are yearning for the cozy past or rediscovering our rustic roots, the answer is right here on the pantry shelves of friends including the home of neighborhood canning queen, Felice.

"Canning is not about being super precise or uptight," she told me. This flawless, no-nonsense mother of five was decked out in chunky pearls as she captivated an audience of novice, apron-clad kitchen collaborators, myself included. It was canning season in Sonoma County and not one of us, apart from our hostess, had seemingly much of a clue as to how to go about sealing the deal on a vintage glass jar of her signature Ginger Pear Chutney.

"The point is to make the most with the quantities of fruit and other produce on hand," she explained.

We were laughing uproariously at our lack of produce preservation prowess when we ought to have been taking notes, though our good-natured hostess assured us as she seamlessly glided from glistening counter to stove top that the art of reviving the canning process is all in the garnishing of the basics. "New lids and seals are essential," stressed an unflappable Felice, after sterilizing recycled glass jars in a bubbling stovetop pot. "Some people sterilize in the dishwasher, but that's not a satisfactory temperature by my standards," she said.

She clearly knew her way around the process from planning to final presentation. Down to the adorable, vintage fabric swatches she and her young daughter had hand cut into squares to decorate the lids of that year's offering, largely supplied by the fruit of a girlfriend's abundant backyard pear tree.

Merriment and mirth is a core ingredient of a casual kitchen gathering to bring in the harvest haul of an overly productive fruit tree, as it has always been. Not to mention mugs of steaming coffee and fresh egg-salad breakfast sandwiches on Della Fattoria bread, with oven-warm scones and dollops of homemade jams.

A backyard summer salad of mixed greens and peaches with a little bit of local, crumbled goat cheese — a gift left on the Red Bench.

Chatter turned to hints of vineyard peach conserves, fig and pear jam and spiced beer jelly. Grapefruit and honey spreads and cucumber fridge pickles are quintessential comfort food for the coming season.

"Why make something that is not seasonal?" asked Felice, who has been canning and preserving her way around northern California's harvest bounty for the past 20 years.

A fan of traditional household paraffin wax for topping her preserves, her most impressive instruction came in her demonstration of how to pop the pesky air bubbles on the waxy protective layer.

"Put the lid on, but don't tighten until the air has escaped," she said. "If you don't hear the popping sound of the lid, it hasn't properly sealed.

Felice recommended keeping canned produce and fruits for no longer than a year. "Enjoy it at home, give it away, share," she said. "It's a marvelous way to make the most of so much wonderful, fresh local produce."

Whether utilizing for jam making or other tasty, seasonal recipes, the black mission fig, or more appropriately, the "Franciscana," when subjected to a cooler climate hillside locale in the San Francisco Bay Area, tends to ripen of its own accord. Sometimes it ripens early in the season, sometimes twice, but rarely, in my experience, as late as November 5th.

Busily scurrying about the hillside during the evening's preparation for an extremely delayed grape pick, I paused to pluck three newly ripened figs from barren branches that looked like they'd given up on production for that year.

Surprisingly, this varietal, introduced to California by the Franciscan missionaries in 1768, appears to appreciate a growing season's extremities. Crimson red and luscious, these lovely, first to ripen, late blooming figs were the signal that the 2010 syrah crop would be equally windswept and interesting — packed with quality characteristics unlike any previous year's haul.

The easiest and tastiest way to serve figs, other than freshly sliced in a bowl of (Straus) Greek yogurt, is to split into quarters, bake in the oven with a dollop of fresh, soft goat cheese and wrapped with a sliver of prosciutto. Drizzle a little olive oil on top before baking and sprinkle chopped basil to serve.

Long distance readers of my online *Southern Sonoma Country Life* know what's in season via frequent updates of my fabled (propped up for posterity, despite its occasional collapse under the elements) little red bench that presides over my front porch.

I'm thinking that the little red bench really ought go "green" given the annual onset of such spectacular hauls of edible deliveries and donations.

Everyone should have a spot on the porch or front doorstep for friends and neighbors to drop off little (and sometimes, quite large) care packages of excess garden bounty, home canned jams and jellies, pickles, blooms, or over ambitious baking endeavors. Sonoma County's wonderful wet spring weather tends to cause a cacophony of color to explode in early veggie and rose gardens around the region and this is my favorite time of year in which to open the door to red bench bounty.

Massive armloads of fresh leafy greens and herbs grown in blooming Petaluma backyards grown from quality seeds, piled alongside Meyer lemons by the couple dozen are some of my top finds of gifted goodness when returning home from some outing or errand.

The little red bench is a symbol of the quality of care friends and neighbors take in looking out for the general well being of a generous, nourished community.

Mrs R. Kopf's Preserved Pears
The Egg Basket Cook Book, 1927

8 pounds of pears cut into cubes
6 pounds of sugar
grated rinds and juice of two lemons
plus juice of two more lemons
ginger root

Cut pears, add sugar.
Let stand for 24 hours.
Add lemon, lemon rind and ginger.
Cook in jars in a bath of boiling water until clear.
Seal.

Miss Emma Daniel's Fig Jam
The Egg Basket Cook Book, 1927

9 pounds of peeled figs

7 pounds of sugar

6 oranges, pulped

2 oranges, shredded

5 lemons, pulped

2 lemons, shredded

Cut fruit into small pieces and simmer for two hours.
Jar and seal.

Rose Kolkmeyer's Fig Pickles
The Egg Basket Cook Book, 1927

6-10 pounds of fresh figs (not too ripe)

1 gallon of water

1 teaspoon of salt

6 cups of brown sugar

1 pint of white vinegar

2 tablespoons of whole cloves

1 stick of cinnamon (in a bag)

Simmer figs in salt water for one hour. Drain.
Make a syrup from brown sugar boiled with vinegar, cloves
and cinnamon. Simmer figs in the syrup for an additional hour.
Fill glass jars and seal.

Back roads rule. Heading back to Petaluma
from neighboring Novato, avoiding the freeway at all costs.

Chapter 20

take me home, country roads

In its proximity to the coast, I have found a home away from home with some unlikely similarities to the Fens of my formative years. Known for its geographical location as "just a head above water," the East Anglian flatlands from which I hail, in its pre-drained original wetland environment, was a haven for the region's early marshmen's rudimentary methods of fishing and wildfowling and living off the land.

Just as pioneer families and Gold Rush investors sized up native lands of northern California in the mid 1800s, seventeenth-century Dutch engineer Cornelius Vermuyden seized the opportunity to systematically drain the marshy English Fens to maximize use of unrivalled nutrient rich soils that lay below. By constructing early river banks and waterways and protecting the low laying region from coastal tides, Vermuyden transformed what had been known as an inhospitable, mysterious Holy Land of abbeys and cathedrals into one of the most significant, cultivated farming regions of the world.

Likewise, I'm constantly mindful of our and future generation's responsibilities in good stewardship and future sustainability of these lands that have given so much to so many.

Back in my childhood stomping grounds of the Fens, today's cultivation of arable land, livestock, poultry, bulbs and flowers, dairy and vegetable production far exceeds a layman's expectations given the region's geographical size. In fact, thirty seven percent of England's vegetable crops, twenty four percent of the country's potatoes and huge volumes of sugar beets, bulbs and flowers contribute more than any other product or industry to the economy of the Fens.

Fenland farms grow sufficient wheat for an estimated 250 million loaves of bread each year. As with their contemporaries here in Sonoma and Marin Counties, more and more Fenland farmers are turning towards local production of small volume craft foods, sold in farm stores, farmers markets and specialty stores. It's encouraging to be a part of a global community of simplified eating habits. Just as the East Anglian Fens are being regenerated to protect the landscape from potentially catastrophic tidal surges and to encourage a continued return of native fish, birds, flowers and insects, American coastal communities must continue their quest for self preservation.

Back in 1857, according to the *California Farmer and Journal of Useful Sciences* (in the July 15th edition), little was known of the vast resources of California, outside of the circle where it affects those most immediately interested. "If we talk of the Dairies of California to our citizens, they hardly suppose there are a dozen in our State of any magnitude," the journal quoted. "We have spent the past week at Petaluma and Santa Rosa valleys, visiting the farms, stock ranches and dairies of those splendid valleys and we wish to lay some of those facts before our readers. We have many very interesting reports to make, but cannot give all at once, lest too much of a good thing would be too rich. We wish every citizen of our State could ride over these splendid valleys and see the coming prosperity of our State."

A visual, roadside reminder of the region's agricultural past.

The report went on to list the shipments of butter, cheese and eggs from Petaluma for the months of April, May and June 1857. "Here is wealth, real wealth — the product of industry and on these we rely for the permanency of California. Petaluma merchants are not troubled when steamer day comes, their debts are paid by the produce they receive and send forward and the gold of the city is sent back to the county, to enrich it, instead of sending it out of the county."

How many communities across the United States have fulfilled such a promise and maintained it for over 160 years, reinventing the farm wheel in such a way to be back at the forefront of agriculture in today's highly competitive food production arena?

An invitation to a subsequent of Suzanne's inventive "Forager's Dinners" brought me, on a personal level and in the writing of this book, full circle.

So thoroughly have we embraced the old ways of our countrified ancestors here in this small corner of northern California, the memory of my own grandparents' cast iron bathtub on occasion being filled to the brim with a startling catch of slimy eels seems not such a spectacle of the past.

A quest to forage for locally grown, caught or hunted ingredients for a fall forager's pot-luck at Suzanne's place had me thinking a lot of my resourceful grandmother's slippery Fenland seasonal specialties.

Where the watery, peat marshes of the Fens were once inhabited by those who fed their families by eeling, fishing and wildfowling on long, narrow, barges, Coast Miwok native Americans lived largely by the same, gentle cultivation of their natural habitat.

It is deeply encouraging to witness an increasingly widening acceptance of the basic theories of self reliance, of sustainable gardening and farming, a return to the buying and selling of local products and getting to know those who farm and craft our food, our wine, our bread and our beer.

It is this interconnectedness, I believe, that makes for the strongest, most resilient of communities. One that appeals to transplants such as myself, to those who have been raised with the integrity of the land on which their ancestors farmed and one that stands as a world-class role model for farm towns to follow on the road to revival.

It had been six months since Suzanne's hunter/gatherer tribal dinner. Just enough time had passed for my mind to fully process the experience.

In tune with the season, November's invitation was thankfully more sedate:

> *"Join us at the table for a foraged feast that's infused with terroir and paired with quintessential California wines."*

"Plucked from the wild or harvested in the backyard, dinner will preserve the season's earthy flavors in a memorable evening of delicious foods, great wines and inspired company. If you are game, you will be tasked with foraging food and using it as the signature ingredient in your selected course."

Fully plated, a sit down dinner for 16 people was planned to take place at trestle tables in the familiar surrounds of Suzanne and Bill's kitchen.

I opened my email the morning after the invitation had been sent and discovered that I was amongst the last to have responded with a preference of which of the eight courses Timo and I would be assigned with. It fell to us to take on salad.

Initial thoughts were to wonder where, in and around our friends and neighbor's yards we'd remotely forage for salad ingredients at this late stage of the year. Wild greens might have been more of a possibility in warmer months. And then I got to thinking that fruits and nuts were in abundance at this time of year. A salad doesn't have to be green.

I had, actually, lots of thoughts about all of this. I mused on the idea that in an otherwise fragmented society, foods grown and produced in the area take us back to our source — to accessibility, to purity, to nourishment. By tapping into our farming roots we step into a shared world where different craft foods and artisan products combine, telling our collective story.

We began foraging in earnest about a week before the dinner. Gail and Michael's prolific walnut tree out in Chileno Valley was my first port of call, followed by the last of the season's beets from immaculate raised vegetable boxes in my neighbor Merle's back yard. Large, juicy oranges were plucked into a paper bag from the yard of an empty heritage home I'd spotted close to downtown. Little sprigs of freshly sprung mint I snipped from my own backyard pots by the fountain, on the day of the dinner.

I'd hoped not to take advantage of a permission to purchase one ingredient, if essential and proving impossible to forage. The wild fennel we unearthed along a hillside path by the water tower that overlooks the city of Petaluma, was way past its prime and so shaved fennel and delicate green fronds were the one buy we succumbed to in order to complete our fall salad, dressed with house olive oil and a splash of freshly squeezed juice from one of the foraged oranges.

Suzanne tends to mix up her guest list each time she throws a foodie affair of some ingenious design or another, so, as usual, I wasn't too sure who we'd be up against in order of small course offerings.

Right off the bat, immediately following Suzanne and Bill's appetizing welcome of shaved egg salad with eggs from their backyard henhouse, green tomato jam, local cheeses, garlic toast, dried apricot ribbons and the most perfectly constructed, homemade rye crackers, was first course warrior for the primo plate position, Dr. Gary.

Imagine our faces, as sixteen forager/diners sat down to bowls of a steaming, fresh array of seafood in a poached cioppino over polenta.

Dr. Gary paired this wonder with Woodenhead Russian River Half Shell, an early fruiting white wine known as French Colombard, regaling a rapt audience with tales of his kayak-foraging expedition to the choppy coastal shores just north of Jenner. Added to his exquisite haul of wild rockfish and Ling cod, a few fine non-foraged clams from Hog Island.

Proving just the thing to refresh the palette, Timo's artful arrangement of our citrusy fall salad and equally light pairing of a Sonoma County MacMurray Ranch Pinot Gris went down well with a crowd anticipating so much yet to follow.

A cream of chestnut soup followed, made with foraged nuts from a multi-generational Mendocino County ranch. Cooked in bacon grease and served with a topping of pea shoots and turnip greens gleaned from the organic gardens at Santa Rosa Junior College by Robert (a sustainable gardening instructor) and Kate, I would have settled for this creamy, smoky delicious soup as my main course meal any day of the week. All the more endearing to hear of the couple's fall foraging trip to Mendocino marking the second anniversary of their first date. The soup was paired with a Stagecoach Vineyard Sequoia Grove Syrah.

Two sets of small plates made washing up between courses a breeze, offering a little bit of essential breathing time in between offerings as pairing partners plated up the next course.

After the soup, baked, scalloped sweet potato pots appeared, topped with pancetta and a Caymus Winery Pinot, courtesy of John and Collette, were followed by scene-stealing platters of individually handcrafted raviolis with wild porcini.

Foraging fanatic Dave, who'd proved himself king of rare, wild crop sourcing for the spring season tribal dinner, explained how this was indeed the ultimate delicacy for the esoteric fungophile. According to Dave: "The rarity of fresh, wild porcini is restricted to a mere two, tiny acres in Sonoma County."

"Porcini, or *Boletus Edulis*, as it is otherwise known is the crème de la crème of mushrooms, small and tight with a strong, turgid flavor," said Dave "Selling for thousands of dollars a pound to the discerning chef."

Dave makes a hearty zinfandel on his Sonoma County property, which he paired with two raviolis and a slivered garnish of yet more porcini, drizzled further with a reduced porcini sauce.

Trail Farms' Carmen produced a surprise plating of sliced sweet potato with fig salsa and goat cheese topped with fresh, orange-hued calendula flowers she introduced as "lovely and ecstatic" —a flavorful representation her Northern Carolina roots.

Theatricals, Barton and Kirsten not only served up a striking persimmon salad with pomegranate seeds, apples and honey crisps, dribbled with local honey and Meyer lemon, but also a rowdy chorus of crowd-pleasing, sing-along rock classics in between courses.

Formidable players on the competitive foraging stage, stalwart participants, Trinity and Frank took the presentation level up another notch with small, individual, savory onion mushroom and persimmon pie, beurre rosé sauce garnished with crème fraîche and quince paste adorned with pastry hearts and paired with Oak Knoll Syrah. Considering the amount of outrageously good food we'd consumed over several hours by this point, this outstanding pie still made it to the top of my list of most memorable bites.

Last, but not least and thank the heavens, not anything too heavy duty, farmers Tara and Craig's freshly "caught" simmering pears poached in wine came to table at the stroke of midnight, or thereabouts, with the perfect closing line that: "the best moment for a piece of fruit is when it literally drops off the tree."

acknowledgements

There's nothing like a long-haul flight at 35,000-feet above earth to sort the mental wheat from the chaff. It was on a 14-hour return trip over the Pacific Ocean to California that I decided the time was right for me to write this book.

It was the spring of 2012 and I had traveled to Sydney, Australia to welcome the much-anticipated arrival of my newborn nephew. Walking daily over the period of a couple of weeks through a maze of unfamiliar neighborhood streets, grocery basket in hand, nourishment of family in mind, had been an adventure that I'd relished and savored.

On the plane ride home, I scribbled my original outline for *Fog Valley Crush* in a crumpled pocket notebook. In shopping and cooking for my sister and family in food-centric Sydney, a certainty had cemented itself as to how satisfying it is to live and work and cook day-to-day, back home in one of the most bountiful and delicious regions of the world.

I started my first draft, a hefty compendium of all-things hyper-local in the artisan food, beer and wine arena, a few days after settling back in to daily life in Northern California.

Nine months later and during the penning of my first draft, I returned once again to Australia, this time to be with my sister and family for the last, unfathomable few days of my darling nephew's valiant battle with a rare and ultimately devastating infant heart condition.

Later, back home in Sonoma County, I took my broken heart and made a loving pledge to honor my brave little nephew's magnificent spirit as well as my sister's devotion and incredible inner strength. I focused myself, continued on with writing and rewriting and have completed a book that is, in a sense, every bit about the beauty of living life well. Not a day passes without my celebrating my late nephew's sweetest of souls in my steady purpose for positivity in prose.

I am, of course, indebted to my parents John and Elaine and much-loved family in the UK for gifting me a deep love and appreciation of community, a strong sense of self and a sturdy set of wings with which to fly. These particular attributes continue to serve me well.

To my mother-in-law Giuseppina — Nonna, "tante grazie" for every constant kindness over the years, not least the gift of your unrivaled traditional Italian cuisine.

Kindred souls, Meloni Courtway, Suzanne Alexandre and Susan Villa each appear throughout this book as bright, shining benchmarks of brilliance in the best of the region's home and commercial cooking. Thank you for your graciousness and support in allowing me to exploit your remarkable talents at stovetop, garden and table.

Elaine Silver, extraordinary woman of words. Your gentle, coaxing, magical brand of friendship and book midwifery has been vitally instrumental in the safe and hopefully sound arrival of *Fog Valley Crush*. For being the first to wholeheartedly embrace its early concept, your unswerving encouragement, deep editorial insight and stamina to pace me to the finish line — a million thank-yous. Here's to more adventures together in Fog Valley.

Linda Walden, dedicated, detailed first reader, thanks to you, too! For the dearest of friends and neighbors (Lesley McCullaugh, Gail and Michael Foulkes, especially) who have so graciously and patiently awaited reading what I've written about them inside the pages of this book, you are the best.

The late, much-missed Robert Brockman, muscle man of many a harvest season — wine pressing, dear friend, will never be the same without you.

Maven of print and design, Lorna Johnson, and illustrator extraordinaire, Nicky Ovitt, I simply could not have produced this gorgeous book without the two of you. It took on a personality of its own and has evolved in as "organic" a way possible for a work of words and images. What an amazingly calm and talented dream team for me to work with and to think that we didn't have to leave town to do this! Humblest of thank-yous to you both.

Multi-media marvels, Rocco Rivetti and Gilles O'Kane took Fog Valley by storm with camera and tripod to produce the best mini-film trailer a book could ask for.

The number one, or rather, "numero uno" reason for my having made it through far too many revisions to count is the indefatigable Timo, my tenacious, tireless spouse and handy in-house winemaker! Credit due, you nudged, cajoled, rallied and, when I wondered many times at the sheer magnitude of an entire book, you downright stubbornly refused to falter in your support of this persistent writing habit of mine. "Sei il sole della mia vita." You started this one when you planted those vines.

Fog Valley Crush was written in large part at my kitchen table. My three sons, Rocco, Luc and Dominic were raised with my tapping away at a keyboard, surrounded by tea cups and dodging a passing parade of flying soccer balls, amplified marching band practice and reptile rescues at all hours of the day and night. This one took a lot longer than the typical assignment. Throughout it all, you've tag-teamed as favored kitchen-company to keep me on my toes. You bring me balance. You bring me joy. For capturing me so at ease in my author's photograph, Dominic, you are the bomb.

The community that has inspired and supported this book is one that is shaped of all sorts of people from a myriad mix of backgrounds, philosophies and mindsets. Three cheers for the melting pot! This one is for you.

recipe index

sources

A History of The Fens, J. Wentworth Day

All About Beer Magazine

BBC World News

Britannia History

California Digital Newspaper Collection

Chicago Tribune

Coming of Age: The Status of North Bay Artisan Cheese Making

Ecology Center

Extra Virginity, Tom Mueller

Food and Wine Magazine

The Egg Basket Cook Book 1927

Favorite Recipes of the St. James Ladies Guild 1979

Hog Island Oyster Company

Household Science in Rural Schools 1918

Journal of Ecosystems

Larousse Gastronomique

Marin Independent Journal

Modern Farmer

Mother Jones

National Geographic

National Park Service — *The Archeology of Sixteenth-Century Cross-Cultural Encounters in Point Reyes National Seashore*

New York Times

Olive Oil Times

Petaluma Area Chamber of Commerce

Petaluma360.com

Petaluma History Room

Petaluma Historical Library

Petaluma Magazine

Petaluma Post

Practical Winery and Vineyard Journal
Remodelista.com
San Francisco Chronicle
Santa Rosa Press Democrat
Saveur Magazine
Sonoma County Historical Society
Sonoma County Vintners
Theoliveoiltimes.com
Travel and Leisure Magazine
Twitter
University of California Davis Overview of Winemaking
Wall Street Journal

song titles/writers

Keep My Skillet Good and Greasy	Uncle Dave Macon
Wide Open Spaces	Susan Gibson
Home on the Range	Brewster Higley
Small Town USA	Justin Moore
Family Tradition	Hank Williams, Jr.
Sixteen Tons	Merle Travis
I Think I'll Just Stay Here and Drink	Merle Haggard
Don't Fence Me In	Robert Fletcher and Cole Porter
Bring on the Rain	Billy Montana and Helen Darling
Baby's Got Her Blue Jeans On	Bob McDill
Mammas Don't Let Your Babies Grow Up to Be Cowboys	Ed and Patsy Bruce
Big Ole Brew	Mel McDaniel
Wildwood Flower	Maud Irving
Walking After Midnight	Alan Block and Donn Hecht
All the Gold in California	Larry Gatlin
Cafe on the Corner	Mac McAnally
The Grand Tour	George Jones
Down on the Farm	Jerry Laseter and Kerry Kurt Phillips
Mama Sang a Song	Bill Anderson
Take Me Home Country Roads	Bill Danoff, Taffy Nivert and John Denver

piccolo regalo

Almond Cake
2 beaten eggs
1 stick of butter, melted
1 teaspoon of almond extract
1 cup of sugar
1 cup of flour

Mix eggs and melted butter; add almond extract.

Stir together the sugar and flour.
Add to the eggs/butter. Mix until smooth.

Bake in a greased, lined, 9" round cake tin
at 350° F for 25 minutes.